The
Body
Electric

THE
BODY
ELECTRIC

A Personal Journey into the Mysteries of Parapsychological Research, Bioenergy, and Kirlian Photography

Thelma Moss, Ph.D.

J.P. Tarcher, Inc.
Los Angeles
Distributed by St. Martin's Press
New York

Design: John Brogna

Manufactured in the United States of America

Published by J.P. Tarcher, Inc.
9110 Sunset Blvd., Los Angeles, Calif. 90069

Published simultaneously in Canada by Thomas Nelson & Sons Limited,
81 Curlew Drive, Don Mills, Ontario M3A 2R1

10   9   8   7   6   5   4   3   2   1
First Edition

Excerpted from the *Los Angeles Times,* July 28, 1979:

> At a seminar on science and religion at Massachusetts Institute of Technology, it was stated that the "popular image of a scientist as a lone, dedicated researcher in pursuit of truth is now dangerously obsolete." In fact, the researcher's "arduous, isolated work may be only a means to fame, fortune and power."
>
> It was further affirmed that "genuinely creative scientists are about as rare in the scientific community as genuine holy men in the established church. . . . But without them, the whole structure would rot."

It is to those few that this book is dedicated.

CONTENTS

ACKNOWLEDGMENTS

To the International Kirlian Research Association, 411 East 7th Street, Brooklyn, New York—whose executive director, Edward Graff, has kept alive and flourishing the research into Kirlian photography. For everyone who wishes advice, literature, references, schematics, etc., address your requests here.

To Victor Inyushin, Victor Adamenko, Henry Andrade, George Lozanov, Florin Dumitrescu, Benson Herbert, Dennis Milner, Larissa Vilenskaya, Gertrude Schmeidler, and so many more around the world who are pursuing each in his own way the same sparkling nonmaterial goals.

To Uri Geller, my thanks. When people ask me, as they invariably do, if you are a fake, I answer I don't know, you may very well be. But your videotape is not. (See Chapter 10.)

To the laboratory volunteers at UCLA—Clark Dugger, William Emboden, Kendall Johnson, Jack Gray, Francis Saba, John Hubacher, Vicki Silva, Leland Moss, and the many others, without such workers—no creation.

The
Body
Electric

1
Why PSI?

On Being Initiated into
Mysterious Realms of the Mind

THE FIRST MYSTERIOUS EVENTS

I would venture a guess that nearly every parapsychologist is drawn to the field because, at some time in his life, he had at least one experience, mysterious and powerful, which he cannot deny, bury, or explain away. My own experiences came rather late in life, after I had enjoyed the worldly pleasures of an acting career, a husband, and the birth of a son—all of which had left me, inexplicably, with a nagging feeling of unfulfillment.

In that era of the late 1940s and early '50s, many sought solutions to their spiritual dilemmas on the psychiatrist's couch—now become a trite piece of furniture, even for TV comics. But during that period, I struggled hour after tear-stained hour to overcome a chronic, neurotic depression. Unsuccessfully. In his rugged, kindly way my husband suggested that I try my hand at writing. At about the same time my psychiatrist suggested a course in body relaxation. I pursued these two disparate activities side by side for many months. Then, just about the time I was finishing my first screenplay, I experienced a mysterious (paranormal?) sensation in the relaxation class.

Those classes were given by Charlotte Selver, later to become celebrated in humanistic psychology. But in those days Charlotte worked in a lonely studio on West 57th Street in Manhattan—

where she bemused her students by asking them to "lie down and let the floor support you...*give* to the floor." Her instructions did not mean much to me until I began to feel how my body kept resisting the floor, rather than sinking into it. The more I tried to "give to the floor," the more tension I felt traveling and sticking through my arms, legs, feet, and toes. I remember the shock of discovering I could not move my toes at all, so frozen with tension were they.

Then, one day, somehow all at once the tensions in my spine, neck, stomach all seemed to melt away and I felt as if I were dissolving...and I became one with the floor and with the studio...and with Manhattan and the world and somewhere...within...is there another space?...?...I was in another dimension, another reality, a timeless yet familiar space. Only gradually did I drift back to the world, and to the class, with which I had lost contact.

This experience proved only a prelude to what happened a few weeks later when, in the process of "giving to the floor," I felt a release which was like a flow of energy...almost an electrical sensation, which traveled around the diaphragm and chest, dissolving something. It was as if that flow of energy opened some sort of channel through me, for now there rippled inside and spread outward a flow of emotions...as if an artist were playing upon my body as an instrument from which emerged a series of sobs, groans, laughs, and sighs, one after another and sometimes in chords, all issuing through me but seemingly not of or from me, an effortless flow of strong emotions which I could observe but was powerless to stop. As I seemed to split in two—Observer and Performer—I experienced a gorgeous feeling of release in that fountain of previously unfelt emotions.

All through the week I kept reverting back to that mysterious happening. From where had those emotions come; into what realm had I wandered? I was loath to discuss the experience with anyone because it sounded crazy—to be split in two, one half observing the other half as if it were possessed by emotions from nowhere. But as I pondered and puzzled, a clue appeared.

THE DAY A BOOK FELL OPEN

Sometimes when early for Charlotte's class, I would stop and browse in a quite ordinary book store on West 57th Street. This particular day I found myself in front of a section of books on the occult which I had not noticed before. For no reason of which I was aware, I reached up for a book, which fell open in my hands to a description of an experience almost exactly like mine: emotions flowing through and out of a young woman as she relaxed on a bed. Thrill of recognition. But what was I recognizing? The book, *Gestalt Therapy*, contained several similar accounts, but its author, Fritz Perls, gave no explanation other than "release," which explained nothing to me.

In the weeks that followed I ransacked that occult-book section and found other, seemingly random clues to a search I did not know I had started, a search related somehow to experiences of "transcendence," "cosmic consciousness," "mysticism," "union," and "miraculous cures." These were phenomena that all of my life I had dismissed as nonsense. But now I had had an experience, within myself, which I could not explain. What *was* it? Would it happen again? It did, but not in Charlotte's class, and not for a very long time to come, because the screenplay I had written was suddenly to go into production in London, with my husband producing and with Alec Guinness and Peter Finch performing in it.

LONDON ADVENTURE: CRASH LANDING

Off we went, husband, son, and I, for many months of excitement in an austere London, still food-rationed, still bombed-out in Grosvenor Square. Every now and again during those months I would encounter a book which would remind me of the Search. Like the newly published *Doors of Perception*, by Aldous Huxley, which described the author's experiences with a drug that "altered the mind." Huxley's descriptions seemed to recall those same mysterious dimensions that I had felt in Charlotte's class. Maybe I could find them again, with the drug that Huxley had taken? But in 1953, in London, mescaline was nowhere to be found.

Then, with shocking swiftness, our newly minted movie—Chesterton's *Father Brown*—had its London premiere, and I gave birth to a daughter, and my husband died of cancer. The shattering significance of stress in mental health was just beginning to be recognized then, along with the concept that each of us has a breaking point. My breaking point arrived after I moved to Los Angeles with my parents, in the form of a depression more desperate than any I had known, a depression culminating in two suicide attempts. Eventually I was put into a hospital and given electroshock therapy. The first series did not work; the second series did (different hospital, different doctor). During that period my body was electrified time and again to the point of convulsions, while for weeks and weeks I lived in oblivion, sans memory, sans feeling, sans sensation. Then one morning, out of the bleak and the blank, a whiff of coffee that smelled *good!* First good feeling in more than a year. Followed by more good feelings. And more. It was as if something within me, literally, had switched from negative to positive.

Here was another mystery: how could electricity, shot through the brain, so totally change one's emotions? Somehow this was not unlike the experience in Charlotte's class, when emotions unbidden had coursed through me like a current of electricity. This was the second time that emotions had been central to a phenomenon which I did not understand. What had the electroshock treatment done? How did it work?

I kept asking the doctors, but none of them could explain why the treatment is effective in relieving depression. That did not make sense at all, for I had been brought up in the religion of science where for every effect there is a cause, and for every cause, an effect. But now these doctors, these scientists, were saying they were using a treatment for which neither cause nor effect was understood?

As I was to learn again and again in my later life as a psychologist, many times a medicine or therapy will work for reasons that no one can explain. The art or science of medicine has learned to take from wherever it can—from folk remedies (digitalis), from laboratory accidents (LSD), from a witch doctor's potion (curare). If the medicament or technique has a specific, practical use, it becomes an accepted therapy. Not for a moment does that mean that the doctor knows why. How does digitalis, acupuncture, aspirin, or hypnosis work? The humble M.D. will twinkle and shake his head; the not-so-humble will give a many-syllabled explanation signifying nothing. The fact remains, no one can explain why electroshock is effective against depression.

FROM ELECTRIC TO PSYCHEDELIC SHOCK

Over the next few years, 1954 to 1958, I became a functioning member of Los Angeles show biz, writing potboilers for movies and TV and liking it not at all. That Something kept nagging, reinforced by the odd book that kept appearing. One day, for example, I found on my own book shelf *Advanced Yoga*, by Ramacharaka, a book I would have sworn had not been there before. I read it with puzzlement and fascination, for through concentration and meditation, it was claimed, certain states of awareness could be achieved in which one transcends time and space and can achieve telepathy, or even travel into other dimensions of reality. A reminder of that lost but still vivid experience of finding an opening in space and time.

And then a new book by Aldous Huxley was published, *Heaven and Hell*, describing the different realms of mind that drugs like mescaline can lead one into, Heaven being an ecstatic, mystical experience and Hell a horrific one, so horrific as to be christened a "model psychosis," meaning a temporary, drug-induced insanity. Even as I finished the book, I learned that not only was Huxley currently living in Los Angeles, but he was to appear on a television program hosted by Oscar Levant, a friend of mine.

I managed to invite myself to the studio, where I heard Huxley speak eloquently about the mystical attributes of the "psychedelics" (a newly coined word in 1957). Unfortunately, he left before the end of the program, and before I could meet him.

Later that night, at a party, I mentioned how fascinated I was by the "psychedelics" and vowed to have such an experience, even if it meant traveling to the wilds of Mexico for the sacred mushroom.

"What's wrong with the wilds of Beverly Hills?" asked a young man. "There's a group of doctors on Lasky Drive experimenting with one of those mind drugs."

"Which drug?"

"One with initials. LFT or LST..."

Those initials meant nothing to me, since Huxley's experiences had been with mescaline, but nevertheless, I phoned the Beverly Hills doctors for an appointment.

I soon learned that these doctors were not at all interested in Huxley's mysticism. They were gunning for psychiatric remedies, using LSD to burrow more quickly into the unconscious. Nor were they interested in me as a candidate for therapy until I submitted to a series of interviews, a battery of psychological tests, and presented a specific psychiatric problem, frigidity. Only then was I accepted for their LSD project.

To the dismay of family and friends who had just recovered from my breakdown and melancholy—so soon, they cried, to be toying with drugs reported to drive people crazy!

ME AND LSD

One of the requirements for this experimental study was a detailed report of each LSD experience, to be written the day after the session. This report-writing proved invaluable in keeping clear the gorgeous imagery of those hours, which began with the very first session, when I found myself almost immediately merging into that other dimension... sinking gradually to the bottom of the sea... which was really not the sea but infinity... a realm I knew, though had so long forgotten... I had been there, here, so many times... in this secret silent place... and in that space, place, at the bottom of the mind-sea... there appeared... what was it?... a huge... clam?... yes, a huge closed-up clam... which I recognized was me.

Symbolic, of course. The closed-up clam, symbol of frigidity. That was the Freudian interpretation, valid and convincing not only to the doctors, but to me. And from the richness of the imagery in those extensive reports, I wrote a book on LSD therapy, from the Freudian point of view, complete with Oedipus, orality, anality, childhood traumae, and symbols of the unconscious. These came one atop another, like revelations, for in spite of my years on the psychiatrist's couch, I had never been convinced of the existence of an unconscious mind, much less its symbolic meanings. Now, under the drug, these erupted, full-blown, and their meanings were instantly clear.

But of far greater interest than the Freudian stuff were the eruptions from what seemed a deeper realm of mind. Such as the time I saw myself in vivid clarity as a legless beggar whipped by a desert sandstorm and heard part of me say, "I died here." And the time I saw myself being locked into an Egyptian tomb with my dead husband, and even as I was screaming the horror of being buried alive, another part of me was thinking, "But wives weren't buried alive with their husbands in Egypt, that was India!" The doctors treated these happenings as more of my unconscious dynamics—i.e., the crippled beggar was a symbol of my helplessness in the storm following my husband's death, and being buried alive in my husband's Egyptian tomb a similar symbol of helplessness. Which interpretations I accepted.

Years later, as a psychologist, I was to learn that any number of interpretations can be imposed on an experience, depending on the theory—Jungian, Reichian, Pavlovian, Wolpian—and that each interpretation can be made to fit the theory, if not the patient. For these Beverly Hills LSD therapists, Freud was the Way, with his twin motifs of sex and aggression ("We fuck and fight," my doctor used to say), and for them there was nothing beyond.

AUTOMATISMS

But in time I became dissatisfied with that dim view of the psyche, and kept searching. And, slowly, perhaps because of that search, wondrous things began to happen. As I wrote more and more fully about each session, the writing began to flow with less and less effort, until the reports seemed to write themselves. As a prelude, perhaps, to the time I woke in the middle of one night, reached for a pen and paper, wrote something in an uninterrupted flow, then fell asleep again. The next morning I was stunned to see that I had written, without conscious thought, in cohesive rhythm and rhyme, the first poem of my lifetime.

This automatic writing of poetry continued, sometimes in the middle of the night, sometimes during the day. Effortless rhythms, streaming out of me (like the emotions?). There developed a powerful sense that I was receiving these rhythms from another plane, and it also felt as if the rhythms were the basic stuff; the words simply giving content for this earth's dimensions. But the abstract *rhythm* is the reality, the true content.

For months, rhythms and words flowed through and out of me in much the same way my emotions had in Charlotte's class. I could appreciate, at last, what I had read about the automatic writings of St. Theresa, Stainton Moses, and Patience Worth (a twentieth-century St. Louis housewife who composed automatically in thirteenth-century Anglo-Saxon). I contemplated how a poet or a playwright sometimes completes a major work over a weekend of "inspiration"—and claims that he has done nothing but hold the pen. I had accepted this as a form of humility; now I saw it as a simple statement of fact.

Was this automatic poetry of mine paranormal? The question was easy to answer. Since the writing of poetry was new within my life experience, it was paranormal—for me.

Other experiences came during LSD sessions, powerful and bewildering. Once, at the start, I saw a fire begin feebly inside me, and it grew so strong so swiftly that it propelled my body across the bed on which it had been lying and flung it against the wall. And the fire grew even stronger, blinding me, bouncing my body from wall to wall with its unleashed energy. Somehow again this was like the emotions that had flowed through me, but this was a vastly more ruthless force. What was that force? I kept asking the doctor, but he just asked if I would like the experience stopped, for I was still being catapulted from wall to wall. I managed to nod, and he to inject me somewhere with a tranquilizer. I came back down, badly shaken by that enormous energy. Where had it come from; what had it been? (Years later, I learned of the Kundalini power that may be released at the base of the spine, which can, at times, cause the spontaneous combustion of a person. I wondered if I had been given a sample.)

And "messages" started to come through me during the sessions via "automatic talking." Once I heard myself hold forth on levitation as a viable phenomenon—and felt a sudden energy lift my body from its prone position to a standing position in one effortless movement. The doctor watched as I sank prone again and rose again, several times. But never did my body lift completely off the ground, a necessary condition for true levitation. On other occasions the automatic talking insisted that thoughts could be transmitted from person to person, and I felt I could receive such thoughts from the doctor. He agreed to an experiment (which was uncharacteristic of him). During that experiment, I could pick up no thoughts of any kind from him. Several other "revelations" about levitation, telepathy, and out-of-body travel proved not at all verifiable.

Somehow, for me, truth and lies and absurdity and grandeur were all mixed together in the psychedelic experience. In an effort to separate them, I would return for the next session, and the next, hoping each time that with this next session the truth would be revealed. It wasn't until several years later, when I had moved to the other side of the couch and was serving as LSD guide for a colleague, that I saw the hook in that "next time." For that colleague, too, kept exploring the hope that the next session would bring a revelation. On one particular night, he added carbon dioxide inhalation to the LSD, and after a time he leaped to his feet, triumphant.

"Write this down!" Peremptory command replacing his usual mildness. "The universe...the *universe*..." He paused to make sure he would say it exactly right. "The *universe*...is my grandmother's silver service!" He stared at the glory of the vision as my stomach turned over and over with the thought that this man had entrusted me with his psyche and I had let it erupt into a psychotic episode. (It wasn't, but it took some time before he saw that his vision was a silliness.)

Another time, a high school chum of my son called to tell me about his revelation.

"I got the answer! From LSD!" said Mickey.

"What is it?" I asked, not wanting to hear.

"Running." Pause. *"Running!"* I couldn't respond. "All the time I was on acid, I was running, and I knew!"

"Knew what?"

"I just knew."

"Mickey..." It was useless, but I had to try. "Please, be careful."

After many confounding excursions, I came to realize that truth and lies, for me, were hopelessly confused in my psychedelic experiences. And I came to believe that the Search for an unknown energy could no longer be pursued through drugs. It was necessary to learn as much as possible about the realms of mind and energy that had been unleashed in me. And the best way to achieve that, so it seemed, was for me to go back to school.

2
Graduate School—
The LSD Side

Learning Much That I
Did Not Want To Be Taught and
Much of Importance
That Was Not in the Curriculum

GETTING IN

t's hard to believe that at the age of thirty-six I applied to only one graduate school (UCLA, one of the "best") and was one of sixty accepted from a pool of 600 applicants. Of these sixty, we were told on Welcoming Day, thirty would flunk out or quit before the end of the year. I had already been told by a friendly professor that I was not the image, being a middle-aged woman, for one thing, ignorant of the hard sciences, for another, and altogether ill-prepared for the incredible grind that is graduate school.

He was quite right. I had already spent more than two years in university Extension taking all the prerequisite courses for a career in graduate school, but during that time I had discovered how deeply educational methods and material had changed in the generation I had been away. Introductory Psychology, for instance. I had taken a course with that title as an undergraduate, where the name Freud was unknown or ignored and the content of which bore no resemblance to the course of the same name in Extension, which gave an overview of Freudian theory so complete that I saw my LSD therapy (which had seemed so brilliant) had merely followed the Freudian line.

The other psychology courses offered through Extension (Child

Development, Theories of Personality, Abnormal Psychology) had been so interesting that I had put off the grimmer prerequisites until almost too late. When I did begin Elementary Statistics, it was like listening to a foreign language. I anxiously appealed to the professor, who was pleasant enough and suggested a refresher course in analytic geometry.

"Analytic—?" The two words together were a foreign phrase.

"No analytic geometry?" The professor frowned. "Then start with trigonometry."

"Trigonometry—?" Fainter voice.

"Advanced algebra?" the professor asked, hopefully. I shook my head.

"In my high school we only went from algebra to geometry."

The professor smiled gently. "Good luck..."

It became clear I would have to start at the bottom, with simple algebra. It was a tough climb, every rung of the way, until I got to trigonometry, which was such a tangle of cosines and tangents that I stepped down to advanced math and learned how some infinities are larger than others and got on speaking terms with $>$ (more than) and $<$ (less than) and $\simeq$ and $\neq$—a sign language which, I learned to my chagrin, my son had known for years. All the while I kept asking, why? Why study math and calculus and analytic geometry for a career in clinical psychology and exploring the unconscious? "Necessary," I was told again and again, but was never given a satisfactory reason *why*.

MEMORIES, MEMORIES

Several of the required courses depended on pure rote learning. Like physiological psychology, for instance, which demanded a familiarity with the names of the twelve cranial nerves, the fourteen endocrine and exocrine glands, the branches of the sympathetic and parasympathetic nervous systems, and the specific crannies of the cerebral cortex. We even had to memorize the word for an "aid to memory," which is "mnemone"—a term I remembered long after I had forgotten the names of the twelve cranial nerves, whose mnemone begins, "On Old Olympus Towering Tops..." Having been a quick study as an actress (I could remember lines with ease), I scored an A, to the dismay of the professor, George Seacat, of whom I asked a letter of recommendation to the graduate school. A man of considerable dry wit, George complained that he had been forced by academic rules to give the A, but that nothing could force him to recommend me, since it would be a waste of his time and mine.

"T.," he said, shaking his trim, crew-cut head (he always called me T. Moss), "T., you'll never make it. You're just not the image. And even if they did accept you, you wouldn't last six months. You're no chicken, are you?"

Even though I admitted to being a hen, George wrote the letter. Years later, I served under him as an intern in a veteran's hospital, and some time after that, when I applied for a job at the Neuropsychiatric Institute, George was asked to give his opinion of my ability. Long after I was ensconced at the NPI job, a colleague showed me George's reply, which went something like this:

> I feel eminently qualified to write on T. Moss' prospects. I told her she'd never make it into graduate school, and if she did, she'd never get through the first year. And if by a miracle she got the degree, she'd find it hard to land a job. So, regarding the NPI position, what can I say? She's not right, according to any of the accepted standards. Look at her ESP research! But she'll undoubtedly cause a flap after you hire her.

George was on target, right on down the line.

THE FIRST MONTHS

From the very start, graduate school was a jungle, with statistics a particularly fierce dragon. We beleaguered clinical students would stare, wild-eyed: analysis of variance and non-parametric statistics for a career in psychotherapy? In fact, the whole class proved so hapless with statistics that special evening classes were organized. Almost everyone came to the classes, which almost no one seemed to understand. Not even the professor. One night he was explicating a problem from the test that most of us had failed, and he stated that X represented the number of cells into which balls (as in a pinball game) could land.

"No," a student objected. "X is for the number of balls, not cells."

"No. X is for the number of cells." The professor repeated his statement, but without further clarification.

"It's for the balls!"

"Cells!"

"Balls!"

"Cells!"

"BALLS!"

"That's what I say!" I heard my voice cutting through the frayed tempers—and the room exploded with laughter.

The mid-term statistics exam found me close to fulfilling George

Seacat's prophecy. I scored 10 points out of a possible 100, and marveled that I scored so high, for I was still having difficulty distinguishing > (more than) from < (less than). I glanced away from my score of 10, right into a 92 on the paper of the student sitting next to me. A score of 92 was almost unprecedented. Exams in universities are purposely constructed so that *no one* can get more than 80 or, rarely, 90. I had learned that fact of academia in my first Extension course, where on the mid-term (my first exam in fifteen years) I realized that I couldn't answer more than half the questions. When the bell curve of the exam results was posted on the blackboard, I saw that the highest score was 32 out of a possible 45. After class I expressed my shock to the professor and asked if anyone ever got a perfect score.

"Not on *my* exams!" the professor answered with some pride.

I realized this was a point of honor. Faculty does not want students to feel they have mastered a subject, perhaps because the "known," in psychology changes so much from year to year. Start with Pavlov and Freud, but soon it's Jung, and Wolpe, and biofeedback, and behavior modification, and where, oh where, is the tenure of known knowledge? Like Alice and the Red Queen, faculty and students both must run very hard just to stay in the same place—which remains just a short distance from ignorance.

STATISTICS IN PSYCHOLOGY

Staring at my exam grade of 10, I knew extreme measures were necessary. So I turned to the student next to me, with the 92.

"Do you tutor?"

He shrugged. "Dunno. Never have."

"Will you? Me?"

Benson did.

At first, all I could see was a morass of equations without *meaning*, and I asked Benson—who at twenty-three was three times as knowledgeable in academic psychology as I was at thirty-six.

"Why, Benson? Why statistics?"

"It's *bubkas*." (His favorite word, meaning—I believe—"nonsense.") "Just memorize the stuff and forget it after the exam."

"But why learn it at all?"

Benson grinned. "You know the expression, *in vino veritas?*" I nodded. "Well, 'In statistics, truth.' Do an experiment and you have to show, from the numbers, whether what you've done is significant. Which is *bubkas*."

"But how can numbers tell you if something is significant?"

"*Significant* is a statistical word." Benson explained patiently how all science uses that particular word. For the results of an experiment to be "statistically significant" the numbers must show that you have a 20-to-1 shot (this translates as p < .05, or "the probability is less than 1 in 20 this could happen by chance.") A 20-to-1 shot, Benson went on, is good, but not nearly as publishable as a 100-to-1 shot, or better still, a 1,000-to-1 shot (p < .001).

"Come on!" I thought he was pulling my leg. "How can anyone get a 1,000-to-1 shot?"

"You'd be surprised how easy it can be. Which means it's *bubkas*."

(In later years, I was to learn from my own experiments that 1,000-to-1 was surprisingly achievable, which made me agree with Benson that it was *bubkas*.)

After a time, Benson introduced me gently into the mystique of experimental designs, which behavioral science borrowed from agricultural studies.

"Look," Benson would go with small words, nice and easy, "the aim of psychology is to predict and control behavior. Remember those key words. We want to *predict* and *control* behavior, whether it's rats, or memory, or sleep, or stomach aches."

"Predict and control memory?"

"Let's work on a design in memory, okay?" I nodded. "I come in and I say to you, 'Thelma, I have here a new drug which will *significantly* improve memory!'"

"Prove it."

Benson grinned. "Right on! Now, what kind of experiment will prove it? Your turn."

"Well, we'll need two groups, won't we? The Experimental Group that gets your drug, and the Control Group that doesn't get your drug. And..." I was thinking this through, slowly, "... and both groups, before taking your drug, have to be tested...I mean, to show that they can memorize about equally, in the same period of time...?"

"You're getting smarter. And how do you do that?"

"I give up."

"You're getting dumber. You get a bunch of college sophomores, match them for IQs, and divide them randomly into two equal groups. Then you ask everybody in both groups to memorize the same bunch of nonsense syllables!"

I groaned and laughed at the same time. I had participated in a nonsense-syllable experiment when I was in Extension. All psychology students have to do time—three hours—in "laboratory work." Probably a necessary form of blackmail. My three hours had been spent memorizing "ack, dib, zyl, gla, eng, bix, xem," while different tones were being played.

"Okay! What next?"

"We find out that both groups learn about the same number of nonsense syllables in the same time period. That's the baseline. Now what?" Benson tossed the design back to me.

"Now the Experimental Group gets the drug, and the Control Group gets nothing, and—"

"No good," Benson interrupted.

"Of course!" I had remembered the emphasis that was being placed, that year, on the "placebo effect." It had been learned, to the sorrow of pharmacology, that when an Experimental Group got a new drug, and the Control Group got nothing, the new drug was generally very effective. But then some wise man decided to give the Control Group placebos, which are fake pills made to look exactly like the real pills but containing no active substance. Then things got really hairy, because the groups that took the fake pills sometimes did just as well, sometimes better, sometimes worse, than the Experimental Groups. Why? What did that mean in terms of human behavior? No one knew, then. And $30 million of research later, no one yet knows. But it is a remarkably important question.

"Okay!" I had the next step. "The Control Group gets the placebo. Then both groups are given another series of nonsense syllables to memorize. And, if your drug is any good, Benson, there will be a statistically significant difference between the amount of syllables the Experimental Group learns, far more than the Control Group."

"You're almost as smart as I am."

But I wasn't, in spite of Benson's heroic efforts. He taught me much that was valuable—especially that the science of psychology has made such a religion of measurements and statistics that if an experiment cannot be demonstrated in the lab, under controlled conditions, then the experiment is generally considered *not* to be a proper subject for psychology. But not even Benson could get through to me the proofs of theorems *re chi* square, and analysis of variance. And the more I struggled, the deeper I sank.

Flunked Out

Halfway through the first year there came a bad personal time, with a death in the family and an orphaned child, and I was forced to be away from school. During that absence another statistics exam was given. When I returned to class, I went immediately to Mort, our professor, and asked for the make-up exam. Mort took me aside and, in as kind a way as he could, told me that during my absence a committee had met to evaluate the standing of various members of the class, and the members had decided to drop me from the program. I was struck dumb, and Mort went on, *in apologia*, about how poorly I had done in his class. I managed a nod. Then, probably because he is a kind man, Mort suggested that I appeal to the chairman of the committee, the only person in the department who could reverse the decision.

The chairman was Dr. John Seward, a gaunt, Lincolnesque man with gray hair and stern eyes that could suddenly twinkle with fun. A distinguished rat psychologist, he was teaching our class Learning Theory with erudition and charm.

"Most of us," he had once remarked in class, "come to psychology to learn about Mother, but all we learn about is rats."

And he made sure we learned about rats, too, for he required several term papers on one or another aspect of rat behavior. I remember, quite seriously, choosing the ejaculatory behavior of the male rat, for which studies the female vaginas had been sewn shut. By a quirk, the problem of sexual behavior in the rat arose in class, and since I had just acquired new-found wisdom, I raised my hand to share it. When Dr. Seward called on me, I sat up in my seat in order to better describe the male's mating behavior (short thrusts, withdrawing completely after each thrust). Dr. Seward stared at me with some consternation as I sat up, and called out:

"There's no need to demonstrate! Just tell us about it."

And everyone had shouted laughter.

Now, I was en route to "tell him about it."

A REVERSED DECISION

When I arrived at Dr. Seward's office, I saw immediately that I had missed his office hours for the week. I knocked at his door anyhow, but of course there was no answer. What to do? As I stood in a sweat of failure and rejection, the door at the far end of the hall opened and in strode Dr. Seward. Of all improbabilities.

Which is as often the way of fact as fiction. Dr. Seward not only materialized at that unlikely moment, he invited me into his office for an unhurried and courteous discussion about why I had missed the statistics exam and, more particularly, why I wanted a Ph.D. I don't remember what I said, but I do remember—and was amazed to discover it—that I was desperate to continue with that dreadful education. There was something in psychology, or in what could be learned about the mind, that I could not define but knew was connected to the Search. At the end of the interview, Dr. Seward rose, saying, "I will reverse my decision."

A reprieve—and one more chance to prove George Seacat wrong ... and to learn something of value?

ANOTHER FAILURE

Every student in our class was required to take certain Core Courses (Statistics, History of Psychology, Learning) and the most crucial of these Core Courses was #206, which required each of us to design and execute an original experiment in an area of our particular interest. This performance, inescapably, would show the faculty whether the student was skilled in the research methodology so vital to psychology.

It was interesting to see the variety of studies planned by my classmates, ranging from rat behavior and nonsense syllables, of course, to the newer pastures of dream research (a study facilitated by the recent discovery of Rapid Eye Movements, REM, which indicate when a sleeping subject is dreaming). Other research projects involved implanted electrodes. (Dr. Olds had electrified psychologists by demonstrating that stimulation of just one neuron in a rat's brain—the "pleasure center"—would cause him to press a bar incessantly, until he dropped dead from exhaustion.) And as for me, what could I devise of especial interest to me?

Why, LSD, of course. I still wanted to know what were those deep centers of the mind that LSD laid bare.

Back then, in 1960, LSD was almost unknown on campus, and it was not difficult to design a study to "examine changes in visual perception through the administration of a psychotomimetic drug." (I had learned that fringe studies could sometimes be approved if the psychological jargon was slick and thick enough.) Each student's design had to be approved each step of the way by the faculty, whose duty it was to stress again and again the need for *controls* in laboratory research. As a result, of course, the thinking of the student doing the controlled experiment was effectively controlled—a form of academic brain washing. In any event, the faculty at last gave approval to my experimental design, in which each subject would be asked to draw a picture around an inkblot *before* taking the LSD, and then, two hours *after* the LSD had been ingested, at the presumed height of the experience, he would be asked to draw another picture around another, identical inkblot. In this design each subject acted as his own Control, meaning that each subject performed the same task before (Control) and after (Experimental) the independent variable (LSD) was introduced.

It would be out of the question to repeat my experiment today, for now all studies using human beings must be approved by the university's Human Use Committee, even for a simple paper-and-pencil test. What chance a mind-blowing hallucinogen? But in 1960 there was no problem at all giving drugs to people, provided that the subjects were willing and that the administration of the

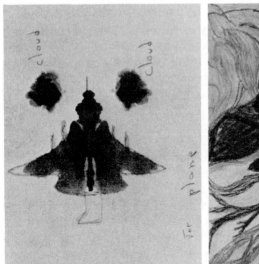

Fig. 2-1. *(Left)* Before taking LSD, this lady said she "couldn't draw a straight line." *(Right)* During LSD experience and for weeks afterward, she continued to draw and draw and draw.

drug was supervised by a medical doctor. I was lucky to have as my sponsor Dr. Oscar Janiger, a pioneer in LSD research, who offered for the study not only his offices but his LSD. Think of it—legal, free, pure LSD, and there were almost no takers! At the start I was browbeating fellow students; toward the end I was beating them away from those little blue pills.

The results of the study were wondrous, almost every subject revealing deeper creativity, deeper insights during the drug state (Fig. 2-1).

Equally wondrous were the reactions of the faculty. In spite of the committee's initial approval of the experimental design, now there was nothing but criticism. One professor insisted that I should have had a placebo administered to a Control Group. How, I asked, could a fake pill be given for a drug that causes hallucinations? No one could answer, and I was sent from one member of the faculty to another, only to find that they not only disagreed with my experimental procedure, but with each other. Though it was never stated overtly, I believe the unorthodox nature of this research (creativity through *drugs*?!) made it taboo.

Once more a decision to flunk me was made and reversed—on the proviso that I repeat the Core Course in experimental design the next year. But in spite of that LSD fiasco, the drug continued to be a major influence in my graduate school career.

ANOTHER COUNTRY HEARD FROM

Over the next several graduate years (there were to be six in all), LSD grew into a prime campus phenomenon, bringing the hippies and their counter-culture of acid rock, light shows, instant gurus, and ashrams. But much of this was still below threshold during my second year, when my book on LSD therapy (based on my Freudian-interpreted experiences with the Beverly Hills doctors) was published, reviewed, and ignored by the therapeutic community.

Around that time, I noticed a bulletin-board announcement that a psychiatrist from Czechoslovakia was to speak on LSD in psychotherapy at a veteran's hospital. None of the students in the psychology department was interested, so I went alone. In a small lecture room, sprinkled with a bored, captive audience who seemed not to have heard of the drug, I sat spellbound as Dr. Stanislav Grof described his technique of therapy, which was so much like my own had been. Freudian therapy, in Czechoslovakia? Where it was impossible to buy a book by or about Freud, where Freud was never taught in schools and Pavlovian conditioning was the only accredited psychology?

Immediately after his lecture, and before I could reach him, Dr. Grof was whisked away. I vowed to discuss his research with him, even if it meant a trip to Czechoslovakia. As it happened, it did.

FIRST PRAGUE JOURNEY

That summer, during school recess, I made a pilgrimage to Prague to learn how the Czechs were exploring deeper levels of the mind through LSD. I was careful, beforehand, to write Dr. Grof of my existence, of my book, and of my arrival date. Unfortunately I could not tell him of the hotel at which I would be staying, since that information was withheld until my arrival in Prague. (This was a not-unfamiliar experience with Intourist, that indomitable Soviet travel agency.) Dr. Grof had not replied to my letter when I left, but I expected, naively, that there might be a message from him in Prague. I was met, at the very gates of the chic Prague airport, by the Intourist guide, who had no messages and apparently no knowledge of Dr. Grof. In fact, she seemed to have little knowledge of English, or her job, which she had just begun. And she looked particularly uncomfortable when our limousine stopped at the hotel—the worst of my experience.

I entered the side-street hotel through a cracked glass door, which revealed a dark and narrow lobby. Behind the brown-black, grimy wooden counter was a hunchbacked dwarf, who served as both registrar and bellman. No English spoken. The Intourist guide registered me over my protests, which she did not seem to hear, and at my shouted insistence inquired if there were any messages. There were not, and she left. The dwarf escorted me up five flights of stairs, carrying my luggage, because the elevator was out of order. The room I had been assigned, without bath, was so narrow it could admit only one person at a time. Smell of musty linen, grit of poorly washed floors, limpness of once-white organdy at the windows. One bare and dim electric light bulb hung from the ceiling. And on the only table, an old telephone with separate ear piece on a hook. But there was no one to call, not even room service.

I had allotted three days and nights to this Prague visit, hoping it would be enough time. I sat the first day away in that room, afraid to leave it in case Dr. Grof called. But when the evening dragged its way through the window, I went down to the dining room, its eight tables empty save for three men, at one far table, drinking beer. The waiter, who spoke no English, brought a menu, printed in Czech. I ordered beer by pointing to the glasses at the occupied table. But since no one there was eating, I couldn't point to food. I shrugged at the waiter, who shrugged at me, wrote something on his pad, and left.

As I waited, a family—father, mother, son about seven and daughter about five—came in and sat at the table next to mine. There developed a quiet, serious discussion between the father and waiter about the menu, as the children looked on solemnly. At length a choice was made, the waiter left, and the father looked relieved. The family sat, speaking little and in muted tones. I guessed these were farm people, on a rare visit to the city (family problems? health?).

To my surprise, my food arrived on the same tray with theirs, and the waiter served me first. I felt my stomach constrict at the sight of the greasy gray meat, partly hidden by greasy gray gravy, and overcooked vegetables without color (cabbage? potatoes? turnips?). As I wrestled with the nausea, I looked over at the Czech family. They were being served the same food I had, but the children's eyes were wide with wonder as the platters were placed before them. This was Oliver Twist being served all the "more" he had ever asked for.

I ate my bread, giving thanks for the lesson, then climbed the five flights to my room in a healthier mind, deciding to read the night away by the light of the 40-watt bulb. It was well past nine o'clock when the silence was shattered by the bell of the ancient telephone, which not only could ring; it could reproduce the sound of a voice, speaking English. It was Dr. Grof, who had phoned every hotel for tourists and had nearly given up.

We met that night in the dismal lobby, now made brilliant by the appearance of two handsome young psychiatrists, Dr. Stanislav and his brother, Paul. Both escorted me around Prague, to a night-club, then to a university beer hall, and then through the streets of the exquisite city. All the while we eagerly discussed our mutual infatuation, LSD, which was now being manufactured by the Czech government (and of excellent quality, they assured me).

The three allotted days were not nearly time enough to learn about Grof's research. He was head of Prague's Neuropsychiatric Institute, where LSD was the favored therapy for the severely neurotic and even psychotic. We visited the Czech NPI, and Dr. Grof showed me some drawings done under the influence of the drug. These were explicitly Freudian in content, and I asked how he had arrived at this Freudian Gestalt. He replied it had occurred in his own LSD experiences, and had been repeated in his psychoanalysis.

"Your *analysis?*" I was startled.

"In Czechoslovakia," he replied seriously, "there is one psy-choanalyst. But he must be very quiet and do his work discreetly. I was fortunate that he treated me."

Dr. Grof went on to say that he had gone beyond the classical Freudian regression of genital, anal, and oral stages and was exploring Rank's theory of the birth trauma and intra-uterine expe-riences. It was this that prompted me to ask if he had come upon any psychic experiences with the drug. But he had not. In essence, the trip had been intriguing, but the Search was still on.

(A few years later, Dr. Grof immigrated to the United States, where he published extensively about his LSD research and, later, about the more mysterious aspects of the human condition.)

LSD AMONG THE ALCOHOLICS

I returned to school where, in spite of my failed LSD study, I was invited to participate in a large research project. Funded by the Na-tional Institute of Mental Health, the project was to investigate the possible use of LSD as a therapy for, of all things, alcoholism.

The study was to be conducted at an honor camp, in the moun-tains outside San Diego. This meant that for more than a year, a group of psychiatrists, psychologists, social workers, and one graduate student were to spend a twelve-hour work day, on Satur-days, for no fee. We did it for the sake of science, for the sake of publications, or (probably for most of us) for both those sakes.

Much energy and large sums of money were spent on that project, out of which emerged one sorry finding: that LSD, as it had been administered, was less therapeutic than the "active placebo" we had used.

"Active placebo" is a paradoxical term, since by definition a placebo is an inert substance. But since, that year, placebos were in, we were faced with an almost insoluble problem: what kind of placebo could be given for a drug that caused hallucinations? There was also a problem of ethics: how much harm might be caused by giving a placebo to a chronic alcoholic who deeply wants to be cured and has been hyped that a new, mind-blowing drug might do it for him? We decided on a drug with an effect somewhat like LSD. This, our active placebo, was methylphenidate, a form of speed—which blew *our* minds.

Because it came to pass that, in our entire eighteen-month study, our *only* cure came from a man who had been given the active placebo. He never knew that, of course, and he spent months (if not years) proselytizing at honor camps around the state about the miracles of LSD. His placebo-induced cure centered on his regressing back to the age of six months and finding himself held aloft for inspection in a hospital amphitheater because of his odd genitalia. After this classically Freudian revelation, he went off booze and stayed off. Last we heard of him, two years later, he was still campaigning for the drug he had never taken.

Eventually this long and difficult research project yielded two tedious research papers, both published in obscure, prestige journals, with long titles and an even longer list of authors, mine among them. This was a feather not only for me, but for the psychology department, who could claim a published student.

Although I had done considerable writing on those papers, I saw them as full of pomp and statistics, signifying very little. As for impact on the scientific community, there was none at all. This was commonplace, even expected, I learned. The big job was to get the papers published. And that included having the paper typed according to rigid specifications, then sent to the editor, who assigned it to three expert consultants, who weighed the paper's merits and demerits and voted on whether it was worthy of publication. This process, which can take months and even years, is called "refereeing" a paper. If the article is accepted, then the author must pay for the privilege of having it published. This is not because the journals are greedy, but because they are starving for lack of readers. I vividly remember a colleague's lament: "We spend our lives gathering data for studies that may be published in journals that nobody reads."

FRUITS OF THE STUDY:
FIRST INTERNATIONAL CONFERENCE

One of those slim papers with the heavy title "Dimensions of the LSD, Methylphenidate, and Chlordiazepoxide Experiences" sent me to my first International Congress of Psychotherapy. I was chosen to present the paper solely because I had private money to pay for the trip. So off I went to Wiesbaden, no expenses paid. That was a heady week, mingling with scientists whose publications in the fields of psychotherapy, Jungian analysis, LSD, and behavioral modification were required reading in graduate school. And Wiesbaden is a delightful German resort, boasting casinos, spas, and a stunning conference center containing long tiers of tables equipped with microphones and earphones for simultaneous translation into three or more languages. It was obvious that most earphones were plugged into the English channel, the English language having ousted French as the international tongue. At the tables sat hundreds upon hundreds of behavioral scientists from thirty-odd countries, all committed to the study of mental health. Some were old hands, very selective about which papers they heard and which wines they drank. Some were young seekers after truth, glued all day to the earphones and all night to bottles of beer at an outdoor cafe.

My particular interest was, of course, LSD in psychotherapy, and the best research in that area was presented—not to my surprise—by the Czechoslovakian delegation, which was headed not by Dr. Grof (who was no longer in Prague), but by the current commissar of the LSD now manufactured in Prague. The Czech drug was reputed to be of superb quality. This was of considerable interest because of the increased, illegal production in the United States of adulterated, sometimes deadly brews and tabs called LSD. I mentioned this to one of the Czechs, who offered me some of his country's product for a modest price. The Czech's cut-rate offer was a transparent ploy; he wanted American dollars, and I wanted samples of the pure drug. But we also genuinely hoped that this exchange might enhance our knowledge.

I learned much from the Czech doctors, not the least of which was their use of art in therapy. They brought with them an exhibition of paintings done by their patients under the influence of LSD—the first "psychedelic art" formally presented, and somehow reminiscent of my early inkblot studies in that fiasco of a Core Course in experimental design.

The Czechs and I spent our last day in Wiesbaden boating on the filthy Rhine River, drinking delicious Rhine wine. As the commissar mellowed with the wine, he told me with wonder of his experience with a suicidal patient who was being led through an LSD session. Suddenly the patient sat up, panicked, for he was seeing his fiancée at that very moment in her apartment, swallowing a lethal dose of poison. He became so violent in his alarm that steps were taken to locate the lady, without success. The doctor, feeling a little foolish, took the patient in his own car to the fiancée's apartment —just in time to have her stomach pumped of the poison she had swallowed.

ESP with LSD. Here another clue had surfaced, just when the Search seemed almost buried under graduate school's hard labor. Would it ever be possible to conduct controlled experiments with the drug, to learn whether LSD truly facilitated ESP? Or, much more to the point, would ESP ever be an accepted research area in the restricted fields of psychology?

3
Graduate School —
The ESP Side

More on Scientific Methodology and Ideology... Or, in Words of One Syllable, More on the Rules of the Game

ESP APPEARS ON CAMPUS

Never, in any graduate class, was psychical research mentioned. Once, in an undergraduate statistics course, a professor referred to parapsychology's "improper use of statistics" which was interwoven with a joke about "reading someone's mind," a feat more properly left to magicians. It gradually became clear that the official (if unstated) credo was that parapsychology was not a proper subject for scientific or psychological study and was therefore taboo. Somehow, the science of this Modern Age and the religion of the Middle Ages seemed very much like each other, with their autocracies and their lists of heresies.

Once, in 1963, I attended a seminar on taboo topics in psychology, where parapsychology was listed, but passed over, in favor of two other heretical subjects: homosexuality and suicide. (In '63 these were taboo! In '73 they were old hats, overexploited by the mental health professionals and the media alike.) That same year brought an unusual request from university Extension: would the psychology department sponsor a program on ESP at Royce Hall, the largest auditorium on campus? The psychology department would *not* and further commented that with ESP as the topic, Extension would be lucky to get one hundred people into Royce Hall. For whatever reason, Extension persisted, found a sponsor, and the debate, "ESP: Fact or Fantasy?" was announced. The distinguished cast included on the Fact side the past president of both the American Psychological Association (orthodox) and the Parapsychology Association (unorthodox), Dr. Gardner Murphy—who, over a long and eloquent career, had managed to champion psychical research without doing damage to his reputation as a dean of American psychology. The Fantasy team included UCLA's eminent Learning psychologist, Dr. John Seward, the very man who had saved me from being flunked out of school.

Naturally, I was eager to attend but did not think it necessary to arrive early. I was wrong. Royce Hall's 3,000 seats were filled, and standees thronged the isles. This was unprecedented: psychical research had never before aroused either academic or popular interest on campus. There was an air of surprised excitement in the auditorium, which turned into something of a whirlwind when Dr. Seward announced, in his opening statement, that he was changing sides from Fantasy to Fact. With not a little embarrassment he explained that, in spite of vehement protests that he knew nothing whatsoever about parapsychology, he had drawn the short straw for the program. Once committed, Dr. Seward had taken refuge in the research library, thinking that an evening in the stacks would give him the necessary ammunition. That evening turned into many, during which time he fed on so much fine data that he could no longer "in all conscience" uphold the negative position. I listened with pride in my professor as he gave meticulous précis of well-designed studies, complete with journal references, just as he had done in our Learning course.

On the Fact side, Gardner Murphy—in keeping with his high-button shoes and blue serge suit—spoke with almost nineteenth-century eloquence, somehow derived from a few scribbles on scraps of paper. Dr. Murphy was not only literary, he was inspiring, and at the end of his talk there was a tumult of applause—which he stopped by stepping in front of the proscenium and, hand upraised, peering angrily into the audience:

"There's always applause! There's always enthusiasm! But are any of you going to do research in this field? (Silence) Well, are you?! How about it?"

I heard myself shouting, "I am! I will!"

It's the only time I can remember being carried away to a spontaneous public avowal. Which I kept.

A PILOT STUDY

The next year ('64), still propelled along the Ph.D. path, I was sent to Wadsworth Veteran's Hospital in West Los Angeles for field training. I was required now, not only to do research in a hospital setting, but also to work with clinical patients, both under strenuous supervision. At Wadsworth, research emphasis was on human emotion as seen through an elegant polygraph that could record eight different body functions simultaneously, among them the electrical activities of the skin (GSR), the brain (EEG), the heart (EKG), and the muscles (EMG).

One day my supervisor, Allen, showed me a typical polygraph recording of the eight body functions from one subject. This started with a baseline taken when the subject was lying down, relaxed, after which the subject was startled by a loud and unexpected noise (the word "Noise" was written over a blip on the chart). Immediately, the neat red squiggles of the baseline, on all recorded functions, went berserk.

"There," said Allen with a pleased Irish grin, "is the inner man!"

I laughed, and was charmed. I was also reminded of a research article by the Czech psychologist Figar (did the Czechs have a corner on unorthodox science?). Figar had used just one polygraph measure—to record blood flow, via the plethysmograph. In his study, Figar had charted a mother's blood flow while, at the same time, her son's blood flow was being recorded in another room. Unknown to the mother, the son was given, at random times, a difficult mathematical problem to solve—a task which causes stress and constricts blood flow. These constrictions were clearly seen on the son's chart, a routine finding. But not at all routine was the fact that the mother's blood flow showed the same kind of constrictions as her son's—and *at the same random times*. The findings suggested, if nothing else, that emotions (as blood flow) had been transferred somehow over a distance from son to mother.

On first reading this study, I was struck by the similarity between this laboratory experiment and the many anecdotes in psychic literature where ESP arrives when the Transmitter is undergoing stress (like the son) and the Receiver is relaxed (like the mother). A typical account describes a husband injured in a bad automobile accident, which the wife sees in her mind's eye as she dozes in front of the TV.

My mind began to smoke at the idea of conducting an experiment like Figar's with Allen's polygraph—and burst into happy flames when I saw, for the first time, the lab's prize possession: an isolation booth. This glorious device had originally been designed for sensory deprivation studies. A subject, put inside the booth with both thick doors shut, could be kept in complete darkness, almost complete silence, and deprived of just about every stimulus —so deprived that within two or three days he might begin to experience visual and/or auditory hallucinations. The popularity of sensory deprivation studies gradually yielded to LSD studies (a quicker, easier way to hallucinations) conducted by Wadsworth's chief, Dr. Sidney Cohen. Along the way, Allen had found it fairly simple to hitch a subject to a polygraph inside the booth, where his body functions could be recorded under rigorously controlled conditions (temperature, humidity, air flow, etc.).

The isolation booth was ideal for Figar's experiment. So, when Allen asked if I had a particular research project in mind, I showed him Figar's study. Allen read it carefully, frowned, and asked me to construct a design that would replicate, and improve on, Figar's work. This was encouragement of a sort. I pondered slowly, thinking back to Benson's meticulous tutoring in experimental design. When I felt prepared, I went to Allen with several suggestions.

First off, I knew Figar would be roundly criticized by American psychologists for having only one pair (mother and son) in his study, for it is *de rigueur* in American science to use *many* subjects, divided into Experimental and Control Groups. I suggested that the Experimental Group be made up of pairs of people with strong emotional ties (like mother and son, twins, etc.) and the Control Group with pairs of people who had never seen each other before. Allen nodded, "Go on."

I went on to suggest that instead of just the plethysmograph, we take advantage of the polygraph and look at several measures, perhaps respiration, heart rate, GSR. Allen nodded again, though I noticed that the lab technician, Walt, looked stricken, for he would have the complicated problem of hooking up eight leads from two different rooms to one chart recorder, in pairs, one above the other. (Walt did it, and became a major source of strength over the next several years.)

Still expanding on Figar, who had used only the one emotion of stress, I suggested three more emotional stimuli: *Sex*, which would be slides of nudes combined with hot jazz; *Fun*, slides of Disneyland, with Judy Garland singing "Over the Rainbow"; and *Fear*, slides of poisonous snakes, climaxed by a loud and unexpected scream of terror. Allen was now beginning to take notes, a good sign. So I suggested one more source of data—which was that the stressed subjects (or Transmitters, as they came to be called) be asked to record on tape their reactions to each of the four emotional episodes—which might confirm or deny whether they were really feeling stress, sex, fear, or fun. (In contrast to the squiggles of the chart recorder, the taped responses would be *subjective*, at that time a novelty in psychological studies.) While the Transmitters were experiencing their emotional episodes, the Receivers in the other room would be lying down, relaxed, and tape recording free associations of what they thought might be happening in the booth—where, of course, the Transmitters were totally isolated.

Allen frowned. "Why? What d-d-do you want that d-data for?" Allen sometimes stuttered. "You're not gonna look for ESP...?"

I nodded. Allen was silent. But at length, he agreed. After all, this was to be a complex study, requiring knowledge of electrophysiology, controls, double-blind techniques, measurements, and statistical techniques—all considered essential in the education of a graduate student in psychology. Since this was primarily a learning process, Allen decided he could tolerate the ESP aspects, which proved to be something that he and the staff could poke fun at. Walt, in particular, enjoyed calling me "crazy Thelma" behind my back, and even to my face, which I rather enjoyed.

Statistical Analysis

During this research project Allen made sure that I would learn about double-blind techniques by using a devastating ploy. When at last I brought him all the raw data, the masses of red-lined chart paper that contained all the physiological information, Allen immediately requested that I take a ruler and measure off two-inch strips of the chart paper for all four physiological measures and all pairs of subjects. Then he asked me to number each one of the strips, starting with 1 and ending with 396. Then he picked up a pair of scissors, gave me a pair, and together we cut into individual squares each of the 396 pieces of chart paper—a process akin, to me, to the murder of a child. Finally, Allen put all those squares of paper into an empty wastepaper basket.

"Now, to initiate you into the mysteries of the r-r-randomization process."

I sat, almost frozen, as Allen lifted the wastepaper basket high in the air, turned it upside down, and dumped the scraps of data on the floor. Then he tossed them with his feet, again and again into the air.

"Se-see? It's simple," he chuckled. "Now you put them back in the basket and start measuring each pair of responses, in m-m-millimeters, to look for similarities."

Hour after hour, week after week, I measured those damn squares of paper, never knowing of course which were the Control Group or the Experimental Group, which the base lines, and which the stress or emotional situations; this is the nature of the "blind" technique. Not that it made much difference in this experiment, because the simple fact was, I could *not* find any similarities: *none* of the pairs of people in my study—closely related or perfect strangers—had responded like Figar's mother and son. Dead end of a long and difficult study. The lab staff were friendly with their jokes about getting published in the mythical *Journal of Negative Findings*. And Allen was pleasant about how hard I had worked and how much I had learned. But I was anything but content.

I could see one last, small straw to reach for—those taped reactions of the Transmitters as they watched the episodes of Disneyland, etc., and the free associations of the Receivers. If I wanted the tedious task of transcribing the tapes, I could find out if there was any similarity between what the Transmitter had felt and what the Receiver had given as free associations. I transcribed.

And I found, astonishingly, a few triumphant ESP responses from the Receivers which even the most entrenched skeptics in the lab could not deny. As an instance, while the Transmitter watched the Disneyland episode (slides of the Matterhorn, cable cars, the Mad Tea Party, etc.), one Receiver had said, "So many things. The Swiss Alps, especially the Matterhorn. And those little cable cars. And ice cream cones. And little boys. But mostly the Matterhorn." Another Receiver, also to Disneyland, "[Laughs] You won't believe this, but I'm seeing myself in a great big tea cup . . . going round and round, so fast . . . [Laughs]. That's all." And as the Transmitter struggled to find the answers to mathematical problems, one Receiver said, "I see a blackboard with someone writing on it . . . in chalk . . . just writing a lot of numbers."

I was convinced this was an indication of ESP, which is presumed to be a form of *thought* energy. Allen was impressed enough to suggest looking for that basic requirement, a statistic. With my unerring talent for misunderstanding statistics, I expressed pessimism, for though there had been a few splendid "hits," they were all too rare to give the statistical significance of a 20-to-1 shot. Besides, I didn't know how to get a number, or measure, out of those verbal responses.

Allen chuckled. "It's t-t-time you learned." He stuttered more when he was pleased.

During that Wadsworth Hospital internship, Allen taught me much, often against my will. But on this occasion I was willing, and he taught me about judges to whom—one at a time, independently of each other—I would give all the free associations (randomized, of course) together with the Transmitter's responses to the episodes (similarly randomized), and ask the judge to match the response to the episode. After eight judges completed their matchings and the statistic was computed with the appropriate equations, we achieved p < .01—a 100-to-1 shot! According to the current scientific canons, we had demonstrated the existence of ESP. Oh, but I was exuberant! And oh, but there was consternation at the V.A. lab!

Shortly there came the pronouncement that the pilot study should be replicated—another canon of rigorous research. It is vital to repeat and repeat and repeat an experiment, and to achieve similar statistical results every time. And of course, the more replications by other researchers in other laboratories, the more meaningful the findings. At last, when many replications have yielded similar results, the research can be taken out of the laboratory and used in a practical way in the world... at which point it is no longer basic research, but applied science.

REPLICATION WITH GINGER

For the replication, I was sent to Joseph A. Gengerelli, the highly respected experimental psychologist at UCLA who had tried in undergraduate courses to teach me statistics. Ginger (fond, apt nickname) was genuinely interested in my project and gave surprising advice:

"Stack the cards in your favor," was the way he put it. I must have looked my dismay.

"Dammit, we're not doing anything immoral or illegal! Just fattening." He chuckled as he unpeeled one of the candy bars I had brought him. Ginger was a scholar of the old world, out of place on the '60s UCLA campus with his silk cravats, his hearing aid, his meerschaum, and his uncharacteristic fondness for dime candy bars. He chewed carefully, feet up on his desk, looking out of one of the rare windows in the psychology building.

"Science is hard," he continued. "And it's proper to do everything you can to obtain the results you're looking for, because you probably won't get them, no matter what you do. If you're honest." He looked away from the window, directly into my eyes. "Are you honest?"

"I think so."

"You know if you're honest or not, dammit! Do you fudge data?"

"No."

He looked at me steadily as he wiped bits of chocolate from his fingers.

"Famous scientist, Lamarck. Ever heard of him?"

I had. He was the man who fought Darwin's idea of evolution through the survival of the fittest, Lamarck's idea being that animal traits made future shapes—i.e., giraffes evolved long necks because they were constantly reaching up to nibble leaves at the tops of trees.

"Lamarck had a disciple. Professor who worked with a certain species of fish. Premise was that after generations in a special environment, those fish would develop speckled backs. Something like that. Details not important." Ginger puffed on his pipe and I waited. There was, usually, one point in his stories that was important. "The professor got his speckled fish, just the way he expected he would. And he published. Refutation of Darwin, you see."

"Brilliant."

"Not the point! It turned out his research assistant had hand-painted the speckles on the fish. Because he didn't want to disappoint his beloved professor."

"Good lord!"

"Professor couldn't take it. Committed suicide. You can't cheat in science. Remember that. You can't cheat in science."

Ginger truly believed that, and so did I. (It wasn't until years later there came the scandals of cheating scientists—in cancer research as well as parapsychology.)

Ginger showed me how to stack the cards in my favor—without cheating—by purposely selecting the best psychics I could find to serve as subjects, instead of a "random sampling" of college sophomores shanghaied into the lab. And by contriving the best possible emotional episodes—which meant keeping Disneyland and the Sex from the pilot study, and discarding the Snake and the Math problems, which had not been too successful. And by inventing new emotional episodes and trying them on willing passersby to see if they were effective.

Ginger also imposed further controls. In addition to the Experimental Group (pairs of people strongly related to each other) and the Control Group (pairs who had never seen each other before), he asked for a second Control Group (no pairs at all, just the Receivers, without anyone transmitting to them). This last group would be asked to give free associations, believing there was a partner in the isolation booth. I protested that this was a dirty trick for the volunteers (as I had earlier protested about giving alcoholics a placebo), but Ginger had no patience with such ethics. This was science.

"Okay, forget ethics," I agreed. "But how can we get a statistic from someone giving free associations, without anyone to match them with?"

"Random number tables." Ginger stared at me dourly. He had taught me random number tables, but expected ignorance.

I took a deep breath. "The Receiver gives four different free associations, as if to the four episodes, 1,2,3,4. But no episodes have been shown. So, after he's finished, we go to a random number table and find a sequence, like 3,1,4,2. That will be arbitrarily the episodes in a sequence that *could* have been shown to him. And that's how his responses get matched."

Ginger grunted. "Not bad."

Random Number Tables

Books as huge as dictionaries have been published with nothing in them but numbers, columns and rows of numbers. These are random number tables. To find a random sequence, you just open the book at random—but you must be very very careful about being "random!" There are hundreds of ways to open a book "at random" and it is important to select the right random page, the right random number to start from, and the right way to read the numbers: across, or diagonally to the right, or diagonally to the left, or backwards or vertically...

The random number game is taken with deep seriousness in science. In fact, though it is hard to believe, major scientific journals have rejected articles because the method of selecting the random number tables was not considered "random" enough. The fact is, random numbers are at the core of the sophisticated puzzle-making that science currently approves. Ginger knew the randomizing game well and complimented Allen's double-blind maneuvers.

Eventually we worked out a neat and complex design, only to discover I would not be permitted to do it at Wadsworth, for the lab there did not want any further contamination with ESP research. This was the first outright rejection I had received from the establishment because of ESP. There were to be many, many more, but as is so often the case, the first time was the worst time.

Eventually, months later, I found laboratory space and began the study. And halfway along, I found a distinguished volunteer Transmitter.

Dr. Gardner Murphy, Experimental Subject

That year of '64, the American Psychological Association held its annual convention in Los Angeles, and Dr. Gardner Murphy was one of the invited speakers. He was also guest of honor at the local Psychical Research Society, where I met him for the first time and discussed with him my ESP study with "emotional episodes."

I am astounded, in retrospect, that I never thought to tell him that his plea to the audience at Royce Hall, years before, had been the inspiration for that ESP study.

Dr. Murphy seemed intrigued by the novelty of the "emotional episodes," for the typical ESP experiment has only *one* stimulus for each trial, usually an emotionless geometric shape (a star, cross, circle, or square).

In fact, Dr. Murphy was so intrigued that I found myself asking if he would like to participate in the study and, astonishingly, he said he would. I promised to fetch him at his hotel at nine o'clock the next morning, which meant that when I returned home, past midnight, I had to find Dr. Murphy a partner. It was several hours and many irate friends later when Sam Culbert, a fellow student, agreed to participate as Receiver. And it wasn't until the next morning, as I was randomly selecting the sequence of episodes, that I felt that surge in the stomach when something unforeseen and awful strikes into awareness—in this case, the realization that I was soon to show the dean of American psychologists some pornographic pictures. I swallowed hard, and proceeded with the experiment. When it was over, Dr. Murphy commented with a smile that it was an "interesting experiment"—and he never mentioned the nudes.

Fellow-student Sam Culbert proved a surprise, as Receiver, by providing (in spite of his skepticism) some of the best free associations of the entire study, my favorite being this short one, to the sex episode: "I seem to see a boat, rubbing against the side of a pier." At first this looked like a highly distorted and ambiguous representation of the sex act, but it was correctly matched by every one of the judges, all of whom (still stacking the cards in my favor) were clinical psychologists who would be apt to recognize such symbolic imagery. Years later, Sam invited me to lecture his students at the Graduate School of Business Administration, and with his permission I told them about that particular response. They burst into spontaneous laughter and applause. Perhaps it's not so distorted and ambiguous after all, that rubbing against the side of a pier?

UCLA SYMPOSIUM

The data for the replication study were still being matched by the judges when the startling news came that UCLA Extension was planning to offer a two-day symposium on ESP! This was in '65, two years after that immensely successful Royce Hall debate which, I believe, was a harbinger of the waves of interest—and commercial appeal—that were to flow from the psychedelic movement toward humanistic psychology and a more holistic medicine. It was a further surprise to learn that the chairman of the symposium was to be Dr. Sidney Cohen, head of psychiatry at Wadsworth and commissar of their LSD drug research. I was still an intern there and was working away in my office when Sidney appeared at the door:

"We need someone to present an original research paper at the

ESP symposium. Have you written up your nonsense yet?"

"No, but I could. In a week."

"No hurry. A week and a day is okay."

We smiled at each other. I had talked to Sidney perhaps a dozen times during the internship, and each encounter had been just as abrupt. I had never suspected that Sidney might be interested in the ESP research!

When the paper was written, I sent it to him through proper channels, and it was returned the same way, with a note:

"Well written. Should be well received."

Among Professional Parapsychologists

As it turned out, my paper was *incredibly* well received, not only by the 1,000 paid attendees—which meant a huge box office success for Extension—but also by that small, steadfast network of American parapsychologists, with whom I was to be in touch over the next decades. Ginger, serving as moderator, introduced that rarest of creatures, a parapsychologist who was also a full professor of psychology at a major university—and a woman! Gertrude Schmeidler was one of the true pioneers of the science. Also on the panel was a brash young man who talked openly and, I thought at the time, insanely, about people getting out of their bodies. This was Charles Tart, a newly minted Ph.D. who, within a few years, would add to the American language the initials OOB (out of the body) and ASC (altered states of consciousness). Presiding one full day was Gardner Murphy, vastly pleased that he had participated in my study, which proved to be the hit of the symposium.

In the audience was the distinguished psychoanalyst Dr. Jule Eisenbud, who had yet to do his remarkable research with psychic photography, and who told me how reminiscent my research was to the dream telepathy experiments done by psychiatrist Dr. Montague Ullman and psychologist Dr. Stanley Krippner at Maimonides Medical Center in New York City. This was research I had not yet heard about, but which would mean much in later collaborations. In the audience, too, was engineer/physicist Douglas Dean, dangling his plethysmograph with which, he told me to my delight and chagrin, he had successfully replicated Figar's study between mother and son—the very study I had failed with so wretchedly at Wadsworth!

Symposium Aftermath

Before the symposium I had been an unknown graduate student struggling toward a dissertation. After it, as a successful exponent of unorthodox science, I was suddenly a rather dangerous celebrity in academia. For the media had widely publicized the event, giving special emphasis to my original research paper. Almost overnight the "emotional telepathy study," as it came to be called, became widely known and quoted. To the dismay of the Psychology Department, for now I could ask that ESP be included in my dissertation, which classically is supposed to deal with original research. I did ask, and I was permitted a study on "non-verbal communication, subliminal perception, and ESP" under controlled laboratory conditions. This was the first time in thirty years, I was told by the founding father of parapsychology, Dr. J. B. Rhine, that "ESP" had appeared in the title of a doctoral dissertation in psychology.

Before the dissertation was completed and the doctorate secured, I was invited to present my study at the annual International Parapsychology Conference in New York City—where the paper was requested for publication in the dignified, if neglected, *Journal of the American Society for Psychical Research*. I was deeply pleased, of course, even though that journal lacked the prestige of orthodox scientific journals. The editor of the JASPR spent an entire afternoon with me reviewing the paper—and then decided not to accept it because the statistics were doubtful. The refusal was unexpected and not a little painful. Back at UCLA, with no knowledge of that episode, Ginger suggested sending the piece to that most prestigious of psychology journals, the *Journal of Abnormal Psychology*, where it was promptly published, with no requested revisions. I cherished the letter of acceptance from the editor, which read in part:

> "I tried my best to find fault with the method, or the statistics, but could not. And I have nothing but the deepest respect for the junior author. [That was Ginger!] Congratulations.

Not long afterwards, I received the Ph.D.

4
The Rules at the NPI

On Becoming a
Professional Psychologist in a
Neuropsychiatric Institute

T. MOSS, Ph.D.

A few months after becoming a doctor, I was offered a position at UCLA as a medical psychologist at the Neuropsychiatric Institute, which occupies a wing in the Center for the Health Sciences. The Center also houses the Brain Research Institute, the Medical School, the Eye Institute, the Institute for Nervous Diseases, and the School of Dentistry, all within one massive structure—reputed to be the second largest interior of any building in the United States, the Pentagon being the largest. On taking the job, I was assigned a windowless, unadorned cubicle with fluorescent lights overhead illuminating off-white walls, ceiling, and floor. At that time, when the building was new, it was forbidden to place a rug on the floor or pictures on the walls; but over the years that law was slowly bent out of shape and then smashed to sparkling bits by psychedelic posters, mod paintings, sunshine carpets, and wood panelling in ever more desperate attempts to hide those antiseptic walls.

Those walls! Not even the labyrinths of Mycenae could have been more intricate or misleading, and the commonest complaint—from staff members as well as all those patients who could not find their doctors—was the feeling of being a rat in a maze. At almost every intersecting corridor there was a prominently displayed map with the exclamation YOU ARE HERE! over a brilliant red circle, information which never never seemed to orient anyone.

This maze was to be my testing ground for the next six months, during which time the Department of Medical Psychology, which belonged to the Department of Psychiatry, and the Department of Psychiatry, which belonged to the Medical School, and the Medical School, which belonged to UCLA, and UCLA, which belonged to the state of California, which paid the salary—all were required to observe my work and decide whether I possessed the required skills for the job. If so, I would be guaranteed the job for the rest of my life. (Unlike death and taxes, that guarantee did not endure.) At the time of being hired, I inquired about laboratory space for research, which now seemed the direction the Search had taken, and I was told that lab space would be made available if I presented a satisfactory research proposal.

SEARCH FOR A LABORATORY

During the six-months' apprenticeship, I hunted for lab space, which simply did not exist. On each floor of the NPI, there could be found long corridors of closed doors on which hung signs, screaming DON'T ENTER: RADIOACTIVE! or KEEP OUT! or DON'T OPEN THE DOOR! MICE ON TEMPERATURE CONTROL! On one or another pretext I managed to gain entry into lab after lab, each unsuited to my purposes, until one day I came upon a small lab in which, occupying almost all of its space, stood a very large isolation booth. It was of khaki metal, forbidding in its dimensions, nicknamed the "frozen meat locker." As I stood staring at that glorious device, I knew I'd come home.

SQUATTER'S RIGHTS

Naturally, that lab was already being used by two psychologists— for EEG and EKG studies of schizophrenics, for drug studies, for implosion therapy, perceptual studies, etc., etc. Happily, none of those studies was done at night and, having been expertly trained in nightly infiltration of laboratories in the psychology department, it was almost routine for me to take down and replace equipment before and after each experimental session. It was not long, though, before I was discovered *in flagrante* and a hotbed of departmental meetings flared up to determine protocol.

In time it was decreed that the lab would be shared by all three of us medical psychologists. The one who carried the most clout (and tenure) was a full professor doing extensive research on the psychotic patients on his ward. This benign, hard-working scientist had a steady stream of schizophrenics entering the isolation booth during the day. The other, younger psychologist was an expert electrophysiologist, who used the polygraph to study the functions of schizophrenics and depressives. The committee decided that these two men were to divide the daylight hours between them and that I could use the lab in the evenings and on weekends. This was exactly how we had worked it before, except now it was official.

Our triple play was in effect for only a few months when the electrophysiologist suddenly decided to return to his native Iran, leaving the polygraph behind in the lab. Shortly afterwards, the full professor was offered a better job at another university and took it, bequeathing to the lab a beige armchair and a leatherette couch. There I was, with full squatter's rights to the lab with the frozen meat locker, the polygraph, the works.

BROTHER, CAN YOU PARADIGM?

Those six grueling graduate years had transformed me (or so I believed) into a respectable statistical psychologist. Thus, when my research began at the NPI, I followed respectfully the yellow brick paradigm of dependent and independent variables carefully selected, the null hypothesis precisely set, the raw data fastidiously gathered to be analyzed via *chi* square, binomial theorem, or analysis of variance.

Only very slowly did I see how very silly it all was.

There had been hints of absurdity before. In my first project with Allen at the V.A., I did a complex study of the "conditioning of involuntary responses"—a research area fresh out of the Soviet Union at that time which swiftly developed into our American "biofeedback." This new work seemed close to what parapsychology calls psychokinesis (PK), or the influence of mind on matter. One early, brilliant study by the American Neil Miller showed that rats could be trained to send more blood flowing to the right ear than the left, and vice versa. Naturally the rat isn't thinking, "Now more blood to the left," but he has been trained to respond to a signal so that his blood will flow in a specific way through his body—and blood flow had traditionally been considered a function over which we have no control.

It wasn't long before similar experiments were tried with people, and it was learned that they, too, like the rats, could be trained to direct the flow of blood. In one impressive study, Dr. Elmer Green of the Menninger Foundation showed that people could direct blood from their heads into their hands, increasing the temperature of their hands by many degrees. In the process, several people lost their migraine headaches—neat evidence for psychosomatic medicine that no drug is necessary for the relief of migraine.

It was a study in this genre that led me down the garden path to the absurd. I had come upon a Soviet experiment in involuntary conditioning, based on the well-known physiological fact that every time we inhale, our blood vessels constrict. In the study, a subject was hooked to a polygraph and told to inhale deeply each time the command "Inhale" was given, and with each inhalation, vasoconstriction appeared clearly on the chart recording. After many commands to "Inhale!" were given and recorded as constrictions, the subject was told *not* to inhale when the command was given. He did *not* obey the command to inhale—but each time the command was given, the constriction appeared, just as if he had inhaled. The Soviet scientist claimed conditioning to the word "Inhale."

This was unwarranted, I argued with Allen, since the subject (there was, typically of the Soviets at that time, only one subject in the study) might have been responding emotionally in the same way that a soldier would who, after obeying his commanding officer's orders time after time, is suddenly told *not* to obey. The soldier's blood vessels would surely constrict—but with emotional conflict, not conditioning.

To test my hypothesis, Allen had permitted a replication of the Soviet study, during which I spent weeks shouting to twenty different subjects, "Inhale!" (obeyed and not obeyed), along with selected Control commands. In the entire study, nineteen of the twenty subjects never showed any constriction *except* for the expected reflex when they inhaled at the command to "Inhale!" But with just one subject, every time I shouted, "Inhale!"—whether he obeyed or not—his blood flow showed the most precipitous constrictions I had ever seen. Apparently the lab technician had never seen anything like it either, because he stopped the polygraph to check it but found it was working perfectly. We recorded many more roller-coaster constrictions from the subject—who happened to be my son.

As a matter of absurd fact, my son's downward swoops of constriction were so huge that their measure, in millimeters, was large enough to give me my first 1,000-to-1 shot ($p < .001$). (At Allen's suggestion, the experiment was written up and submitted to a distinguished journal, under the heavy title, "Conditioning or Conflict? Effects upon Peripheral Vascular Constriction," published eighteen months later in *Psychosomatic Medicine* 26 (1964):267-273.)

Big strokes for the middle-aged lady intern. Which did not go unchallenged. For at a staff meeting, the laboratory technician commented that if my son had not been a subject, the data for the study would have been a dud.

"That's t-true," agreed Allen pleasantly. "But that's the nature of statistics. We are l-looking for the *average* response of a g-group of subjects."

"But it wasn't the average response!" the technician argued faultlessly. "Only one subject out of twenty responded that way. T.'s son!"

"R-right. T.'s son was one of the twenty subjects. We get an average by adding up all of the r-responses of all of the s-s-subjects, and divide by twenty, the number of subjects. There's n-no other way to compute an average."

The technician shook his head as if to clear it. "But that's not right! Dammit, it *wasn't* the average response, it was just the response of her son."

Allen nodded. "And his score is p-part of the average."

I did not enter the discussion, because I would have had to agree with the lab technician. The only person to show that response had been my son, and his response probably had nothing at all to do with conditioning but with his teen-age rebellion against authority. I might have seen that if my vision had not been clouded with desire for that imminent publication. I needed more lessons in objectivity. And I got them.

The Lessons in Psychological Testing

It came to pass that my chief duty at the NPI was "service"—which translates to mean incessant psychological testing of in- and out-patients. The assignment came as a shock, because in graduate school, we had had to take six courses in statistics but were permitted only two courses in psychological testing, with the professors intimating that this was a sorry task for the profession.

In fact, to show how false and unreliable (not to mention silly) these tests could be, the students were required to take them. I was especially appalled by the Minnesota Multiphasic Personality Inventory (called MMPI for short), consisting of 566 statements, each to be answered True or False, with no Maybe permitted. (This is called Force Choice, and can be infuriating to the person forced to make the choice.) For example, one statement read, "Washington was a better president than Lincoln." How answer that, with no data and no opinion? I arbitrarily checked False, and at our next class asked how that particular item was used to rate personality. We were told that there was no rationale for the 566 items, which had been put together almost randomly many years ago by psychologists who then tested them on many, many patients. Through constant shuffling and re-shuffling, the items were finally sorted into scales that measured, in numbers, traits like depression and schizophrenia, etc. (Not that the schizophrenic scale measures schizophrenia, nothing so simple; rather, it combines with other scales to arrive at various diagnoses.)

Certain psychological tests—I had learned during my internship—give as good an index of brain damage as neurological tests (which is not saying much). There is one seven-minute test, the Bender-Gestalt, which is downright brilliant for discovering, sometimes, why Johnny can't read. This test consists of simple figures, like a circle touching a diamond (◯◇). If a child who has not been able to read is asked to draw that figure, he may draw a perfect circle, but he will draw the diamond with equal skill *to the left, rather than the right*, of the circle (◇◯). He *sees* things reversed, and that defect causes reading problems which, once identified, can be corrected.

But in general, I agreed with the professors that psychological tests were one of the less reliable tools of clinical psychology.

Consequently, I was not at all prepared when my new boss told me with his clipped Canadian accent how important psychological test batteries were in my new job. "I should point ote—" Morris said earnestly, "that a full battery is required, projectives as well as paper-and-pencil."

"The MMPI, too?" I asked the question with a knowing smile.

An abrupt, single nod of the head. "Withote dote, one of the essential tests."

I choked on a laugh. Morris glanced at me sharply. "We have one of the best interpreters of the MMPI in the country. He gives a seminar, and I suggest you take it." Morris, with his gray hair, gray moustache, and gray suit was like a gruff, gray Father Bear. I took his suggestion.

And was very glad I did. For I learned that Alex Caldwell had indeed penetrated to the core of the MMPI. It was as if he *sniffed* the scores on the test to arrive at his diagnoses, which were uncannily accurate—and had little to do with the formulae he taught us. I had met with that kind of expertise once before, at Wadsworth Hospital, where psychologist Gertrude Baker could pinpoint, from the Rorschach test, in what area of the brain a tumor might be found. Neurosurgeons from all over the V.A. would bring her their difficult cases and would receive invaluable advice about where to cut into the brain.

It seems that psychological tests are as good as their interpreters—the best of whom make up their own rules. Eventually I learned to write up a good test battery, but nothing like Alex Caldwell or Gertrude Baker. Here was another lesson showing that statistics could only give us numbers, and that intuition transcends that wisdom by far.

Still Another Lesson: The Statistics of ESP

Backed up by the smashing success of the telepathy experiment, I plunged into variations on the theme of Transmitter being shown emotional episodes and Receiver giving free associations. Once, lacking lab space, I used my garage in a wondrously significant (p<.001) long-distance study from Los Angeles to New York to England, with three groups of Receivers gathered in each city. But a second long-distance telepathy study—L.A. to N.Y. to Edinburgh—was a statistical dud. And from then on, the statistics of the experiment played hide-and-seek with significance. Although in every single study there were always a very few excellent ESP responses, there were never enough to guarantee significance. And I learned that careless decisions by the judges could tilt the wheel from significance (p<.05, publishable) to non-significance (p<.06, non-publishable). In discussing this phenomenon with colleagues, I learned that many psychological studies are prone to this statistical pitfall, so that for any one study, various statistical models may be called into service with the idea that if one statistic doesn't work, another may. (As someone remarked, there are lies, and damn lies, and statistics.)

Eventually we racked up almost as many non-significant results as significant. But the statistics notwithstanding, in every one of our sixteen studies there were some startlingly accurate ESP impressions. It became obvious that statistics could do nothing to enhance or explain the phenomenon, which remained elusive. And the Search seemed to have reached a dead end, at least in terms of laboratory studies.

Some of the best ESP came outside the experimental controls. Right after one session, when the tape recorder was still on, the Transmitter happened to say, "Funny. After I finished sending, I suddenly saw a tremendous burst of fireworks in my head—I don't know why, the fireworks didn't have anything to do with what I was sending." The Receiver, five floors below, had taped at exactly that time, "Just after the time was up, I saw in my head a burst of colored fireworks—but they didn't seem to have anything to do with anything." Here were two people, in a telepathy experiment, having exactly the same image at the same time. But since the image was not one that was being used in the study, the event could not be counted as data. ESP outside the rules of the game was no ESP at all.

And Still Another Lesson in the Absurd

Three years at the NPI had brought a routine of testing, teaching, and research, to which had been added a series of parapsychology conferences more and more global. The most alluring of these had been in Le Piol, a gem of a village on the French Mediterranean, to which had come the most distinguished parapsychologists of the Western world—as well as hard-nosed scientists like former UCLA professor of physiology Dr. Donald Lindsley and the celebrated Dr. W. Gray Walter whose research into the brain and EEG had been required reading in graduate school.

That particular conference, in 1968, gave for perhaps the first time serious scientific consideration to LSD, meditation, and altered states of consciousness as aids to para-normal powers. From then on, there began to appear in our Western labs yogis from the East to show that they could alter their EEG patterns at will, as well as their skin temperatures or heart beats—exactly what the new discipline of biofeedback was exploring! Somehow ESP, LSD, meditation, and biofeedback all were coming together for the scientific community as well as for the general public—the latter liking very much the approval of science.

At UCLA, university Extension was at the forefront of this *zeitgeist*, having learned back in '62 that parapsychology was profitable. So it did not come as a big surprise when Extension asked me to teach a course in parapsychology, which had been approved by the American Medical Association—and for credit! But I was astonished to learn that, four weeks before the first class, the 420-seat auditorium had been fully booked—with the opening night finding a near-riot at the doors as hundreds of jostlers, checkbooks in hand, clamored to get in. This was perhaps the beginning of the moneyed public's headlong rush into encounter groups, marathons, psychic fairs, acupuncture, holistic medicine, and the rest. These were the courses that attracted the public that paid the money that kept Extension in business.

But the course in parapsychology had to be organized and a syllabus invented for approval by academia. Which meant I had to do considerable study in the formal aspects of teaching parapsychology. I was shocked by what I discovered. The fields which most interested me—meditation, transcendental experiences, mysticism, and the whole range of *bioenergy* experienced—were not within the scope of parapsychology as defined back in the 1930s, at

Duke University, by Dr. J.B. Rhine, the pioneer of parapsychology as a laboratory science. Dr. Rhine had limited the field to these four: telepathy, clairvoyance, precognition, and PK (psychokinesis, the movement of objects via the mind). Each of these had been put through the statistical loops and double-blind hoops of controlled experiments, with cards and dice as the preferred tools in the experiments.

I had resisted the use of ESP cards up until this course, but now they seemed appropriate, not only to discuss Rhine's pioneering research in academia, but also as classroom experiments, for students no longer liked to be lectured at; they liked to participate and experience for themselves.

I demonstrated an experiment in telepathy to the class by asking them to write down a series of guesses about which of five symbols (circle, square, cross, waves, star) was being transmitted by someone in another room, who was given one card at a time from a deck of twenty-five cards, thoroughly shuffled before the experiment begins. In twenty minutes it is easy to transmit four decks of cards, or 100 trials. Then another 100 trials for clairvoyance (no one looks at the cards, which are shuffled and remain untouched until all guesses have been made), and another 100 in precognition (the cards are not even shuffled until all the guesses are recorded and collected; this task requires guessing what the order of the cards *will be* —hence, going into future time). This comes to a sum of 300 trials from 400 students, or 120,000 trials. Repeat the trials with the following year's class, making 240,000 trials, and you have a splendid number for a statistician to feed a computer. The larger the number of trials, the smaller the score need be to show statistical significance. When the results came back from the computer, we were faced with this shocker: the students had scored so far *below* pure chance that the statistical significance was more than a trillion to one (p < .000000000001).

(Scoring *below* chance can be a real effect. For example, if you *always* lose at roulette, someone betting *opposite* to your bets will *always* win. So there is something other than chance operating. This "something other" has been called by parapsychologists "psi missing"—the opposite of psi, which is doing significantly *better* than chance. Psi missing means doing significantly *worse* than chance.)

But what did that mean, in terms of these experiments? Simply, that instead of scoring 5 hits out of every 25 guesses (which is what a monkey would get, randomly putting the 25 cards in 5 different boxes), the students had scored 4.8 hits out of the 25 cards. By averaging that small bit less than chance, the odds became a trillion-to-one shot. I remembered what Benson had said about the easiness of getting a 1,000-to-1 shot. And I remembered he had said that statistics were *bubkas*. An absurdity.

The Rules of the Game

I had at last learned that following this yellow brick paradigm had not led me either to insight or knowledge. Again, the search for something beyond time and space seemed to end in a blind alley of controls, double blinds, randomization, and replication—none of which seemed ever to reach the heart, the *sniff* of the matter.

5
Breaking Loose

Around the World in Search of Psi, with Special Emphasis on Explorations in the Soviet Bloc Countries

THE APPEARANCE OF SOVIET PSI

Just when I was feeling most churlish about the statistical straitjackets of academic parapsychology, there was published a book, in 1970, called *Psychic Discoveries Behind the Iron Curtain*, which galvanized me out of those research ruts. The authors, Sheila Ostrander and Lynn Schroeder, had gone to an International Parapsychology Conference in Moscow and had found—or so they had written—that the Soviet Union, that most materialistic of countries, was deep into the mysteries of such ephemeral realms as biocommunication and psychotronics (their words for ESP and PK). Professional parapsychologists deplored this book as "sensationalistic" and "fictionalized," for they could not accept reports of such phenomena as the "skin vision" of Rosa K. (who was supposed to "see" colors, and the printed word, with the tips of her fingers); or the "psychotronic generators" of Pavlita in Czechoslovakia (who claimed that he could energize those generators to do work through the bioenergy emitted from his fingers); or the telepathy under hypnosis (claimed to be put on television by Czech psychologist Dr. Zdenek Rejdak).

More captivating by far, though, than any of these accounts were the reports and photographs of a new "electrical photography," named after its Soviet inventor, Semyon Kirlian. The photographs showed what were called "energy fields" around plants and people, and even a "phantom" of part of a leaf that had been cut away before the picture was taken. As I stared at, and studied, those Kirlian images, I grew somehow more and more certain that here was something, somehow, connected with the Search. Perhaps those photographs were making visible those invisible forces or energies which carry thoughts and travel deep into awareness...?

The more I studied those pictures, the more I began to entertain an idea, almost too daring to consider...until I finally sat down and wrote two letters. The first was to Professor I.M. Kogan, of the Moscow Society for Radio, Electronics, and Biocommunication (read this last as "telepathy"). Just the year before I had invited Kogan to present a paper on his research into "the informational aspect of telepathy" at an ESP symposium at UCLA. He had accepted, sending his paper immediately for translation. Which was lucky, because when he did *not* arrive it was possible to read his paper, in English, *in absentia*. (Kogan's research, I noticed, was discussed accurately in *Psychic Discoveries Behind the Iron Curtain;* so I was not willing to dismiss the book as "fictionalized.")

Now I wrote Kogan another letter, this time asking if it were possible for me to meet with him in Moscow to discuss his research. My second letter was to a Professor Inyushin (of whom I had never heard until this book) asking if I might visit him in Alma-Ata to discuss his research with energy fields and Kirlian photography.

Having been alerted to the vagaries of Soviet scientists (like Kogan's "no show"), I did not expect replies; but replies came, promptly, from both. Kogan in Moscow suggested a two-week period in November, and Inyushin, in Alma-Ata, cordially invited me to visit him and explore his research, some of which he sent under separate cover. It was clear, from his monographs, that he was doing studies on the energy fields that surround plants and people, using that mysterious Kirlian photography as his major tool. This was fuel for the flight.

And more fuel arrived with an invitation to present a paper on meditation at the First World Congress on Yoga in New Delhi, scheduled for December. Suddenly, after all those years of statistical dead ends and double-blind alleys, there was a sense of being led back to the Search, which seemed now to be pointing toward energy fields and altered states, with emphasis on meditation. (Meditation, I was beginning to learn, is perhaps the core around which all these mysteries revolve.)

But to go around the world, a leave of absence from my NPI duties was needed, and such a leave could be granted only by the chairman of the department, the newly appointed Dr. Louis Jolyon West.

Jolly

Jolly, as he liked to be called, was a formidable, hippo-like executive whom I seldom saw. Once it happened that just the two of us were standing, waiting for elevators to take us in opposite directions (symbolic, if you like). Jolly seemed less massive than I remembered and I ventured that he had lost weight.

"Weighed myself this morning." He smiled ruefully. "I weigh one pound less than an eighth of a ton." So saying, he disappeared into his elevator. Characteristically, it took me some time before I translated that information into a number: 249 pounds of chairman.

Jolly was gargantuan in many ways: ambitions, research interests, grantsmanship. (He acquired more large grants than anyone else at the NPI—with graphs on his walls to show it.) When Jolly was first being considered for the NPI chair, he gave a masterful lecture to the staff, featuring his research with American Indian runners whose 200-mile marathons had been monitored with his portable electrophysiological equipment; his research at the South Pole where sensory deprivation studies had been undertaken; and his research with LSD—he was notorious for having killed an elephant with an overdose of the drug, and he dared to show a slide of himself staring down in disbelief at the carcass of the defunct beast. Even that feat was overshadowed by slides of his specially designed computer, programmed to give sundry mechanical psychotherapies from B Mod to crisis intervention. Someone in the audience asked if the computer had been programmed for psychoanalysis and Jolly answered, "Of course. For psychoanalysis, we pull the plug."

This received the loudest laugh, for psychoanalysts are famous for saying little or nothing to their patients.

When Dr. West joined the NPI he was careful to study each of our resumes (called *curricula vitae* in academia) and to discuss them in individual interviews. I remember having a fantasy that in my interview he would first be incredulous, then curious, then sympathetic to the parapsychological publications that were proliferating. Instead, he looked directly at me and said, "There's no such thing as ESP."

Before I could think of an answer (though no question had been asked) he continued, "You probably know Monty Ullman." I blinked and nodded. (I had just made tentative plans to meet Monty and his wife in Czechoslovakia, for he, too, was planning a pilgrimage for parapsychology.) Dr. West went on:

"Monty's a close friend of mine and a fine psychiatrist. I've always told him that parapsychology was a waste of his valuable time."

I mumbled something.

"Let me say this to you, Thelma. I believe with all my heart that you're wasting your time." He paused. His voice was kind and his eyes looked steadily into mine. "I do not for one moment believe in what you're doing. *But...* I will defend to the death your right to do it."

"Thank you," I said, and smiled at the Voltaire reference. Inwardly I was not in the least sure he'd defend anything, for he was reputed to be a first-class manipulator. But in the years that followed, Dr. West defended and defended, keeping me on the faculty when others tried to get me off. (My research in psi was a constant embarrassment to the staff at the NPI.)

Leave of Absence

I was able to make an appointment with Jolly re the leave of absence, and arrived on time, but Jolly was, typically, very late. And, typically, he offered coffee as soon as he arrived. Which, for an avid coffee drinker, is the best of apologies. We smiled at each other as we sipped the hot brown/black stuff, and I told him about the invitation to the Yoga conference.

"Congratulations."

"Thank you."

"We can't fund your trip, of course. Meditation is interesting, but not yet a research area in psychiatry." (This was 1970.)

I nodded. It had never occurred to me to ask that the trip be funded. "I'd like to stop in Russia, en route. And Czechoslovakia, and Bulgaria. There's research in those countries in parapsychology, or psychotronics as they call it. I've already made tentative appointments with some of their scientists."

"It should be interesting for you. You know my feelings."

"Yes." We smiled and sipped. Could it be so simple? Was he granting me leave? "I expect the trip will take four or five weeks." No response. "Is that okay?"

Jolly nodded and looked at his watch. "Anything else?"

"Just thanks, very much."

He repeated again that he did not believe in what I was doing, but that he would defend to the death my right to do it. Right there and then he had defended it to the extent of granting an around-the-world leave of absence.

Learning Some Russian Rules

Before my departure, it was my rare fortune to meet the authors of *Psychic Discoveries*, who gave me vital telephone numbers and addresses, like that of Czech psychologist Dr. Zdenek Rejdak, in Prague, who knew how to contact the major scientists in Czechoslovakia, and of Edward Naumov, who could do the same in Moscow. Sheila and Lynn also suggested tactics against red tape, which helped to make intolerable situations almost tolerable. A clear demonstration of the rules in this game appeared on my very first stop, which was Prague.

PRAGUE REVISITED

Back in 1965 I had an Intourist welcome, which now in 1970 was repeated, in that I was met promptly at the airport by the Intourist guide and driven in a black limousine to the hotel, the name of which had again been withheld from me. But, unlike that first Prague hotel with broken elevator and broken glass window, this 1970 hotel was a palace, with royal blue carpets and myriad bells to ring for instant valet, chambermaid, and concierge.

Once I was registered, however, the Intourist guide, with steely charm, insisted that Dr. Montague Ullman was not at the hotel where he had asked me to phone him. Nor would the guide phone the hotel to inquire for him. So as soon as she left, I phoned the hotel myself—only to be told by that hotel operator that Dr. Montague Ullman was not registered. Half an hour later, Czech parapsychologist Dr. Zdenek Rejdak rang me in my hotel (how had *he* known which hotel? I hadn't known it myself) and arranged a meeting that afternoon with Monty and himself—in Monty's room at the very hotel where Monty had asked me to call him.

Dr. Rejdak's Regime

Dr. Rejdak proved as knowledgeable and cooperative as Sheila and Lynn had said he would be. Just a few months before, he had organized an International Conference on Psychotronics in Prague and was able to arrange a screening for us of some special events from that conference. These included, just as Sheila and Lynn had written in their book, a television program, shown throughout Czechoslovakia, in which an army psychiatrist hypnotizes a subject who, in trance, was able to identify by the taste in his mouth a substance eaten by the hypnotist in another room. I had read of such "telepathic taste" studies by Sir Oliver Lodge in England, performed more than a hundred years ago, but to see it in a modern TV film was a rare excitement. Equally enthralled was Monty Ullman, himself an expert hypnotist, who had never attempted the study. (In later years, I was to try it many, many times—unsuccessfully.) Another Czech film showed the research of Robert Pavlita and his "psychotronic generators," which precipitated dirt from water and generated enough energy to propel a windmill—all without electricity or other known energies! Just as Sheila and Lynn had reported it. But was Pavlita's work genuine?

In psychical research, that is a question almost unanswerable, for fraud is common, and just about every paranormal phenomenon can be faked by a good magician.

But Monty and I had come in search of any and every clue. So, at dinner in Dr. Rejdak's home (which had an extensive library of psychical research, in many, many languages) we asked for more immediate evidence of Pavlita's generators.

Pavlita, the Inventor

Rejdak was eager to oblige, but money was a problem in arranging the necessary motor trip to Pavlita's home. We then had our first lesson in bending some Czech rules when a bootleg visit, via hired car, was contrived with the use of American bank checks. We drove six hours in incessant rain on narrow muddy roads, with one stop at an inn for a meal of bread and sausage and excellent Czech beer, to arrive at last in the village where we were warmly welcomed by the Pavlitas in their apartment.

Both Pavlita and his daughter worked with various generators, which Pavlita insisted were powered by human energy fields. Once "powered" (through what seemed to be magnetic passes from Pavlita's temple to the generator), the instrument performed its particular functions, such as running a toy windmill. Monty and I were particularly impressed by one generator which seemed able to magnetize wooden matchsticks so strongly that both Monty and I were able to pick up with the matchsticks an assortment of objects —bits of wood, paper, paper clips, etc.—all clinging together in a bizarre necklace through some mysterious power of attraction. What caused that magnetic force? We wanted to know, but Pavlita answered with a shrug. We were to learn again and again that scientists in various disciplines were finding phenomena for which they had no explanation. Monty and I were reminded of the definition of parapsychology in the Soviet Encyclopedia:

> What is referred to as parapsychology should be subdivided into two areas. One is phenomena that realistically exist but have yet to be scientifically explained. The other is fakery advertised as supernatural occurrences by mystics and charlatans; these people need to be exposed and discredited.

In the next day's cold autumn light, Monty and I discussed what we had seen, focussing on the chief question: could we believe the phenomena? We agreed the major obstacle to belief was the fact that Pavlita would disappear into a back room, emerging with a new generator to demonstrate. We were not permitted to go with him. What went on in the back room? We had to consider that what we had seen could be a legitimate phenomenon—or a magic trick. As so often happens, we could not be sure, in this instance, where the truth lay.

The Ullmans and I parted in Prague, planning to meet again in Sofia, Bulgaria, to investigate Dr. Lozanov's Institute of Suggestology and Parapsychology.

SOFIA

Once again, with prompt efficiency, the Intourist guide met me with a black limousine at the airport to take me to my hotel. And once more, with that steely charm, the guide told me that there was no Institute of Suggestology and Parapsychology in Sofia; nor was there a street in Sofia with the name given me by Sheila and Lynn, on which they said the Institute could be found. As soon as the guide left, I took a short walk from the hotel, following the directions Sheila and Lynn had thoughtfully provided. And within ten minutes, just as promised, I arrived at the street, and the Institute, which looked exactly as it had been described in the book.

I entered the building, introduced myself, and learned from associates that Dr. Lozanov had received my letter but was in Moscow—and *might* be returning the next day. Feeling not a little frustrated, I left the Institute and went on foot to the hotel where the Ullmans were staying. This time I was not alarmed when told by the clerk that the Ullmans were neither registered nor expected, and simply sat down in the lobby to wait. Within the hour Monty and Janet came strolling in, as pleased to see me as I them. It can be lonely for American tourists on their own in a Soviet country.

The next morning, a welcome call with the news that Dr. Lozanov had arrived and would meet with Monty and me that afternoon. Dr. Lozanov proved to be a small, alert, peppery man who took pleasure in feeding us excellent Bulgarian chocolates along with copies of his many research papers, in Bulgarian and Russian. Of more immediate interest than his articles was his invitation to observe an all-day class in Suggestology which, he explained (as had Sheila and Lynn), was the learning of a foreign language through selective *in*attention. In other words, the students are directed to listen to music and *not* to pay attention to the Russian lesson which was being given along with the music. This principle of learning with the unconscious mind was working marvelously well according to the students with whom we talked.

Unfortunately, that same day Janet Ullman developed a seriously infected tooth, which forced the Ullmans' early departure. After Sofia, I was on my own.

MOSCOW IN NOVEMBER

Not too much snow, and not too cold, but all the same it was into a white city that the Intourist guide brought me, in that same black limousine, to the Intourist Hotel, just one block from Red Square. I was given an elegant room, high in the tower, overlooking the street where I could watch the October Day celebration of their revolution (which happened in November). This was an endlessly long parade which included floats from every Soviet republic, and interballistic missiles which rolled into Red Square, starting at 6 A.M., ending late that night.

The hotel boasted several luxuries, including a Brazilian coffee bar (coffee was more popular, it seemed, than tea in Russia, wherever I went), which also served fruit juices, like mango and cherry and apricot, but never orange or pineapple; the mango was superb. And even more exotic than the stained-glass nude in the nightclub was the handsome green telephone in my bedroom—which was also a mockery. For there are no telephone books to be had in Russia, and no information service. I ransacked my luggage for that formal letter of invitation from Professor Kogan...

Yes! There it was, the telephone number, under the heading of "Society of Radio, Electronics, and Biocommunication." I dialed the number, was greeted by a Russian-speaking lady, and was transferred from one person to the next until at last I heard a woman's voice in English:

"Dr. Moss?"

"Yes!"

"I have for you a message. Dr. Kogan asks me to tell you that he is out of city and will not return until you leave."

Choleric, I was, not to mention disheartened, for I was now 12,000 miles into limbo. All the same, my fury may have accomplished something, for two days later I was contacted again by that same woman with a consolation prize: a meeting had been arranged with a distinguished Soviet Academician (the highest scientific rank in Russia). I was taken for that meeting in a very long black limousine, which drove from the hotel around the block—about a quarter-mile—to the Society, where I was escorted into a large, oak-paneled conference room. The Academician, and two interpreters, rose and bowed and offered me a seat. I was asked many, many questions about parapsychology, which I answered to the best of my knowledge. None of *my* questions, however, was answered even vaguely. At the end of this one-way screening, the Academician, who was of the old world, courtly and courteous, kissed my hand and commended my courage on this lonely journey into the unknown. Which did little to relieve my anger, bafflement, and frustration.

Skin Vision

Happily, the telephone number provided by Sheila and Lynn for Soviet parapsychologist Edward Naumov in Moscow proved correct, and through Naumov, I saw much I would otherwise not have seen. He took me to the Russian film described in *Psychic Discoveries*, which was a remarkable demonstration of "dermo-optical perception," or the ability to sense colors and even printed words through the tips of the fingers. Several women were shown as they held their fingertips *above* a metal container, and then identified correctly the color of the paper concealed within. This was, of course, impressive, but even more so was Naumov's offer to arrange a private, informal demonstration of skin vision.

At the demonstration, I was handed cardboard cards on which had been printed letters of the Russian alphabet, which I was asked to decipher with the tips of my fingers, eyes closed. I could feel only the smooth cardboard surface. Then a volunteer was blindfolded (blindfolds can be easily penetrated and are therefore not a satisfactory control) and, by touching the surface of the cards lightly, she deciphered the letters easily.

Was she really seeing with her fingertips—or was this a magic trick, with blindfolds? (I did not learn the answer until two years later when a totally blind volunteer, Mary Wimberley, came to the lab and learned to discriminate letters in exactly the same way.)

Victor Adamenko, Biophysicist

It was Naumov who arranged a meeting with Dr. Victor Adamenko, a prominent biophysicist, in a Moscow restaurant. And only much later did Naumov explain why I was never to see the inside of anyone's home, or laboratory, the entire visit in the Soviet Union: according to the Russian rules, no one is permitted to be host to a foreigner unless he has a visitor's permit, and no one I met in Russia had a visitor's permit. Therefore, all meetings were in my hotel room, or in restaurants, or in theaters.

So it was in a restaurant I met Adamenko, the young scientist who had already done so much research in Kirlian photography. In fact, he had just completed his master's thesis, which included the history of electrical photography. This news—of his thesis—had stunning impact, since it was being strenuously argued in America that there was no such thing as Kirlian (or any other kind of electrical) photography. Adamenko assured me he had worked with Kirlian photography for a very long time, since he had lived next door to the Kirlians as a child and sometimes helped in their research.

He himself, Adamenko said quietly, had been the very first to photograph the "phantom leaf"—an effect which Kirlian adamantly refused to believe for a long time! Adamenko felt strongly that this electrical technique revealed energy fields around both living and non-living matter.

With a sly grin, Adamenko went on to tell me that the *Journal of Biological Photography*, which is published in the United States, had printed an article on electrical photography in 1939, an article he had found in the Moscow public library—an article that had escaped everyone in the United States who was arguing whether Kirlian photography did or did not exist!

Before I left Moscow, Adamenko gave me a copy of that article, in which the authors claimed to be photographing an unknown radiation. I asked if he believed this was true, and he gave a two-edged answer; as a physicist, he was inclined to believe that the authors had photographed the "cold emission of electrons," but as a parapsychologist, he felt that another kind of radiation was present, perhaps a bioenergy, about which little is known. When I asked if he could explain further, Adamenko drew from his pocket his "tobiscope," a pencil-shaped instrument with a small bulb at one end which lit up whenever it touched an acupuncture point (which, at that time, I did not believe existed). Adamenko illustrated neatly on my arm, moving the instrument along the skin where, at odd moments, the bulb would light up. He explained that the light went on because of a difference in electrical flow at those points on the skin. This was no proof, of course, that the bulb was being lit by acupuncture points. It was equally plausible, without further proof (taking the point of view of the Compleat Skeptic), that a tiny switch was being manipulated to light the bulb when desired. The only way to be sure was to have a tobiscope of one's own with which to experiment. I asked for schematics to build one for myself, but Adamenko skirted the issue. (I was to learn, from repeated experience, that there never was available, or delivered, the schematics, designs, or instruments of Soviet inventors.)

An Unexpected Side Trip

Naumov and his colleagues suggested a day's flight to Leningrad, where it could be arranged for me to meet with Russia's most famous psychic, Mme. Kulagina—in my hotel room, of course. To help with the travel plans in Leningrad, Naumov offered to have a Soviet friend join me on the plane, but it was necessary for me to arrange the flight myself. Through Intourist, of course.

So I presented myself at the Intourist Agency in the hotel, where I was interrogated about why I wished to make this unscheduled trip to Leningrad. Eventually I was sent to Intourist Headquarters, where the journey was officially approved. As the beautiful Intourist agent handed me the plane ticket, she asked casually,

"Are you flying alone?"

"Yes."

She gave me a dazzling smile. "We know you are not, but it is all right."

For once, an Intourist agent had tipped her mitt.

Leningrad

It was in the Victorian, velvet-draped elegance of Leningrad's Astoria Hotel that I met the world-famous Mme. Kulagina, her engineer husband, and Mme. Vasiliev, sister of the late pioneer Soviet parapsychologist Dr. Leonid Vasiliev. There had been many experiments done at Leningrad University with Kulagina, first by Professor Vasiliev, and now by Professor Sergeev. And under controlled laboratory conditions, Kulagina had been able to move objects by making passes over them, or sometimes just by staring at them. She had no idea how she achieved the effect, but Sergeev had found drastic changes in her EEG while the objects were moving. On another occasion, she had been able to start the heartbeats in a dead frog. Kulagina affirmed that such demonstrations were exhausting and sometimes made her physically ill. Since I knew she had given a demonstration for Monty Ullman just two weeks before, and since I had seen several of her experiments on film, I did not ask for a demonstration.

Actually, I was more interested in the anecdotes of Mme. Vasiliev, apparently a gifted psychic in her own right. It seems, in times of crisis, she could find for her absent-minded brother a crucial missing passport, or a jeweled tie pin. This she could do, she said, by somehow willing herself into a trance, in which her mind was silenced, thus allowing her body and hands to be guided to the lost objects. Since I had read exactly similar accounts in the annals of the American Society for Psychical Research (and was later to see them in the lab), this was convincing data—at least as convincing as a demonstration of PK from Kulagina would have been, for without the critical presence of a professional magician, I could easily be duped.

ON TO ALMA-ATA

From Moscow, the next scheduled stop was to see Inyushin in Alma-Ata, at Kirov University—if I could get there, that is. Kazakhstan was a ten-hour flight from Moscow, where the weather had turned winter-awful. There was a twenty-four-hour delay at the airport, twelve hours of which were spent in the Intourist lounge with two professors of geology from the University of Pisa who were trapped on their way to the University of Novosibirsk, in northern Siberia. They invited me to join them in vodka, which cheered us considerably. So much so, in fact, that when we were given a reprieve from the Intourist lounge to dine at the airport restaurant, they declined. I went alone, almost at midnight, and was seated in the crowded restaurant at a table already occupied by a blonde young man in pilot's uniform who was slightly intoxicated and sociable. He told me it was his birthday, and I ordered champagne. As we drank, he confided that as soon as the weather cleared he would be flying his passengers to Alma-Ata! When he learned I was en route there, he told me with excitement that Alma-Ata was his home and that his mother was a prominent psychiatrist and head of the mental hospital there, where she earned a thousand rubles a month. As the dinner wore on, the more intoxicated he became, and the more baffled was I. *He* was going to fly the plane? He assured me he was, and we would be leaving at 3:30 A.M.

After some very good blinis (the only ones I ever found in Russia; I *never* got black bread), I went back to the Intourist lounge, where eventually the professors and I were informed that planes would not be flying until the morning and we would be driven to the airport hotel for the balance of the night. We had seen the hotel, brick and neon, handsome on the outside. Once through the doors, it was a case of picking our way over sleeping bodies to the elevators, where the Italian professors were escorted in one direction by a man, and I in another direction by a lady, who unlocked a door, tossed a sheet, pillow case, and towel on one of the two unmade beds in the room, and left.

The room was small, steamy and damp from a hissing bare radiator that looked out of control. There was a bathroom, floors wet from dripping rusty toilet and sink, no door. I made one of the beds and crawled into it, staring at the snow fluttering down outside the window in the neon-lit night. I wondered, once again, why I was where I was. Suddenly the hotel door was keyed open, to admit a large, stocky woman who said *zdrastvutye* as she stripped off her clothes, then made the other bed, lay down and snored,

snored loudly, snored steadily until without warning in the black of the stormy night she stopped snoring, got up and toileted and dressed, said *do svidanye* and left.

Shortly after dawn filtered through the filthy sky, I was summoned back to the Intourist lounge with the Italian professors. They were told their flight was cancelled, but I was told mine was to leave from another airport where I was taken, by bus, with a full load of passengers ranging from splendidly groomed colonels in the Soviet army to peasant women with shawls over their heads and live or dead chickens in cages or bags. Each of us got a seat on the very full plane, and a hot meal was dished up out of cauldrons. It was far tastier fare than the plastic-packaged airplane meals at home.

We landed at Alma-Ata at four in the morning, and as I stepped into the crisp cold, I was met promptly and efficiently by the ubiquitous Intourist guide, ready with limousine to drive through the well-paved, wide streets, past Alma-Ata's prestigious new hotel, which I was told was "only for Russians." We stopped at a more modest building where I was given an attractive room which was unheated, for the pipes had burst just the day before. I asked if I could be taken to a heated hotel and was told by the Intourist guide that this was the room I had been assigned.

The next morning, with hosannas to Sheila and Lynn for the gift of Inyushin's telephone number, I made almost immediate contact with the professor, who arranged to meet me at my hotel that evening at six. But by seven, there was no Inyushin and no word from him. Not knowing what to do, I wandered into the hall and to the keeper-of-the-keys, an omnipresent lady who sits regally at a large desk on every floor of every hotel in all of Russian hostelry. This particular keeper-of-the-keys in Alma-Ata had neglected to tell me that Victor Inyushin had been sitting for more than an hour in the hall, waiting to be announced.

Somehow in the gloom of the corridor his eyes reached mine and without a word, ignoring the keeper-of-the-keys, he rose, together with his wife and colleague, and the four of us strode to my room, where we closed the door. Almost immediately we were interrupted by an Intourist guide who offered to serve as interpreter, which offer was casually refused by Inyushin. We were alone! Almost the first thing I asked was about Soviet pilots, and I learned that no Soviet pilot is permitted to drink alcohol before a flight, that no psychiatrist in the Soviet Union earns anything near a thousand rubles a month, and that no mental hospital in Alma-Ata was headed by a woman psychiatrist. Had I been taken for a champagne ride by a Soviet psychopath dressed in pilot's clothing? I may never know. Adding another *je ne sais quoi* to the journey.

In the course of that rich evening, Inyushin invited me to visit his laboratory, lecture to his students, dine at his home, and go to the National Theater with him (I was a rarity, he said with a smile; the last previous American to visit the university had been the celebrated American painter Rockwell Kent, some ten years before). But each and every invitation proved as mythic as the tales of the Soviet aviator, for when Inyushin called the next morning, it was with the news that permission had not arrived from Moscow for him to take me to his lab or, as it turned out, even on to the campus. Over the next days we met in automobiles, restaurants, and my hotel room for more and more information exchange.

Inyushin told me that their current research dealt with Kirlian photography as it related to acupuncture and psychic healing. At that time both of these were, for me, on the lunatic fringe: acupuncture was an ancient Chinese superstition, and psychic healing was something shown on Sunday-night TV. (Within the year, I was to be deeply researching both of these fringe areas— with an ever-increasing sense of awe.) To help with my understanding, Inyushin gave me many gifts of articles (in Russian) on parapsychology, Kirlian photography, and "bioplasma"—which was Inyushin's word for an organized or patterned energy field around living (and non-living) objects. To illustrate his ideas of bioplasma, he also presented me—rare gifts!—with many photographs and slides of the Kirlian effect. These were even more beautiful and mysterious than the photographs I had seen in *Psychic Discoveries*—and here were the people who had taken the pictures!

I bombarded Inyushin and his colleagues with questions about what was being revealed in the Kirlian images: what were the bubbles, the coronas, the pearls? They laughed and shrugged and said, basically, that they would very much like to know. But, Inyushin believed, the coronas demonstrated aspects of the bioplasma which surrounds our solid, physical bodies, for such energy fields are the matrix within which our physical bodies grow. This concept is an exceedingly old and esoteric one—but it is also in keeping with the contemporary research of the American scientist Dr. Robert Becker, who, after amputating a rat's leg and placing the stump in a weak electrical field, was able to grow a new leg on the rat!

Remarkably, Inyushin knew of Becker's research. (How had he learned about it? Few people in the United States knew of it.) Here, I was elated to discover, in far far-away Kazakhstan were people as knowledgeable and avant-garde about the mysteries of mind as anyone I had met. We chattered in a hybrid of Russian and English, halfway through the nights, each and every night. For Inyushin's colleagues were young, younger even than his twenty-nine years, and churning with excitement about telepathy, precognition, and out-of-body experiences. And they wanted every scrap of information I could give them about our laboratory research.

In exchange, Inyushin told of his father, an engineer who had spent years working in India, where he had become a disciple of yoga, which Inyushin also practiced, as did several of his colleagues. It was clear that here, in southern Siberia, the principles of altered states of consciousness and meditation were being discovered by these young scientists under the rubric of exploration into bioenergy. In much the same way, I had been discovering these principles, one by one, in my own Search.

It was with much regret that I left these fellow-travelers in Alma-Ata.

TO INDIA, VIA TASHKENT

Intourist offered two exits from the Soviet Union: one by returning to Moscow, the other by flying to Pakistan, via Tashkent. The choice was easy; what more romantic name than Tashkent? And romantic it was, with its sultry desert wind, tropical fruits, incredibly varied population of two million people living in a city completely rebuilt after a devastating earthquake.

The Intourist guide at the airport was, for the first time, a young man, red-headed, talkative, and curious about the United States and me. He asked almost as soon as we met what race I belonged to, and when I answered, "Caucasian," he dismissed that as meaningless. I replied that to my knowledge there were only 4 races, to which he responded rather pompously, "In Tashkent alone, we have more than thirty races, among them Mongolian, Arabian, African, Chinese. I, personally," he continued, patiently, "I am of the Jewish race."

"In the United States," I replied, "we see it differently. We do not speak of a Jewish race, but of a Jewish religion."

"Oh." He smiled, amused. "Yes, the United States government is very concerned with religion."

"Our government's primary concern is not religion, but religious freedom." I was getting irked.

"Oh, yes?" He looked even more amused. "Then why on your dollar bill—you have with you a dollar bill?" I took one from my wallet. "There, you see?" He pointed to the words on the dollar bill. "On your currency—*In God We Trust.*"

Somehow I felt inadequate to answer.

Bombay

It was a shock, departing from the computerized airport of Tashkent and arriving at the open field and barn that was the Bombay landing strip. I was now en route to the Yoga Conference in New Delhi to deliver my paper on meditation, allowing for a two-day visit to Bombay, the first Indian city I was to see. It was a dreadful sight, beginning as soon as we descended from the plane. Beggars were immediately clawing at us, screeching, overriding the officials who tried to hold them back. (I had not seen a single beggar from one end of the Soviet Union to the other.) Then, driving by bus into the city, on either side of the unpaved road, acres of "houses" without roofs, windows, doors, plumbing. Open sewage like running sores. This road, we were told, was the only introduction to Bombay for its international visitors.

While still on the bus, we learned of a total civil airlines strike, which meant no way to the Yoga Conference in New Delhi, and no way to a holy man in Kashmir whom I had hoped to visit. Instead, entreaties and bribes to a network of travel agents for passage home, out of India. And much, much waiting.

I did most of my waiting, smack on the Indian Ocean, in a masterpiece of a Colonial hotel, filled with incredibly carved wood staircases, ceilings, railings, some of which there-and-then were being dismantled to make way for century 21. The lobby was a bedlam of electric drills, construction workers, plaster, concrete. Yet the many bars and restaurants continued to offer meat and alcohol and even male prostitutes for their clientele, many of whom were wealthy Indians. For them, there were prominent signs hung daily from the doorknobs of the guest rooms, warning that the untouchables were inside, cleaning the bathrooms, so that they could stay away and not be contaminated.

And just outside this munificence, this decadence, lay the beggars-in-waiting. Some of these had been deliberately mutilated at birth—a broken arm, a hacked-off leg, a twisted spine. It was not uncommon to see a woman thrusting her maimed baby at a guest coming out of the hotel's swinging doors. It was said to be a poor idea to give money, because then the beggars would come from everywhere with outstretched arms, shouting what sounded like curses. On one feckless walk I dared to take, under a roofed arcade, deformed creatures on the sidewalk and in hand-made carts wheeled and maneuvered around me, preventing my exit, laughing their derision at my alarm. No violence. Just an amusement, dispersed as quickly as it had formed, leaving me shaking with nausea and guilt.

This was the India that greeted me. The same India where so

many had sought, and some had found, holy men to guide them toward a spiritual path. I had hoped for something akin to that, but found only this unholiness.

Still waiting for passage out of India, I sat like a prisoner in the exquisite comfort of the palatial hotel, with its twenty-four-hour room service, staring out of the window where, just a few feet away, another skyscraper hotel had begun to form. Its foundations laid, now the concrete for the first floors was being poured—not by machines, but by people, each carrying on his head a large bowl filled with concrete, step by step up steep ladders to a flat expanse, where they tilted their heads forward, sending the wet concrete pouring from the bowls into the concrete puddle beneath them. Mass production, Indian style, done with grace, heads erect, bowls balanced, dignified. These workers were happy, I was told, for the work and wages, rare in India.

And as I watched, day by day, I became more and more despondent. There had been such hope at the start of this journey, to learn about energy, mind, spirit. . . .

HOME AGAIN, BROKE AGAIN

Around the world in forty days, and what had I learned? Nothing, it seemed. The main thrust—to learn about energy fields through Kirlian photography—had been a major failure. There had never, ever been any kind of demonstration, not even a glimpse of a Kirlian device. The only dim salvation lay in the pile of scientific literature I had been given, almost all of which was in Russian. Here was another dilemma, since translations into English from Russian, especially scientific Russian, are crazily expensive, and I was fairly free of money after the trip, with no possibility of funding from the NPI or anywhere else. So the Russian articles remained unopened for months.

Then, out of nowhere, there walked into my office a young UCLA professor of Slavic languages (specialty, scientific Russian) who at the suggestion of a mutual friend was presenting himself as a near-penniless candidate for psychotherapy. We contrived a superb barter: psychotherapy sessions for English translations. This was an arrangement that lasted for many months, to the satisfaction of us both.

The first articles rendered readable helped not at all, for they were technical tracts in physics, electronics, and biology, almost as undecipherable in English as they had been in Russian. The later articles were more interesting, but offered little practical information about parapsychology or Kirlian photography, although there were a few schematic diagrams and instructions for the building of a Kirlian apparatus which were incomprehensible to me. I sought help from the experts who—almost to a man—laughed. It was impossible, they said, to construct anything from those schematics. One kind friend, a physicist from an eminent think tank, took the trouble to explain that, even were there enough information to build the device, the electronic components described were manufactured only in the Soviet Union.

Other experts in engineering and physics commented with some bitterness that the Russians were known for not giving enough information to duplicate their research. And then there were the direful ones, the electrical engineers, who shook their heads, "God help you! Use voltage like that, and you'll fry. That's as lethal as the electric chair!" Others voiced the suspicion that the Soviets had perpetrated a practical joke and that probably there was no such thing as Kirlian photography. This cry of *fake!* was loudest from professional photographers, who explained patiently that every Kirlian effect, from bubbles to corona, could be created with their magic of "halation," "reticulation," and assorted arcane film chemistries. Once more, the assumption so prevalent among skeptics, that if something can be faked, it cannot be a genuine phenomenon.

Gradually, the Kirlian project ground to a dead end, where it languished for months.

6
Kirlian Beginnings

Being a Tale of Fortuitous Trial and Error, All the Way...

BACK IN THE GOOD OLD NPI

Business as usual at the NPI included teaching another evening Extension class in parapsychology (1970/71) which was even more popular this third time around. Then there came one night when the guest lecturer from Czechoslovakia was a "no show." I filled the breach—with help from the Soviet slides of Kirlian photography which were in my briefcase—by telling of my experiences around the world in search of psi.

After class there was the typical cluster of students with their nimble and numbing questions. As they slowly dispersed, one slight, clean-shaven, balding man with an ear-to-ear smile stepped up eagerly and said, without preface, "I'd like to do Kirlian photography!"

"Oh, so would I!" I answered with not a little sarcasm—and then caught sight of a dark figure leaving the auditorium. It was Jain, a graduate student from Caliornia Institute of Technology who had made a similar remark earlier in the course. I had given him several of the Soviet articles on Kirlian photography, now translated. I called to Jain and asked that he share that material with the eager gentleman, whose smile grew broader. They left together.

I thought no more of that incident in the weeks that followed, chiefly because there was rarely a follow-up of that kind of after-class interest, and also because I had grown disenchanted with the research into telepathy, clairvoyance, and precognition. The search for these elements was foundering in a slough of good design, good controls, and even at times good statistics—but the phenomenon of ESP remained as elusive as ever. This was not what I had expected of the scientific method. After all, if someone synthesizes a new drug, or creates a new psychotherapy like behavior modification, and if it is shown to work in controlled studies to a "significant" degree, then the drug or therapy is taken out of the lab and is used in the community. Yet there was still no such use of ESP in the community, not even after one hundred years of research. In fact, there was still suspense with each new study over whether ESP would show up with significant statistics. In short, our ESP experiments were producing no new information about how ESP works.

THE APPEARANCE OF K.J.

It was, I remember, a warm and caressive spring evening, and I was standing on the patio of the Dickson Art Center before going in for one of the last of the parapsychology classes, when the man with the Cheshire-cat smile approached and thrust something into my hand.

"Look at that!" The smile erupted into a high-pitched laugh.

I looked down and saw a marvelous Kirlian photograph of a leaf. "Where did you get *that?*" I gasped.

"I made it." Another yelp of laughter. "In my father-in-law's garage."

I grabbed his arm, asked if I could show the picture in class, and requested that he stay after class so I could learn his story.

The smiler with the Kirlian picture turned out to be an insurance man named Kendall Johnson (soon to be Ken, or K.J.), to whom Jain had given just one of the Kirlian articles—the one published in the U.S. in 1939 which Adamenko had discovered in the Moscow public library. Oddly, it was just about the only article Ken could have understood, for his education in science and electricity was almost as primitive as mine. Ken had understood just enough to go browsing in an electronics junk shop for parts and to assemble a device like the schematic diagram published in the article—a device invented before electronics burst into transistors and brilliantly colored wires. When K.J. finally put it together and turned on the juice, it worked!

Garage Science

Ken continued to experiment in the garage, where I visited him one Sunday. That day he was not successful in making even one picture, but at other times, he would produce a bonanza—and then he'd race to my home with slides, slide projector, and screen to show them. Most of his photographs were of the leaves and flowers that grew outside his house, and breathtakingly beautiful they were, with all the coronas and bubbles I had seen in the Soviet pictures. Whatever this Kirlian photography might prove to be, it was clearly not a hoax, a practical joke, or a fake phenomenon. I explained to K.J. that my interest was deep, but that before serious research could get under way, it was necessary to be able to make a photograph whenever we wanted one—which meant perfecting his device. Ken agreed and kept on going. It has always been an amazement to me, how Ken worked. He never gave a rational explanation for why he did what he did; he'd just laugh that wild laugh and say something like, "It felt right" or "I dunno, it just happened." Sometimes this could be maddening, for he'd capture a remarkable effect, then not remember what he had done so that he could do it again. Even more maddening: he had little or no background in research and design; he would bring in marvelous pictures of various leaves, but he would have forgotten to make a note of what kind of leaves they were, or what exposure time he had used, or other such trivial but vital data. After a few such incidents, I pounced on him for not keeping any *protocols!* His hurt, bewildered look reminded me of those early times in graduate school when I heard the word "protocol" and thought only of a diplomat at a formal dinner. So I explained that for each photograph there should be a data sheet, stating the name of the object, the kind of film, the exposure time, the wave form, and so on. It was then I came to the basic realization that Ken was almost constitutionally incapable of that kind of grut work. His talent lay in spontaneous improvisation—which sometimes resulted in nothing but black film, because in his excitement he would take a piece of film from the secure darkness of its triple box while the light was still on. But at other times he would capture something wondrous, like that rainbow image of his own electrified elbow, which he had inadvertently touched to a hot wire but managed to keep on film long enough to photograph (Fig. 6-1).

In short order, I found myself inundated with glorious Kirlian photographs which I struggled to name, sort, and file, feeling more

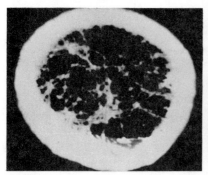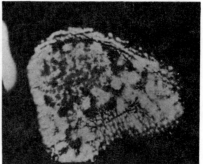

Fig. 6-1. *(Left)* Ken Johnson's elbow in a normal state. *(Right)* The same elbow while Ken suffered a strong electric shock. Both show Kirlian phenomena.

and more like an anxious dormitory mother hoping none of her charges would go astray. Finally, with misgivings, I asked K.J. if he would like to bring his equipment into the lab where we could work together. He nodded (he was often without words). A few days later, he brought in one of his devices, together with a bunch of photographic developing equipment. As he put those things down, carefully, he looked around and said quietly, "This is a cathedral."

That's how Ken talked. Sometimes I badly needed an interpreter (he was no good at interpreting his own remarks), but this time I understood. For Ken, access to a lab at UCLA was the equivalent of religious worship.

The First Instrument

In the three months since the building of that first device, K.J. had learned how to maneuver with electrical photography. And through careful study of the Soviet articles, he was now able to obtain many of the effects about which they had written—all to my open-mouthed wonder, for far from being sophisticated, or even functional, his instrument looked like a Rube Goldberg contraption. It was rigged from electronic bits and pieces, put together with wires that habitually spaghettied out of its grey metal box.

Though Ken learned a great deal during his years at the lab, he was always a loose-wire designer. From the very first I ranted against all those dangling wires which could, and did, cause strong electrical shocks if touched and which could even be lethal, or so I was warned by the experts. There never was any real mishap, although one night brought me close to separation. We had been working in the garage, and I had brushed against one of those damnable loose wires and been badly shocked. I began swearing at

Ken and his lousy technology. Instead of apologizing, Ken said eagerly, "Would you put your finger on film? I want to get you when you're angry!"

Loath to miss the opportunity, I continued to swear, loudly, while Ken took my picture. When we developed the photograph we saw, for the first time, the "red blotch of arousal"—which became a focal point for our research into human emotions as seen through Kirlian technique (Fig. 6-2).

All the same, Ken with his loose-wire devices became rather a figure of fun to the elegant engineers who came to the lab to examine this new wizardry and were faced with Ken's hopelessly amateur instrument.

But the damndest thing was that it worked, and continued to work, brilliantly, when there was no other device, anywhere in the country, that did.

LEARNING HOW TO TAKE A KIRLIAN PICTURE

Once Ken moved his instrument into the lab, I learned how basically simple it was to take a Kirlian photograph. There was no camera and no lens, for this was contact photography, which simply means that a photograph is made by putting an object in direct contact with the film. In one brief session, Ken taught me how to photograph animal, vegetable, and mineral (a finger, a leaf, and a coin).

The technique was easy, and effortless. Typically, we would put a finger pad on film, which was on a metal plate, which was con-

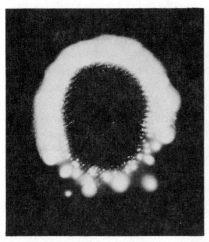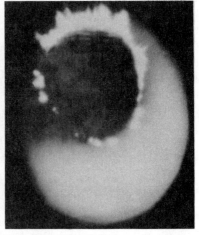

Fig. 6-2. *(Left)* My finger pad in a normal state. *(Right)* Same finger pad, taken while I was angry.

Fig. 6-3. Picture of a person having his finger pads photographed on a Kirlian device.

nected to a power source, and then we would press a button for one second (Fig. 6-3).

But everything else about Kirlian photography was confusing.

What Were We Looking At?

From the very first, the big question was: what does Kirlian photography reveal? What is the meaning of the bubbles, the corona, the "blotch"? We had not only to invent the instrument and the technique for taking the pictures, but also the vocabulary to describe what we saw. Since electrical photography was unknown in America, there were no guidelines to follow, no experts to advise us. There could be no neatly designed, statistically analyzable experiments as with the earlier ESP research. We were on our own.

It was exciting, it was frustrating, and it wasn't long before we were a laughing matter with the NPI community, who kept asking why I had suddenly begun to play with pretty pictures.

Why Kirlian Photography?

Basically, we were working with the Kirlian effect because Inyushin had stressed that it might be showing the "bioplasma" or patterned energy fields, about which Western science knows so little.

Through my personal experiences in body relaxation and LSD therapy, I had felt something akin to "bioenergy" rip through me, once as a fountain of emotions, and once as an avalanche of fire. In trying to understand what I had experienced, I had found again and again in the literature of parapsychology, of mysticism, and of Eastern religions the same basic idea: that interpenetrating everything in the universe there is an invisible energy which can be channeled into a powerful force to carry one's self out of the body, up into the air, and across the seas (the out-of-body experiences); or to change one's level of consciousness into other dimensions of reality (cosmic consciousness, the transcendental experience); or to transmute sickness into health (spiritual and psychic healing). Of course such ideas are contrary to the views of modern science. But should they be?

This was the lure of Kirlian photography for me: the possibility of demonstrating scientifically, in the lab, the existence of a Life Force and an Energy Body.

THE "DYING LEAF" EFFECT

Ken agreed wholeheartedly with this basic research premise, and together we searched in the Soviet experiments for a place to begin. Soon we were struck by the implications of the "dying leaf," in which the Kirlians had taken a healthy leaf and photographed it periodically over time. Gradually, the Kirlian image of the leaf would grow dimmer, until it could no longer be photographed. This phenomenon suggested to the Kirlians that a bioenergy, or life force, had gradually left the leaf after it had been plucked from the mother plant. Since this idea was so central to our research interest, we performed the dying-leaf experiment many times—and each time we found exactly what the Kirlians had described. Usually the leaf lost its image within three days, even though the leaf itself remained green in color. We also found that dead, brown leaves could not be photographed at all, which strengthened our idea that a life force had departed from it.

(Further evidence seemed to come from the Kirlian work with coins and metals, which we also duplicated. These *in*organic materials seemed always to photograph with the same brilliance, presumably because they contained no life force that would ebb away.)

That's Not Bioenergy! That's —

Almost from the start, there were criticisms from the hard scientists, who said there was no need to bring in such bizarre notions as "bioenergy" or "energy body" when a simpler explanation would do. One such simple explanation was an electrical one: coins and metals are excellent conductors of electricity, and therefore will always photograph clearly when electricity is passed through them. Also, water is an excellent conductor, and therefore *moist* leaves will photograph well. But—once a leaf dries out, it is no longer a conductor, and hence no longer able to pass electricity through it. Which explained away the dying-leaf effect. Or so it seemed then. (We had still to learn that some moist materials did not photograph at all, and that some dry materials photographed superbly.)

Phantom Leaf Failures

More important, theoretically, than the death of the leaf was the ghost it might leave behind. If we were able to cut off part of a leaf and in a Kirlian picture show the *entire* leaf (as the Russians had done), there would then be indisputable (?) evidence for the idea of an energy body. So we struggled—oh, how we struggled!—to obtain the phantom leaf, month after month, with hundreds upon hundreds of leaves from various species. Never a sign of a phantom, even though Inyushin and Adamenko had both assured me that the phantom leaf was a genuine effect, and Adamenko had even given me a photograph of one (not particularly convincing), with the advice that the phantom is difficult to obtain.

Characteristically, none of the Soviet literature mentioned the technique to obtain the phantom, so Ken kept improvising strategies, which were at least helpful in teaching us about the Kirlian technique. But we had no success at all with the phantom, not for two years. Oddly, these many failures worked to our advantage, for thousands of times we photographed the precise, sharp edge where the leaf had been cut and nothing more than that. This was an important item in later years when we could produce phantom after phantom, showing clearly the shape of the leaf that had been cut away. When that happened, instead of accepting the bizarre idea of an energy body, our critics explained those fine phantoms as "gaseous emissions" or "moisture" or "water vapor"—none of which had showed up in all those perfect failures.

The Dead Man's Hand

With so much criticism, and so much failure in producing a phantom, I became foolishly defensive. And one day, when I was telling a conservative physiologist that Kirlian photography might be revealing an "unknown bioenergy" and his eyes glazed over with disbelief, I asked if he had a corpse that we might photograph to see if it imaged differently from a living body. He was noncommittal, but a few weeks later, he came bearing a gift wrapped in a white bandage. It was a pleasant shock to unwrap it and find inside a dead man's hand. Treasure! Challenge! Ken and I worked late, very late, trying to solve the macabre problem of getting the dead fingers on film without our live ones contaminating the results. We finally managed, and were disappointed.

One should never hope for results in science, for *hope* can cloud the issues. But I had been hoping we could get more evidence to support our findings with the dying-leaf effect. The dead man's hand did not give it, for his fingers took definite, if peculiar pictures. We wondered, finally, if we might be getting a picture of the formaldehyde that the hand had been soaking in for four weeks —and we decided to cast around for an unadulterated dead body.

The Tale of a Rat

What easier creature for a psychologist to locate than a rat, live or dead? Up to the psychology department we went to see Ginger, who, with a disbelieving snort, donated one of his white and furry friends, together with food pellets and some ether, the latter because rats o.d. easily and painlessly on it. En route with these treasures, an idea: we could give the rat just a little ether, and then when it was under, we could cut off part of its tail (with or without a carving knife, that was K.J.'s problem), and so avoid killing it. Then we could photograph the tail that remained, to see if a phantom would appear of the part that had been cut away.

Naturally, problems arose.

Item: Rats are furry and fur does not take a good Kirlian picture.

Item: Rats are skitterish and will not pose for an electrical photograph.

Item: Rats are sensitive to electrical shock and respond to that noxious stimulus, as to other noxious stimuli, by defecating and urinating. In this instance, on our film.

Eventually, Ken improvised a cage to hold the body of the rat, but with a hole through which its tail could protrude. It is well known, of course, that rats have long, almost hairless tails. What is not well known is that their tails are exquisitely photogenic in the Kirlian way, giving mysterious detail (Ginger could not believe this was the tail of a rat). It is a tribute to Ken's dexterity that he got this photograph of the rat's tail, unanesthetized (Fig. 6-4). It was the only one, because the rat swiftly learned to flick its tail when the electrode approached, and soon we were forced to abandon that game for the ether—which immediately made the photography effortless.

With the rat anesthetized, K.J. carefully amputated a small sec-

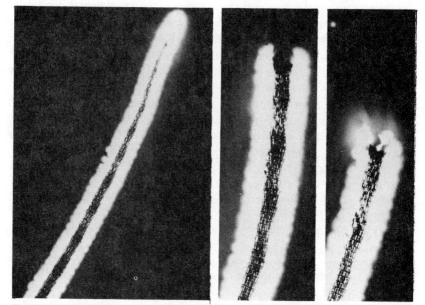

Fig. 6-4. *(Left)* Kirlian image of the tail of a living rat. *(Right)* The same rat tail with part of it amputated. As can plainly be seen, there was no sign of a "phantom tail" in either photograph.

tion of its tail, after which he placed the stump of the cut tail on the film and sent one second of electricity through it. Then he gently removed the film from under the tail and put it in the developer. We waited the four minutes it took to process the film. Would the picture show the part of the tail that had been cut away? It showed a neat, clean, cut-off tail.

We never, ever got a phantom tail, and we tried with several rats and mice. We also took advantage of their corpses to photograph them over a twenty-four hour post-mortem. But, so far as we could see there was no difference at all between the living and the dead. Were we wrong about this photography? Were we searching for an energy body that did not exist, or at least could not be seen with this technique? Doubts certainly grew within us. But at the same time, other intriguing phenomena were beginning to appear.

BIOENERGY AND THE GREEN THUMB

The lab was galvanized one day by a call from the eminent crystallographer/physicist Dr. William Tiller of Stanford University. Tiller had recently returned from the Soviet Union, where Adamenko had described enough about Kirlian photography to make him want to see for himself. We welcomed him to the lab and spent a busy day, the most intriguing part of which was a study that Tiller, himself, devised. He took a healthy leaf and photographed it, then he gashed the leaf and photographed it again. This much was routine; we had found that a mutilated leaf caused the Kirlian image to become much, much dimmer, with gaping holes of black, even in places where the leaf was intact. (This was another answer to the claim that the photograph disappeared because its conductor, water, had dried up; these mutilated leaves were still very moist—but all the same, they lost their luster.)

It was in this lackluster state that Tiller introduced the new twist: he picked up the mutilated leaf and held it between his hands to see if he could "heal" it with his own bioenergy. This was an idea we had never heard of, never thought of. And we watched, fascinated, to see how the leaf would photograph, post-treatment. It seemed brighter to me, but not bright enough to impress Tiller, apparently, for he went on to another study.

Somehow that experiment stayed with me, nagging, until one day I decided to try my hand at energizing a leaf. I chose a geranium leaf, which is much more sensitive in Kirlian photography than the camellia leaf Tiller had used. After gashing the geranium leaf, it became dramatically dimmer in its image and lost most of its bubbles. Then I held the leaf between my hands, as I had seen Tiller do, and afterwards, photographed it again. This time its image was more brilliant than it had ever been, with more bubbles, too. It looked positively rejuvenated. I raced to show it to Ken, who laughed and suggested maybe it was the moisture and heat from my hand that made the difference. Eager to see what another "treatment" would do, I held the leaf again, and took its picture again. Apparently it fell victim to "overkill," for now it barely showed up in the photograph.

But this failure only led me to ponder the old wives' tale that certain people have "Green Thumbs," meaning that plants grow strong and healthy for them, while "Brown Thumbs" cause plants to wither and die. Could Kirlian photography be distinguishing, through these energy fields around a leaf, the Green Thumbs from the Brown Thumbs?

Green Thumb

As if in response to this new question, I soon met a lady who claimed to be an expert gardener for whom plants flourished. I invited her to the lab to participate in a controlled study—our first controlled experiment with Kirlian photography after eight months of trial and error. The hypothesis being tested was that in an interaction between a person's hand and an injured leaf, there would be a rejuvenation of the leaf's energy field, whereas the Control leaf (an injured leaf with no human interaction) would not show any change in its Kirlian energy field.

The first requirement was to find two leaves from the same plant as similar in size and shape as possible (oddly, not an easy requirement to meet). Once we had these twin leaves, one was randomly chosen as the Experimental leaf, the other as the Control. Next, Mrs. Green Thumb and I went into the isolation booth with the leaves, and she watched while I photographed each leaf in prime condition. Then I gashed and punched holes in both leaves and photographed them again. As expected, after the mutilation both leaves became very much dimmer, with blacked-out areas in their Kirlian images. Next, I put the Control leaf to one side, not to be touched until photographed again. And then, carefully, I placed the mutilated Experimental leaf on a piece of film—also not to be touched until photographed again. This was a vital control which Ken had recommended. Any "treatment" had to be at a distance from the leaf to rule out the influence of moisture and heat from the human hand. Next, I asked Mrs. Green Thumb to hold her hand about two inches above the leaf to send it "healing energy." At no time was she permitted to touch the leaf. When she felt the leaf had received enough energy, she withdrew her hand, and I photographed the leaf again, as well as the Control leaf, which had had no treatment of any kind.

The results were wonderfully gratifying. The Experimental leaf had become vividly brilliant and bubbly post-treatment, while the Control leaf had remained lackluster, with black spots. Thus, the hypothesis that bioenergy from a person can revitalize a leaf (the Green Thumb effect) seemed demonstrated. We tried this experiment many times, with consistent results. The concept of energy fields in Kirlian photography seemed once more a real possibility.

Brown Thumb

One day a research associate named Barry asked what we were doing with all those leaves. I explained about the Green Thumb, and Barry laughed, saying he was notorious for plants forever dying around him. Here was a fine chance to explore a *negative* bioenergy! We repeated the same Experimental process and saw, after Barry's "treatment" of a leaf, that its Kirlian image all but disappeared; in fact, on film, the Control leaf looked far healthier than Barry's "zapped" one! Here was our first Brown Thumb, and we repeated the experiment several times with Barry, to be sure of the effect. Barry was generally (though not every time) able to zap the leaf almost into invisibility.

Thus began our Green Thumb/Brown Thumb studies, which eventually numbered hundreds of cases. Most subjects had a Green Thumb, but we found several with Brown Thumbs, and then there were those inevitable people who seemed to create no difference at all.

These studies were our introduction to the possibility of seeing, on film, how an energy that emanates from people can influence the life around it. And this Green Thumb/Brown Thumb effect was to be swiftly followed by other, more powerful demonstrations of the transfer of bioenergy.

7
Unorthodoxies in Healing

Of Acupuncture, Magnetic Passes, and Psychic Healing—All of Which Seem to Depend on a Transfer, or Manipulation, of Bioenergy

NEW JOURNEYS

The next year (1971–72) saw an influx into the lab of very different people offering very different kinds of volunteer research, each unknown to the other, yet all complementing one another and shedding unexpected light on our explorations of energy fields and energy flow—which many in the medical school would have preferred to keep dark. Although these volunteers were working in the lab over the same period of time, it is probably best to look at each contribution separately.

K.J.'s New Inventions

Ken's inquiring and imaginative nature brought many surprises to the lab, generally in the shape of various Kirlian devices using different electrical power sources. Once Ken got his teeth into electricity, he bit hard, and out sparked Kirlian pictures made with a Tesla coil (which is what the Kirlians use), a Van de Graaf generator, direct current, transistors, a Mark X, etc., etc. And, as a sort of regression among these increasingly complex techniques, Ken showed me how it was possible to make "Kirlian pictures" simply by rubbing my feet on a heavy nylon carpet and touching my finger to a piece of film. Just as when you walk down a thickly carpeted hotel corridor and touch a metal doorknob, you experience a spark, so when the finger touches the film there is a spark—and, Ken explained, it is the *spark* that makes the photograph.

After that insight, Ken began to look directly at electrical influences between people by using various meters. One day, with that ear-to-ear grin, Ken came walking into the lab and asked, "Remember Adamenko's tobiscope for finding acupuncture points?"

"Sure. I'd still like to know if it's for real."

Yelp of a laugh. "Let's find out!"

Ken pulled out still another electrical device, a special meter to which was attached a narrow metal probe. He pointed out that when the metal probe was not active, the meter registered zero, indicating no electrical current. Then he began to move the probe over my skin, just as Adamenko had moved his tobiscope in that Moscow restaurant. I watched, and the needle remained at zero —until suddenly, it shot way over, showing an electrical charge of some kind. Ken moved the probe away, and the needle returned to zero; when he moved it back to the same spot, the needle deflected sharply again.

"Acupuncture point," said Ken, blithely.

"Do that again!"

Ken did, several times, finding new "points" as he moved the probe over my forearm, wrist, hand. I took the probe from him and experimented on myself, then on him. The needle continued to deflect at certain spots. What were those deflections? Could they really be acupuncture points? Ken pulled out an acupuncture chart, and the points on the chart seemed, generally, to correspond to the places where the deflections occurred. In further study, we were to find points that were not on the charts, and vice versa. Also, we learned that the points were found in slightly different places with different people.

How could we be sure these were really acupuncture points? In that year of 1971, I knew of no one, anywhere, who knew anything about so arcane a field as acupuncture. So we put the "acuometer" aside, just as we had put aside several of Ken's photographic devices, to be explored later.

An Acupuncturist Arrives

A few weeks after that decision, I was en route to give a lecture on parapsychology to medical students (a rare event) when my eye was caught by a bulletin board announcement of a lecture/demonstration to be given by an acupuncture master. An unparalleled happening on campus. (This was six months before our American doctors visited the People's Republic of China and reported on acupuncture anesthesia, which was, of course, the start of a considerable medical furor.) That announcement must have triggered something within me, because I found myself lecturing to the medical students on Soviet research into acupuncture, which was not my intended topic, and which caused immediate puzzlement.

"How do you spell it?" From a student at the back of the hall.

"Acupuncture?" He nodded and I spelled it.

"What is it?"

I plunged into an explanation of this ancient Chinese therapy, based on the concept that in addition to such well-known circulatory systems as blood and lymph, there exists in the human body a system of invisible channels, or meridians, through which circulates an energy called "chi" (titters from the audience). This energy is presumed to flow into a field around the body and then into the atmosphere (more titters). If this energy flow is blocked, there is illness, which can then be remedied by inserting needles into special, invisible acupuncture points (guffaws).

I dropped acupuncture and went on to discuss laboratory experiments with the telepathic dream, with only slightly more success. I left the lecture hall feeling the talk had been a fiasco. It may have been. But just three days later, that bitter pill gave way to a wonderfully sweet taste when an excited medical student who had been at the lecture tracked me down in one of the NPI labyrinths. The student reported that he had met, in his church that Sunday, an acupuncturist from Taiwan who had given such a skillful demonstration that the student invited him to UCLA. But he needed a supervisor, and would I be willing... would I ever!

There was absolutely no need for supervision. Zion, a young and confident Chinese trained in traditional Manchurian acupuncture going back eleven generations, gave a stunning performance for the large and curious group of medical students, who were determined to be tough-minded. All the same, there was a gasp when Zion plunged a six-inch needle a good two inches into a student's flesh, without the student knowing the needle had been inserted.

I wasted no time requisitioning Zion as a volunteer for my own research. And Zion, being a stranger in a strange land, was pleased with the refuge of a university lab.

The first thing we asked Zion to do was to locate specific acupuncture points on our bodies, with his fingers, in the traditional way. Then Ken took his "acuometer" and touched the metal probe to those points. Invariably, the needle deflected sharply from zero, showing a strong difference in electrical conductivity. We then asked Zion to choose places on our bodies that were definitely *not* acupuncture points, and when Ken touched the probe to those places, the needle remained at zero. Zion became more and more intrigued and began to experiment with the acuometer on his own body, where he knew exactly the location of his acupuncture points. He explained that the location of acupuncture points on patients was, for him, the most difficult part of acupuncture treatment—and he had never, until now, seen an instrument, anywhere, that could locate the points.

We all beamed at each other and made immediate plans to investigate whether an acupuncture treatment would affect a Kirlian image.

Acupuncture and Kirlian Photography

The basic principles of acupuncture stem from that ancient idea of a universal energy—called "chi" by the Chinese—which surrounds and interpenetrates the human body. As ridiculous as this notion had seemed to the medical students, it nevertheless is a concept that has been expounded in many cultures over many many centuries. And it has been given a host of names: in India it is "prana"; in Hawaii, "mana"; in Germany, Reichenbach had christened it "od"; in Austria, Mesmer had called it "animal magnetism"; and in America, Reich had called it "orgone." Currently, in the Soviet Union, Inyushin was calling it "bioplasma."

Suddenly, with Zion, we had the prize chance to find out in our own lab if "chi" or bioenergy could be detected in a Kirlian photograph. This was what Inyushin had claimed to be doing in Alma-Ata—studying acupuncture with Kirlian photography. Now we could explore similarly, by looking to see if an acupuncture treatment would change the appearance of a corona around a finger. We explained this to Zion, who understood immediately and asked what finger we wanted to influence. We suggested the right index finger and Ken volunteered to get the needle.

We first established our base line by taking a picture of the right index finger before any acupuncture stimulation. Then I asked Zion to change the energy flow into that finger—and saw, dismayed, that Zion was going to insert a needle near Ken's shoulder.

"Oh, no!" I stopped Zion. "We want the energy flow to go into his *finger*."

Zion explained that the point near the shoulder lay on an invisible channel that flowed down the arm, into the hand, and out through the index finger (called, in acupuncture, the Large Intestine meridian). Then Zion stuck the needle deep into Ken (who said it didn't hurt, much), twirled it, left it there five minutes, and removed it. Then we took another photograph.

We found a startling change in the corona; the narrow, blotched corona had become dramatically wider, larger, brighter after treat-

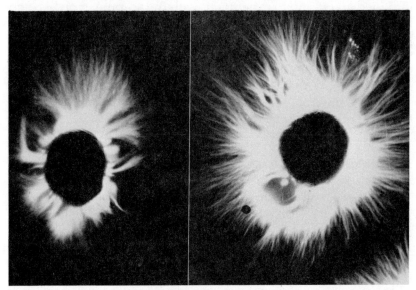

Fig. 7-1. *(Left)* A normal finger. *(Right)* A broken finger on the opposite hand. A vivid picture of an "imbalance of energy."

ment. Could this truly be interpreted as an increase in energy flow? Only extensive experimentation would give us an answer. And extensive research we did, with Zion. And with another volunteer who joined the lab.

Undergraduate Volunteer

For the first time, in that summer of '71, Ken and I were invited to give a public lecture on Kirlian photography in Los Angeles. Looking out into the sparse audience, I recognized the intense, bearded face of John Hubacher, who had taken the two undergraduate courses I had taught on campus. So I was not surprised a few days later when John wandered into the lab and stayed. Without saying much (he was another one of few words), John would volunteer to be a subject, or to develop film, or to make prints, and somehow he soon mastered the Kirlian process and became the lab's photographer-in-residence.

Almost immediately, John made an important contribution to acupuncture research. One day, a visitor with a broken finger came into the lab, and that broken finger was too good an opportunity for John to miss. So he took pictures of both the broken finger and the healthy finger on the other hand (Fig. 7-1). Clearly, the *broken* finger gave a far bigger and brighter corona than the healthy one—a finding straight out of acupuncture theory, which states that in a healthy body there is a balanced flow of energy, but when there is a trauma or injury, the flow of energy becomes *imbalanced*. When we saw this brilliant example of an imbalance of energy flow, we realized that here was another vital area for Kirlian research.

John began a campaign for every broken finger, toe, foot, hand, limb he could find, and we learned from dozens of cases that this imbalance of energy was a repeatable and reliable effect! Here was a triumph for a 5,000-year-old theory, making visible that imbalance, for the first time, through Kirlian photography. (It was odd that the *injured* side generally showed the larger and brighter corona, which was the opposite of what common sense would predict. Shouldn't the injured side show less energy? But then, so much of science contradicts common sense—the world is obviously flat and stationary, tables and chairs are obviously made of solid matter.)

With the discovery of this energy imbalance, John became keen on acupuncture research and thought he could show—as Inyushin's colleagues claimed to show—that Kirlian photography would reveal acupuncture points. He spent nights and weekends with acupuncturists and Ken's acuometer, locating the points and photographing them, both before and after stimulation. The results were intriguing but not conclusive. Only years later, in Romania, did I find John's work vividly substantiated.

Acupuncture Seminar

While this peculiar research was going on in the lab (to the amusement of my NPI colleagues), acupuncture exploded into the world's consciousness. Our American doctors had seen and filmed several operations in China where the only anesthesia used was acupuncture. Medical science went into a furor, some experts claiming a hoax, others invoking hypnosis or the power of suggestion (inevitably) as the explanation, while other "experts"—among them some greedy charlatans—jumped on acupuncture as the new panacea. To look more deeply into this controversy, the NPI asked our lab to present an acupuncture seminar to the staff.

For the occasion, Ken outdid himself, creating an assortment of instruments that could detect acupuncture points. One device consisted of a metal probe connected to an oscilloscope. When the probe touched an acupuncture point, the wave form (∿∿∿∿) on the scope turned suddenly into a tiny circle (o). This rivaled, in sheer eccentricity, the midnight that Ken telephoned to ask if I would like to be the first person in the world to hear "Stomach 36." (Stomach 36, belying its name, is an acupuncture point located near the knee.) When I said yes, there was a moment of silence and then over the phone came the sound of what might have been the lament of a lonely bird. I chortled and asked for more. Eventually Ken told how he had rigged a device to a radio so that when he touched a point with the probe, the radio played the "music" of the point.

Our seminar provided a delightful opportunity to see conservative doctors and psychiatrists taking Ken's probes, listening to the "music of the points," and watching the waves turn to circles on the scope. But, at the end of the seminar, one psychiatrist told me peremptorily that "acupuncture is merely an excuse for sticking needles into people." (I didn't think, till far too late to say it, how often our own doctors stick needles into people. Needles containing poison.)

Those Aren't Acupuncture Points!
Those Are Sweat Glands!

We were challenged, that day, on what Ken's acuometer was actually showing. Some of the doctors argued that those deflections might not be due to acupuncture points at all (and I was reminded of my own skepticism about it, until our work with Zion). When I asked why else the probe would deflect at those spots on the skin, one doctor said it might be that the probe was responding to sweat glands. After all, sweat is wet, and therefore a good conductor of electricity—an argument not unlike the "moisture" theory we'd met with earlier.

To track down that possibility, Ken and I trudged to a psychology professor who had been a pioneer in the electrical physiology of the sympathetic nervous system, which is where sweat is manufactured. I expected the professor to run the probe over his skin, smile, and say something like, "Oh, yes! Did that forty years ago. You're picking up _____."

But he didn't. He probed and probed and finally said maybe we should test for sweat glands. When I asked how, he came up with a keen idea. Find a "sympathectomy"—a person who has had an operation which cuts the sympathetic chain, which *stops all sweating* where the chain has been cut. Now, the professor said, you have a person who cannot sweat. Run the probe along the areas where he cannot sweat. If the probe has been picking up sweat, then the acuometer won't deflect; if it *does* deflect, then it is responding to something *other* than sweat.

We started a hunt for a sympathectomy. But long before we found one, we learned that the drug xylocaine creates a "temporary sympathectomy," meaning that while the drug is working in the body, no sweat is produced. We found volunteers willing to be given a shot of xylocaine which stopped all sweating for four

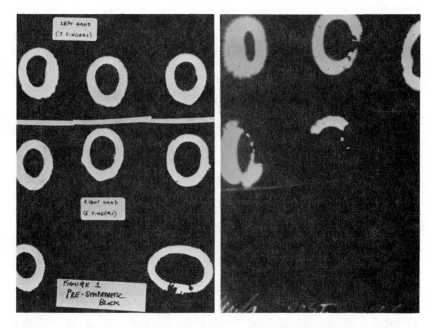

Fig. 7-2. *(Left)* Before "sympathectomy," finger pads of both hands, with coronas of about the same size. *(Right) During* sympathectomy effects. Drugged fingers *(top)* show bright coronas—but the normal fingers *(bottom)* have disappeared! Another example of "imbalance of energy."

hours, and we probed the points on the arm over and over again during those hours. We found that the acuometer *did* deflect, but not as strongly. Ambiguous finding.

But in doing the study, we found a powerful effect we hadn't even dreamed of. (That's science—a series of accidents, finding one thing when you're looking for something else.) We had taken Kirlian photographs before and during the xylocaine injection. Each and every time, we saw that after the drug was injected, the drugged fingers showed up brilliantly, but the non-drugged fingers totally disappeared (Fig. 7-2)! Here was more, fine evidence of acupuncture's "imbalance of energy flow," about which Inyushin, Adamenko, and Zion had told us. Now we could see it, with our own eyes, in the Kirlian pictures. Before the drug was injected, the coronas of both hands were about the same size. But after the shock of the drug there came this sharp imbalance—the drugged hand bright, the other hand nowhere to be seen. After the drug wore off, the two hands again showed the same size coronas, balanced again. We were seeing how trauma creates different amounts of energy flow, just as acupuncture theory says it will. So our acupuncture research continued, for years.

East versus West

Unfortunately we had to work without Zion, who swiftly lost interest. After all, his Eastern training was to use acupuncture to heal the sick, while our Western training was to test acupuncture theory in the lab. Zion could teach us, point for point, the names of the 1,000-odd acupuncture points, where they lay on the twelve meridians, how they related to the five qualities, and so on. But for us, this was just a bunch of trees obscuring the forest. In the same sort of way, Zion was totally bored with the trees of the twelve cranial nerves, the plexi of the nervous systems, the EMG, the EKG, and the tedium of measuring over and over and over again the changes in electricity at points pre- and post-stimulation. So he dropped out of the lab into a profitable practice with a grateful clientele. I remember, late one night, tuning in the TV randomly to find singer Peggy Lee, more svelte than I had ever seen her, telling how her newfound health and figure were due to the acupuncture expertise of "Mr. Zion."

Almost as soon as Zion left, other researchers arrived to replace him. One of the finest was a physician with impeccable credentials, Charles Ledergerber, M.D., obstetrician/gynecologist on UCLA's medical staff. It was interesting to learn that a childhood accident had long ago pointed Charles toward unorthodox healing. At the age of six he had become paralyzed in one arm. His father, a medical doctor, had tried every conventional treatment without success and finally took his son for unconventional treatment by a nonprofessional healer. The treatment involved sending some kind of electricity into the boy's arm. No results were apparent for months, but Charles slowly regained full use of his arm, which was of course vital for his later work as a surgeon.

When electrical stimulation of acupuncture points was introduced into the United States from China, Charles was among the first to explore it. In fact, when he first came to the lab, he had already discovered that electrical stimulation of special points on the abdomen could induce labor at a specific time. (Want your baby Thursday? No problem.)

Charles did many studies with us, the most productive being the arduous weekend when he brought with him Guido Fisch, a medical doctor from Switzerland. We photographed many fingertips before and after needle stimulation, the needle work done by Dr. Fisch. Since we used color film, the photographs could not be processed until the study was finished. The results showed almost all fingertips in royal blue *before* stimulation and with a crimson blotch *after* stimulation. Dr. Fisch was enchanted and wondered if the blue might represent the female *yin* energy and the crimson, the male *yang* energy—both necessary to acupuncture, for *yin* and *yang*

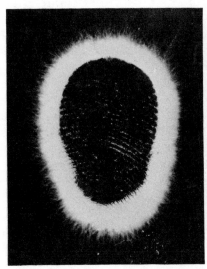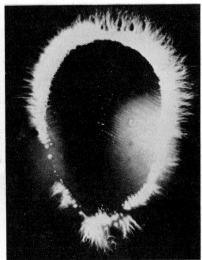

Fig. 7-3. *(Left)* Mrs. L.'s finger pad in her normal state. *(Right)* Same finger pad after Mrs. L. had taken coffee and a cigarette for the first time.

energies, together, are said to compose the "chi" which courses through the body. An interesting idea, still to be confirmed.

During that long weekend, Mrs. Fisch and Mrs. Ledergerber served as subjects, being punctured with needles or simply sitting, waiting. Then, in a twinkling, Mrs. Ledergerber became a heroine. During a coffee break she told me that she never drank coffee or smoked cigarettes (both of which I had been doing steadily). Her husband recommended that she have her Kirlian picture taken right away, after which she should smoke a cigarette, drink a cup of coffee, and have her picture taken again. We all began to laugh at the idea, but Mrs. Ledergerber stopped us cold by saying she would do it. It was startling to see her fluffy, smooth corona before the coffee and tobacco change to that roughed-up, uneven corona afterwards (Fig. 7-3).

Another Impeccable Expert

A very different exploration of energy in the body was being studied at UCLA's renowned Brain Research Institute, through the use of implanted electrodes. In this type of research, slim needles were carefully inserted into the skull, so that a jolt of electrical energy could be sent into a single brain cell—which, it was thought, might set off a specific behavior, like the jerk of a paw, a twist of the neck, or a blink of the eye.

One of these brain researchers came to ask us to take Kirlian pictures of a cat during stimulation of an implanted electrode. This was not possible, we explained, because to stimulate electrically *and* to take a Kirlian picture might electrocute the animal. The doctor wasn't discouraged, however, and he suggested instead that we do an acupuncture study of the cat, before and after needling. We had never taken a Kirlian picture of a cat's paw before, and I was aware that anything could happen. Happily, the doctor had brought with him his assistant, a superb cat handler, who placed the cat carefully in position, then lifted its paw to place it exactly where needed on the film. This was an odd spectacle: the cat with several implanted electrodes sticking out of its skull, held in place by a mortarboard arrangement that looked as if the cat were in cap (but not gown) for his graduation. The trainer caressed the cat and maneuvered its paw into position very, very carefully, for no one knew if the cat would bite, hiss, or leap for the door when the button was pressed.

I took a deep breath...and pressed the button. Buzz. Picture. Cat tranquil, unmoving. The trainer lifted its paw, and I took the film, replacing it with a fresh piece. Two more pictures of the normal paw. Now that we had three photographs that looked very much the same, the doctor stuck a needle into an acupuncture point in the cat's thigh. Cat remained tranquil, even when the needle was stimulated electrically. While the needle was still inserted, three more pictures were taken. Finally, the needle was removed, ten minutes were allowed to pass, and three more pictures were taken. We processed them right away.

We were astonished to find a complete opening of the paw while the needle was inserted (Fig. 7-4). Same opening on all three pictures. On the post-therapy pictures, after the needle was removed, the opening was gone. A fascinating phenomenon, suggesting again that acupuncture theory might be right on when it talks of a *flow* of invisible energy in and out of the body, through the points. Were we seeing an example of an acupuncture point opening up? We would need at least one hundred more studies, with one hundred different cats, before we could claim such an effect. (Later we did the same study with a dog and found the same open-paw effect.) We urged the doctor to return soon with more cats. Sadly, he brought no more cats, for he left the Brain Research Institute shortly afterwards for a Canadian university. It wasn't until an International Conference on Acupuncture in Bucharest, years later, that the brain researcher and I met again. He told me that he had published our brief study in an acupuncture journal, describing the "flow of energy" we seemed to have recorded.

Premature, I thought to myself. But at the same time I knew some of our own research may have been published prematurely,

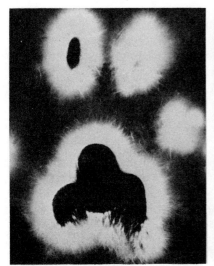

Fig. 7-4. *(Left)* The cat's paw in its normal state. *(Right)* The same cat's paw while an acupuncture needle is inserted, showing an "opening up" of the paw.

which is the way of science in academia today. Publish quickly, or perish quickly.

JACK GRAY AND "MAGNETIC PASSES"

Occasionally, even in 1971, colleagues would ask me to give a seminar on parapsychology for their graduate students, and of course I did. After one such seminar, a student approached me (with some embarrassment) to say that his father was a hypnotist who had had a lifelong interest in parapsychology and would very much like to meet me. I very much wanted to meet him, for anyone with a lifelong interest in psi might very well be dedicated and knowledgeable.

When Jack Gray came to the lab, I saw that he was both. And—a big bonus!—he was eager to do research. At that time in his early sixties, Jack was a practicing hypnotherapist, thanks to the "grandfather clause." This translates to mean that as a young man, Jack had been a stage hypnotist who had sometimes cooperated with medical doctors during the long period when hypnosis was not recognized as a valid therapy by the American Medical Association. When hypnosis was legitimized by the medical profession in 1957, Jack was asked by several doctors to practice his skills on patients who needed surgery but could not tolerate an anesthetic. Jack would induce a deep hypnotic trance, during which the patient would neither feel nor remember anything of the operation. This phenomenon is hard to accept, even when you see it done. In fact, when a demonstration was given to England's Royal Academy in the nineteenth century, in which a man's leg was amputated under hypnosis, the Society proclaimed the operation to be a fake and that the patient was simply pretending not to feel pain! (This cry of Fake! Pretense! Charlatan! is commonly heard with unusual medical practices like hypnosis and acupuncture, just as it is in parapsychology.)

Magnetic Passes

Jack and I were grateful to have found each other; he to be permitted scientific exploration in a university setting, and I to be able to study with a supremely able hypnotist who had actually taught himself the art of "magnetic passes," a phenomenon that had not been discussed in medical circles since Anton Mesmer (the father of hypnosis) had been denounced as a fraud by the French Academy of Science.

I was dumbstruck the first time I saw Jack do the passes, which just looked silly. Jack would ask someone to sit in a chair, then he would wave his hands a slight distance from the body, starting above the top of the head and gradually moving down around the arms and torso, all the way to the feet, at which point he would shake his hands, as if wringing off drops of water. Then he would repeat the process. In a very short time, usually, the subject would close his eyes, relax, and in some indefinable way "go under"—at which point Jack would nod to me, and I'd conduct a hypnotic session, exactly as if the subject had been hypnotized in normal fashion. Time and again Jack would prove the trance by sticking a needle or pin a good half-inch into the flesh (a standard test for depth of hypnosis), and there would be no reaction at all.

My fascination with these passes stemmed from the sense that they might be another instance of bioenergy being transmitted from one person to another, through which all sensations of pain disappear, or total amnesia is produced, or forgotten experiences are re-lived. All of these behaviors were documented in the lab and shown to colleagues, *but we could find no instrument anywhere that was able to record a flow of energy.* And because of that, colleagues argued that magnetic passes need not be a transmission of energy. Then what *was* happening, we would ask? They could give us no other ideas.

Naturally, we tried to find that energy with Kirlian photography, but the data were far more inconclusive than they had been with acupuncture. Instead, I had a different, more difficult lesson to learn about magnetic passes and the transfer of energy.

Dystonia Muscularis Deformans

In the elevator one morning, a grotesque girl in a wheelchair, her arms and legs so contorted it was not possible to sort out her anatomy. But her face, with its aura of curly, blond hair, was lovely. A psychiatric resident was in the elevator next to me, and when the child was wheeled out I turned to him with a question. His answer consisted of the long Latin name, *Dystonia Muscularis Deformans.*

"What's that?"

"Rare muscular paralysis and stiffening of the joints out of shape. Not much known about it."

That sudden inner feeling: something connected that child and me, but I didn't know what.

Within days I was summoned where I had never been summoned before, to a child's ward of the medical center, to look at Jenny, the child with *Dystonia Muscularis Deformans,* for which there is no known cure. The doctors were studying the possibility of an hysterical origin for the illness and were entertaining the possibility of hypnosis as a desperate resort before brain surgery.

I was pleased with this opportunity, for Jack was now coming steadily to the lab and agreed to work with me with magnetic passes, which proved incredibly effective. Not only did Jenny go into a profound trance, but when she did, her body relaxed and the twisted arms and legs lost their dreadful rigidity. Jack asked me to work with her on a daily basis, giving the hypnotic suggestion each day that her body would stay relaxed, and her limbs straight, after the hypnosis ended. He also stressed that I was to "shake the poison" off my hands at the end of each pass and be sure to wash my hands thoroughly after each session. Which I did, faithfully.

Jenny continued to respond remarkably in trance; she could move her fingers easily and straighten her legs effortlessly. The nurses in the ward were impressed and wonderfully helpful; they worked with Jenny, giving her pencil and paper and crayons, all of which Jenny could hold and use, even writing her name—when she was in trance. I felt confident (and so did Jack) that with enough practice, Jenny would become more flexible in her waking state.

We were wrong. Week after week went by in which the doctors and residents would come in to see Jenny's mobile limbs under hypnosis and magnetic passes. But within half an hour after the trance was ended, in spite of strong post-hypnotic suggestions that her mobility would remain, the *Dystonia* twisted her back into that grotesque rigidity. I grew discouraged. And, one particular day, I remember washing my hands with extra care and flicking the water away with a sense of distaste combined with futility. Dinner that night was routine and I fell asleep feeling nothing unusual.

But I woke the next morning unable to move my arms or legs. I felt dizzy, remote. I could not think, except to realize that something was very very wrong. Could I have caught the *Dystonia?* Impossible. It wasn't contagious. But all the same, I could not move, and for almost an hour I struggled just to get out of bed. In another enormous effort, I reached the phone and dialed the NPI to say that I was ill and would not be in to work. That great job accomplished, I sank back into a foggy malaise for the rest of the day. Toward evening, I was lucid enough to think of calling a knowledgeable friend, who recommended I do some visualization and some breathing exercises.

In those days, the use of visualization and breathing as therapy was just about unknown in the circles in which I worked, and part of me considered the idea foolish. But another part of me knew that if I were to continue to explore unorthodox healing and yogic practices like breathing, I had to do it. Another part of me was insisting that I call a respectable doctor of medicine. And there was still another part of me, the Onlooker, who was asking if it were really possible to contract *Dystonia Muscularis Deformans* through magnetic passes. There was nothing in the literature indicating that it was contagious, nothing. (Later, I was to find an esoteric book, *The Science of Psychic Healing* by Ramacharaka, which gives the simple statement that *all* illness can be contracted through magnetic passes.)

So I began the breathing and visualization, and they were inordinately hard work. The first session I could manage no more than three breaths; the next, four; and slowly adding more. By midnight I was feeling slightly better and fell asleep. Throughout the next day, I kept on with the practices and by bedtime had returned to normal movement and normal feelings.

I realized I had had an experience which most people would refuse to believe. (Some would argue that it was "nothing but" a hysterical reaction. If so, it is the only hysterical conversion I have ever known. And it responded swiftly to breathing and visualization, which is something of a miracle, even in that light.)

I never did mention it to colleagues at the NPI, but I did withdraw from Jenny's case, I believe to the relief of the staff. (She was subsequently given the brain surgery, which was of little help.)

The ward psychiatrist had observed some of the sessions under hypnosis with Jenny and had tested for himself how malleable and soft her limbs became in a trance. He had commented on this to a resident, who had researched the illness in the library. This young man came to visit me one day with the information that *Dystonia Muscularis Deformans* responds with malleability under hypnosis. This he could accept because he found it in the literature—it was written.

"I see." I was curious. "And is it written *why* hypnosis softens the muscles?"

"No. Only that the *Dystonia* responds to hypnotic suggestion, but only while the patient is hypnotized."

"Aren't you curious about why that's so?"

The resident looked puzzled, shrugged, and left. Apparently he wasn't curious.

I was. And still am.

THE "LAYING ON OF HANDS" AND A PSYCHIC HEALER

During this research into magnetic passes with Jack Gray, there arrived at my office door a little man with a portfolio which contained letters from medical doctors of several countries attesting to his "healing" of seemingly incurable patients. Though I was involved in a few peculiar research areas already, this man's tale was a bit hard to deal with, even for me.

It seems this little man had worked routinely as a typewriter mechanic. One day, in what seemed like an innocuous lark, he visited a fortune teller, who told him he had "healing hands." He thought little of her words until he was attacked by a headache so blinding that he had to stop his car in the middle of a desert. It was then he remembered the fortune teller. Feeling like a fool, he put his hands to his head—and within seconds his headache vanished and he was able to drive home. After that, with increasing curiosity, he tried the "healing hands" on others suffering headaches, with astonishing success. Gradually he expanded his "laying on of hands" to every kind of medical problem from migraines to mental illness. His successes were gratifying, of course, but a puzzle for which he wanted a scientific explanation. Therefore, he had volunteered his services to doctors and was now offering them to us—in the hope that we could provide his "scientific explanation."

Buyer, Beware!

The first rule for a parapsychologist is to beware the stranger bringing gifts. Particularly such a gift as the laying on of hands, which in 1971 was limited, in the United States, primarily to cults and charismatic TV demonstrations. I did not wish to be rude to this man, but I also did not wish to enter still another fringe area of research. Before I could think of a polite refusal, he spoke of the "electricity" he felt in his fingers when he did the healing, an "electricity" which the patients reportedly felt, too—sometimes like a tingling, sometimes as heat. That struck a chord, for the Soviets had mentioned "healers" in a similar way in relation to a transfer of energy, which they believed was demonstrated through their Kirlian research.

So I was pleased, then, to invite the healer to the lab, where Ken happened to be working that day and also, usefully, suffering an attack of bursitis. We devised a simple study, in which Kirlian photographs were taken of both Ken and the healer before treatment. After that, I asked the healer to do his work—which consisted of nothing at all that I could see except the placing of his hand first on one area of Ken's shoulder, and then another.

I had become accustomed to Jack's magnetic passes, which at least were active in their manipulation of the presumed energy fields around the body. I asked Ken if he felt anything, but he did not. Eventually, the healer said the treatment was finished, so we took Kirlian pictures again, post-treatment. There were astonishing changes, for Ken's corona had tripled in size, while the healer's had diminished. Were we witnessing, with hard photographic evidence, a *transfer* of bioenergy, or healing energy, from healer to patient? (We waited, Ken and I, for a remarkable improvement with the bursitis—which did not come.)

The healer was excited by the pictures and volunteered the next few days to treat volunteers with minor complaints. Some of these volunteers described, without being asked, feelings of extreme heat or a prickly tingling sensation. This happened so often that I volunteered for a treatment but, like Ken, felt nothing at all. (I was to learn this was an individual response, a subjective sensation, which did not seem to relate at all to the effectiveness of the therapy. Some people who felt nothing obtained immediate and lasting healing, while others who felt the "electricity" did not improve.) Much more consistent than the subjective responses were the Kirlian photographs, which showed an increased corona in the patient, post-treatment, with a decrease in the healer's corona.

But soon the healer had to go on about his business. He asked for a few Kirlian pictures and a letter of recommendation to add to his portfolio. I gave him the pictures and a brief note saying he had cooperated in some laboratory research, being careful not to recommend his ability in any way. We had, after all, witnessed no remarkable cures, but merely a few alleviations of minor symptoms.

And that seemed to end a brief laboratory episode.

The Kidney Test

Some weeks later, Marshall Barshay, M.D., walked into the office and asked about our "validation" of the healer, who had shown him our pictures and our letter. I answered with a bit of anger that we had validated *nothing*, and Marshall countered by saying *he* would like to validate the healer and would I be interested in the project. This was truly a startling proposal from an M.D.

"What's your idea?" I asked. (Doctors can be peculiar, too.)

"I specialize in dialysis," Marshall answered. "When kidneys don't function, the patient must go on dialysis two or three times a week to stay alive. No one yet has ever been taken off the machine and survived. Suppose someone did. Would that be a good test of a healer?"

"It would be gorgeous...!"

Not only was this bona fide M.D. willing to conduct the experiment—in the laying on of hands!—but he would try to do it in as scientific a way as possible, which included a complete series of lab tests to look for improvement in the complex variables involved with kidney malfunction. Besides all that, Marshall was enthusiastic and efficient, and in no time seventeen of his volunteer patients, all on dialysis, were coming to the lab every week to have their Kirlian pictures taken before and after treatment. The treatment consisted of the healer simply placing his hands directly on the patient's back, over the kidney area. The study went flawlessly; the patients were happy to be subjects, the healer to be working on a scientific project, and we to be collecting all that Kirlian data— which confirmed that the patients' finger-pad coronas increased in brilliance and width after the treatment, while the healer's image frequently decreased. This evidence seemed to support the idea that the laying on of hands might be transferring an energy from healer to patient.

But the actual *healing* was a different matter. There were undeniable remissions of minor symptoms like headaches, nausea and dizziness—but at the study's end, *not one patient* had been taken off dialysis.

Unorthodox healing remained a big question.

From Magnetic Passes to Psychic Healing

Then out of nowhere, psychic healing came to Jack Gray, who had always considered himself a plain hypnotherapist, using hypnosis as an aid to control smoking, obesity, migraines, phobias, etc. (Hypnotherapy is *not* considered a form of psychic healing, though perhaps it should be.) One urgent phone call to the lab turned upside-down Jack's (and my) image of what he was.

Into UCLA Hospital's intensive care had come the victim of a terrible automobile accident, a twenty-year-old man whose right leg had been smashed into forty-odd bone fractures, including a demolished ankle bone and a score of exposed nerves. Along the way, Mitch had developed osteomyelitis and other infections which were being treated with powerful doses of drugs that were causing problems with his kidneys, his sight, and his hearing. He was also being injected with large amounts of morphine for the intolerable pain. Immediate amputation of the leg had been recommended by a conclave of thirty doctors, who had reported that the leg would always be useless, as well as a source of constant, terrible pain which could only lead to drug addiction—if, indeed, Mitch were to survive.

It was at that crisis that Mitch's mother phoned the lab. She had been told that we were working with hypnosis and begged our help. I explained that there was nothing we could do without the consent of the doctors—and probably little we could do even with their consent. She had already—remarkably—received permission from the doctors for the use of hypnosis as a last measure. All I could do, then, was discuss the case with Jack, pointing out that the hospital was antagonistic to hypnosis (this was still 1971), and should Jack fail, in what seemed a hopeless case, that antagonism could grow worse. But over the years, Jack's skin had grown thick enough to withstand all the slings and arrows of an outraged profession. His chief interest was to be effective for the patient, if he could.

Mitch's Story

Mitch delights in describing his disgust when he was first told about Jack's visit. He knew nothing of hypnotists except what he had seen in nightclubs, and he expected a man with turban and cape and magic wand. Instead, a slight, elderly gentleman in a navy blue suit and tie came into the room quietly and proceeded to walk around the bed at a careful distance from the mangled leg, which was in a cast. Mitch, who had been screaming, "Cut it off, cut it off, I can't stand it!" stopped in mid-yell and cried to Jack, "What the hell are you doing?"

"I don't want to hurt your leg by getting too close. The field around it is very disturbed."

That was the sentence that did it. For weeks Mitch had cried out in pain whenever a doctor or nurse came within a foot of his bed, and he had accused them of striking against his leg. They had insisted they were nowhere near the leg—and now Mitch suspected they may have been getting into his "disturbed field," whatever Jack meant by that.

Mitch also tells of Jack's methods: a combination of magnetic passes, hypnosis, and even telepathic phone calls (late one night Mitch was thinking wistfully about a pizza when his phone rang. It was Jack, who asked, "Pepperoni or mushroom?" and then hung up.) Almost from the start, under post-hypnotic suggestion, Mitch's agonizing pain disappeared so that—unheard of in the hospital—he was off morphine within two weeks and never took it again. This total absence of pain created difficulties for the doctors, who needed its measure to determine procedures, so they asked Jack to bring the pain back. Under hypnosis, again, Jack suggested that Mitch would feel the pain whenever the doctors were in the room. Now that Mitch was relieved of the intolerable pain (except in the presence of the doctors) *and* the mind-confusing drugs, Jack was able to work steadily until the day that Mitch walked out of the hospital on both legs, having regenerated his ankle bone and re-grown nerve fibers—neither of which had been considered possible by the doctors. One of those doctors stated in a television interview that this had happened and was in the medical records, but he had no explanation for it.

And it might be said, straight-away, neither had Jack, nor I. Mitch's case, which took more than a year, seemed to reveal capacities in Jack that he had never explored. He would tell me how he kept seeing in his mind's eye a piece of bone in Mitch's leg that was causing constant infection. Eventually he mentioned this to the doctors, who at first said that was impossible but then did exploratory surgery—and found the piece of bone, which was removed which then stopped the infection. At other times Jack would feel, as he made the passes, movements in the field around the leg, as if invisible "bumps" were being smoothed out. These were subjective sensations, of course, but the results were hard data, now part of the medical records.

Because it was hard data, other M.D.s began to send their patients to the lab for Jack's help, patients who were not responding to conventional therapy. Over the years, more and more patients were sent to the lab and we eventually created a research project in "Psychic Healing" (what else could it be called?) which was both a fascination and a frustration. Sometimes the patients grew miraculously better, recovering from a "hopeless" cancer or paralysis. But more often there would be only slight improvement or, occasionally, no improvement at all. Jack would shake his head in puzzlement at both the cures and the failures, for he could never define what caused the changes when they occurred. It was not just the hypnosis, and it was not just the magnetic passes. Was it something to do with a bioenergy that conveyed information? Or was it a mind energy?

Once Jack murmured to me, with a helpless laugh, "I don't know what I'm doing. . . ." And I answered, "Neither do I, Jack. But keep doing it! And maybe one day we'll find out what it is." (Sad to say, Jack died before that day—which is still to come.)

Over the years, John Hubacher faithfully took pictures of healer and patient, pre- and post-therapy, so that eventually our healing studies filled more than twenty thick notebooks, constituting the most prolific of our research areas. Most of the time, though not always, the coronas of the patients increased considerably after therapy, which seemed to confirm the idea of a transfer of energy from healer to patient.

And so these oddball researches seemed, like Topsy, just to grow. . . all the while drawing odder and odder looks from the colleagues at NPI, looks which seemed to ask: what, *what*, in the name of Freud, has any of that research to do with Neuropsychiatry?

My hunch was, a great deal. Still to be discovered. And somehow, for some time, the work was permitted to go on in the lab with the frozen meat locker.

8
Growing Fame/ Notoriety and Growing Opposition

Psychic Healing and Acupuncture Gain National Interest, Causing an Avalanche of Curiosity About the Kirlian Effect—and a Barrage of Criticism

NEW YORK KIRLIAN CONFERENCE

As our potpourri of projects—acupuncture, magnetic passes, the "laying on of hands"—plowed on, side by side (but never together) in the lab, there came an invitation in 1972 to participate in the very first United States conference on Kirlian photography and acupuncture in New York City, no expenses paid. Ken and I accepted happily.

Since no one knew then what might be lurking around this odd couple of science, the conference attracted a huge audience of Ph.D.s, M.D.s, physicists, biologists, electrical engineers, acupuncturists, students, tricksters, and quacks. Ken and I sat through the glut of papers, hoping for clues to any of the mysteries with which we were wrestling (What *is* bioenergy? Are there *truly* acupuncture points and meridians? What is seen in Kirlian photography?) But as paper followed on paper, data on data, statistic on statistic, I felt again that graduate school syndrome of intellectual constipation. And I saw why the experienced conferee was so selective about the papers he would hear.

When my turn came to present our research, Ken's colored Kirlian photographs were flashed on the large screen for the first time, hugely magnified. And they were breathtaking. Brilliant blues, purples, oranges, reds, yellows of the leaves transformed by Green Thumb or Brown Thumb; of healer and healed; of leaves gradually "dying," over time, in their Kirlian image. We were suddenly a sensation, even though we could not say, with any clarity, what we had photographed. We felt our most solid work was in our acupuncture research, for we could show, again and again, how acupuncture's theory of energy flow and energy balance/imbalance could be visually represented through the Kirlian pictures.

There had been a few interesting presentations on acupuncture theory and practice given at the conference. One Englishman had spoken knowledgeably, it seemed, of "chi" energy flowing along meridians, very much as Zion had explained it. So, as I was at the podium showing an odd Kirlian image of a finger pad, I called on the British acupuncturist (who was, like most acupuncturists of that era, *not* an M.D.) to ask if he could diagnose the ailment, from the photograph, on the basis of acupuncture theory. The Britisher stepped up, denying any knowledge of Kirlian photography but making a diagnosis anyhow—in glib phrases—which was quite wrong. The audience applauded loudly, anyhow, which was a fine lesson in how readily the public can be duped. (Years later, in Romania, I was to observe a medical doctor give an accurate medical diagnosis, based purely on acupuncture theory, from electrical photographs.)

That first Kirlian conference introduced us to a very few other workers in Kirlian research. Interestingly, they were all students who had produced working devices that could take electrical photographs. These students, like us, showed how a leaf died, over time, in its Kirlian image, eventually not producing any kind of photograph at all. And they showed, like us, how the finger pads changed with emotion. The other, older scientists who spoke on the Kirlian effect did so theoretically, explaining what the images showed in terms of electricity. We had heard these comments before—that the Kirlian photograph simply showed conventional "corona discharge," which appears around any object that is electrified in a special way. But none of these critics had taken photographs, or experimented in any way with the Kirlian technique. I was beginning to learn the very basic difference between experimental and theoretical scientist. And I saw again, sharply, that it is students who have the curiosity and imagination to explore.

ASTRONAUT IN ARKANSAS

Almost together with the invitation to the New York conference, I had been invited to address another conference, in Arkansas, on the more familiar subject of ESP. In truth, parapsychology conferences were becoming stale stuff, and I probably would not have accepted—if one of the scheduled speakers had not been Edgar Mitchell, the second man to walk on the moon, who had conducted an ESP experiment during the space flight. Mitchell showed exquisite slides of his trip to the moon, which he accompanied by a reading of his poetry. The imagery of his poetry reinforced the rumors I had heard about the astronauts' paranormal experiences in space. I hoped, there in Hot Springs, to learn the facts.

K.J. and I had already had a brush with psychic events in space, but only enough to whet our interest. Several months before, a man from NASA had come to the lab, asking about Kirlian photography as a "non-destructive test for metal fatigue." He explained that on space flights, metals become "fatigued" and develop tiny fissures which can go undetected—until disaster hits and the craft explodes (not unlike the catastrophe of the DC-10 engine). Standard tests for such fatigue points are virtually useless, because in order to find them, some part of the craft has to be destroyed—a Catch-22 of research and design.

Could the Kirlian technique show the miniscule cracks without destroying anything? The man from NASA brought samples for Ken who, after much intricate trial and error, succeeded. As our reward, we were taken to a NASA Research Center to meet special board members. I remember, on the freeway, asking K.J. and the psychiatrist then working with us to *please* be circumspect and discuss *only* the Kirlian work with metal fatigue. But the psychiatrist quickly plunged into the mysteries of the phantom leaf and energy bodies and the "out-of-body" effect—which, to my utter confusion, sparked the board to probe for further information about how the separation of the physical and energy bodies might occur. I began to realize that the *energy body* was their chief interest...and the only reason, that I could fathom, for that interest would be the "out-of-body" experiences the astronauts were rumored to have had in space. I remembered, with a chill of excitement, reports in the early '60s of the Soviets training their cosmonauts in telepathic communication in case electronic equipment broke down. (Telepathy was presumed to be instantaneous transmission and thus faster than electricity.)

It was at that point that I questioned the NASA board members about the experiences of astronauts in space—and was met with never a reply.

Now, in Arkansas, Edgar Mitchell spoke to me of his profound belief in psychical research, and how he planned to set up a center of education and finance for that orphan branch of science. (It is a sad thing that he was not able to realize his vision.) Yet when I asked about his paranormal experiences in space, he talked freely of his telepathy experiment (which had been reported extensively in the media) but said nothing about any out-of-body experiences he may (or may not) have had.

TWO DISSIMILAR HEALERS

At the Arkansas conference, I also met for the first time one of America's most distinguished healers, Olga Worrall. At that time in her sixties, Olga was in the throes of adjusting to the sudden death of her lifelong partner and husband, Ambrose. For more than forty years, she and Ambrose had freely offered, to anyone who came to them, spiritual healings which involved the "laying on of hands" (but which could also be carried, by thought, over long distances). With Ambrose's death, Olga was shaken but quietly resolved to go on with the work.

In loud contrast was an American healer-come-lately, who explained to all who would listen how he had miraculously cured himself of a terminal illness in a V.A. hospital and had then gone on a pilgrimage to Tibet to learn healing from the "masters." After years of instruction, he was now about to bring his gift to an ailing world—for a considerable fee. In a few demonstrations, I saw that this man had mastered a theatrical technique which involved lunging at the patient with a sharp scream as he placed his hands on one or another part of the body. Some of the people I met claimed a remarkable recovery, but I wondered if that healing technique might more properly be called a shock therapy.

Many months later this American, who now had a Tibetan name, robes, and accent to match, called me to ask if he could do research with us. I could not place him until he gave me his American name. When I expressed astonishment at the transformation, he said in pig-Tibetan, "Much wotuh ovuh blidge!"

Unorthodox healing produces bagfuls of chaff, in which can be found some genuine kernels of wheat. I was to find a few kernels in the lab.

TWO CONFERENCES ON HEALING

That New York Kirlian conference had proved to be something of a sensation on the East Coast, and it was followed in that same year by two West Coast conferences, New Dimensions in Healing, with were even more sensational. I never expected the conferences would be such a hit when I accepted the post of co-chairman, which "honor" includes the chores of organizing the program and selecting the faculty. This was to be a most unusual academic event in that it was offered—in the tradition of show biz rather than science—twice, in two one-night stands on two consecutive weekends. The first "show" played in Northern California, at Stanford University, and the second in Southern California, at UCLA.

Several respected scientists had accepted our invitations, among them a few who had worked for years, in obscurity, on aspects of unconventional healing. Occasionally their research was published in out-of-the-way journals, but the work had remained generally unknown or ignored until the Stanford symposium, when it became Big News.

None of us was prepared for the flood of media people who poured around the conference faculty, asking incessantly for interviews, particularly of those scientists who had done controlled laboratory studies. First among these was biochemist Dr. Bernard Grad of McGill University, who a decade earlier had done beautiful, precise studies showing that a healer's hands could cause swifter than normal healing in wounded mice and richer than normal growth in plants. Following Grad's lead, biochemist Sister Justa Smith (a nun who, in her own words, had kicked the habit) showed, also with controlled studies, that the bioenergy from a healer's hands evoked a much higher growth rate than normal in enzymes—and that the growth curve was similar to that created by a magnetic field. (Once again, scientific research was showing a possible relationship between *magnetism* and *magnetic passes*, which was what Anton Mesmer had claimed, two hundred years earlier.)

Olga Worrall

But by far the biggest and most delayed triumph came to "the little old lady," as the lab came to call Olga Worrall. With her husband Ambrose, Olga had tried for half a century to get hard, objective data that would confirm a "healing energy"—which, in their ministry, had produced countless remissions. They never did succeed, but met instead with constant opposition from scientists, especially in academia, who "knew" there was no such bioenergy. Actually, my invitation to Olga was the very first she had ever received to lecture at a university, and she was loath to accept it because Ambrose, an aeronautical engineer, had always lectured for both of them. So, when I met Olga in Stanford, she was suffering a bad case of stage fright. She asked me to listen to the paper she had written, which was a conventional history of unconventional healing that came alive only when she spoke of her childhood, when her mother discovered Olga was the only one who could stop her dreadful backaches. Neither Olga nor her mother knew

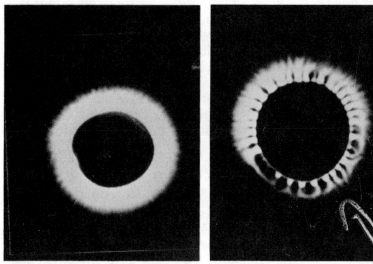

Fig. 8-1. *(Left)* A drop of trypsin in its normal state. *(Right)* The same drop after being "energized" by Olga Worrall.

why Olga's hands stopped the pain, but they did, and so quickly that the child was sent out to ailing neighbors instead of being allowed to play, which she would have liked much better.

I remember Olga's timid delivery at Stanford—and delight in contrasting that memory with a later one of Olga, *sans* script, showing slides of her research from London to Lourdes and regaling her audience with tales of quadrupling the growth of plants in Atlanta from her home in Baltimore. This last phenomenon was recorded on precise charts by scientists who were, and still are, at a loss to explain the miracle, as is Olga.

New Blood in the Lab

When the New Dimensions of Healing symposium reconvened at UCLA, Olga asked that we play hooky the first day (we had heard the papers at Stanford) in order to do some Kirlian experiments. Olga was still searching to find objective evidence of that healing energy. We were joined that day by Sister Justa Smith and Bernie Grad, who asked respectively for Kirlian photographs of enzymes and blood serum, which they hoped would photograph differently after Olga "energized" them.

Ken improvised nobly, never having photographed liquids before. And by the end of that grueling day, we had a goodly supply of blood and enzyme pictures, taken both before and after Olga had

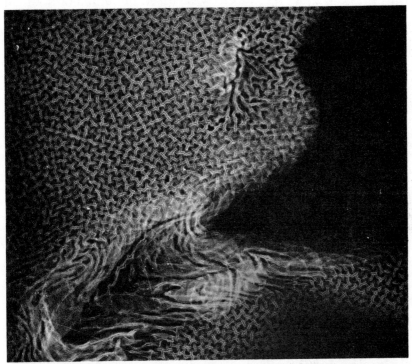

Fig. 8-2. Our first "non-electrical" photograph by Olga Worrall—which she described as "ectoplasm."

held her hands over them (Fig. 8-1). These showed, typically, odd "lines of force" after Olga's treatment. Everyone was pleased, and ready to quit, when Olga suggested one last study. She asked that we put away all the Kirlian equipment and simply sit quietly in a circle, inside the isolation booth (which was now doubling as a seance room!). Then Olga asked for a fresh piece of film, which she held between the tips of her fingers. After a few minutes of quiet, Olga asked me to develop the film, which I took from her and dropped into the tank. We all watched as a textured "cheesecloth" pattern emerged (Fig. 8-2). This was our first experience with non-electrical "bioplasma"—if that's what that highly structured stuff is.

Similar non-electrical patterns were to emerge on film, taking us by surprise. In fact, it happened again, that very night. Long after the rest of us had gone home, Bernie Grad and K.J. worked late making Kirlian pictures. But as they worked, odd "blobs," which took on a precise pattern of slanting rain, began to show up in the developed film. No matter how they positioned the film, and regardless of whether the current was passed through it or not, that precise slant of rain kept appearing. They no longer touched the film, but simply shook hands over it—and the slanting rain appeared. Finally, they did nothing more than take the fresh film from its box and drop it into the developer. Same slanting rain. Ken raced over the next morning to show me the negatives and I thought of ways to explain them away (bad film, poor developer, bad mixing, etc.), all of which Ken and Bernie had thought of the night before and had methodically ruled out.

Was this "slanting rain," like Olga's "cheesecloth," a form of bioenergy which did not need electricity to appear on film? We didn't know (was it the presence of Olga that sparked it?), and Ken spent every spare moment over the next days exploring the phenomenon—which grew weaker, after the symposium, and finally stopped, never to reappear as slanting rain.

But whenever Olga visited the lab, which she did often over the next years, we tried to create more of that non-electrical photography. We never again saw the "cheesecloth," but on one memorable afternoon, she created such strong, swirling "fog patterns" on film that we were tossing fresh film from newly opened boxes into freshly mixed developer—and found the same fog patterns every time. Olga apologized for ruining our expensive film, but I was greatly cheered to see such a strong effect. That peculiar, non-electrical phenomenon had occurred now on several separate occasions, which made it less likely to be an error made by us, and more likely, perhaps, to be related to a special bioenergy.

FIRST NATIONAL ACUPUNCTURE CONFERENCE

Just as there had suddenly arisen a Kirlian conference in New York and twin healing symposia in California, there as suddenly appeared an acupuncture conference in Bethesda, Maryland, sponsored for the first time by the National Institute of Health. The guest list included well-known, highly respected scientists now working in the field of acupuncture—and me. The federal government had expressed an interest in learning whether there was any solid scientific data to support the idea of a flow of energy in the body which could be manipulated by needles or electricity. (This last, electrical stimulation, had just recently been reported from the Republic of China.)

What finer debut for our acupuncture research with Kirlian photography? And what better study than the recent xylocaine-induced "sympathectomy," which had shown brilliantly the imbalance of energy due to trauma—where the coronas of the drugged fingers were bright and full, but the coronas of the normal fingers had totally disappeared. In that study we had struck another lode, because we had seen that the energy "imbalance" of acupuncture theory *also* showed up as a huge increase in electrical flow, which could be measured with a sensitive voltmeter, and which we could report, in *numbers, statistics,* and *graphs!* This was hard, objective scientific evidence. At least, that's what I had thought. But our paper and its photographs and graphs were met with the skepticism which is common to unorthodox research.

All the same, it was a rich meeting, where ideas of a possible bioenergy were at least being entertained by men of merit (who also held many degrees). I remember one scientist who was enchanted that we had found the same "hot spots" that he had discovered with an instrument of his own devising. It was an invention similar to Adamenko's tobiscope and Ken's acuometer. But this scientist, with a discretion I admired, avoided calling those hot spots "acupuncture points," but used the more scientific phrase, "electrodermal points." And electrodermal points they are still being called by many scientists today. (Just one more instance of an appropriate phrase making the unorthodox more acceptable. Some others include "biocommunication" for telepathy, "remote viewing" for out-of-the-body, "non-verbal communication" for ESP.)

Though our research was not applauded by the scientists at Bethesda, it was embraced by the media, and once again our photographs were displayed prominently in national publications like *Medical World News.* Within weeks, we were being deluged with invitations to conferences national and international. Somehow, suddenly, we had fame and/or notoriety.

THE NEW WORLD OF SHOW BIZ SCIENCE: BRIGHT SIDE

And with it we were introduced to the life of the academic superstar, who travels in sun and snow and shade around the world—New Orleans, Hawaii, Edinburgh, New Delhi, Detroit, London, Sao Paulo, Sofia, Bogota, Munich, Mexico City—to conferences whose topics range from psychiatry to sorcery to physics to semantics to pain. Whatever the conference, the same superstars arrive, with all their expenses paid by the organization, which usually throws in an honorarium besides. Such stars settle in, often the night before their papers are to be read, and leave shortly after delivering them, presumably because they are en route to the next conference. No matter the nature of the meeting, the superstars give their standard lecture—but with a different emphasis, depending on the topic at hand. And since every conference has a different audience and a different theme, the stars can give the same lecture a new title, which can then be added to their *curricula vitae*—that list of academic accomplishments which has become the Book of Records by which the scholar is judged. (The *curricula vitae*, or "c.v.," used to deal chiefly with classes taught and papers published but has gone on to enumerate each and every outreach to the media and the public, and has thus become a weighty matter—the more pages, the more prestige.) Since I was a novice to this sort of show biz, it took me a long time to recognize what was happening. Which was fine, for I had not heard many of those multi-purpose texts and profited from them.

The lab also profited from the honoraria which I began to receive. Since the lab was just about the only one doing serious Kirlian research in the United States in 1972 and '73, we had a corner on the lecturing market. Which meant we could ask an increasingly higher fee—an unmitigated blessing. For the lab, *throughout the research*, remained unfunded—except for those honoraria, which in time rose to $1,000 per lecture. This did not make us rich, of course, but it did make possible the purchase of lots of film and the processing thereof, our only major expenses. The lab staff, all of them, were volunteers, and the lab space, all twelve by fourteen feet of it, was given freely for as long as Jolly West defended our right to it.

SHOW BIZ SCIENCE: DARK SIDE

Jolly's defense almost came to an abrupt stop, right after the New Dimensions of Healing symposium at UCLA. The abundant publicity that came with the symposium developed into a troublesome sore for the UCLA Medical School, of which the NPI was but a branch. The media had stressed that the conference had seriously considered not only acupuncture, but magnetic passes and psychic healing—and this the Medical School viewed dimly. Soon, I was called before Jolly West.

When I entered his office, he was studying the symposium's brochure, for which I had written an editorial using the phrase, "laying on of hands." Jolly looked up at me, pointed to the abominable phrase, and said in a kind way that my use of "biblical language" in an institute dedicated to medical science was inappropriate, if not injurious. It was clear that my job was on the line, and I was prepared to be asked for my resignation. But that did not come. For Jolly went on to ask, unexpectedly, how many people had attended the symposium. I replied that I didn't know— perhaps 1,500 to 2,000? I saw Jolly's jaw drop as he reached for the phone to verify that startling number with university Extension, which came through rousingly once again to report that the symposium had received not only kudos from the audience and media, but that a very large profit had been realized from the event. This news seemed to change the atmosphere of our interview, which soon after ended with no (apparent) action taken.

Shortly afterwards, the lab was visited by a delegation of research scientists (M.D./Ph.D. hyphenates) as well as a professional photographer. They asked many questions, studied our techniques and pictures, and even participated in a study. They were polite, and serious, and left after several hours—to write a report (a copy of which was sent to me) suggesting that the research, while unorthodox and odd, might prove of some interest to science.

After which, the work continued uninterrupted until almost a year later in 1973, when there arrived still another invitation to another conference. It was there that all hell broke loose.

FIRST INTERNATIONAL PSYCHOTRONICS CONFERENCE: PRAGUE

This one was all the way over in Prague, and there were no expenses paid and no honoraria offered. Yet it was the only conference I thought really vital to attend. It had been organized by Czech psychologist Dr. Rejdak who, in 1970, had introduced Dr. Monty Ullman and me to the parapsychology of Czechoslovakia and had driven us far into the suburbs to visit that controversial inventor of "psychotronic generators," Robert Pavlita. Now, in 1973, Dr. Rejdak was the chairman of this First International Psychotronics Conference. (Psychotronics was another newly minted word to make more respectable psychokinesis, or PK, defined for this conference as "the interaction of people with objects in the environment.") To this Prague congress would come scientists from several Soviet countries, as well as from the Western world, who would be sharing information of their research into the paranormal. This was the very goal that had sent me round the world, a few short years ago, in vain. I did not know if this conference would prove any more rewarding, but this was where the Search was now leading and I could only follow.

So I mailed my acceptance and began a paper on our newest Kirlian work.

Prague, Third Time Around

With paper in portfolio and with lots of questions to ask Soviet friends who were scheduled for the conference, I flew to Prague for the third time in eight years and, for the third time, paid my own way.

Very different it was, this time. Gone from view was the side-street hotel with the broken elevator and the gray greasy food; gone, too, was the palace of my second visit, with instant concierge, waiter, valet. But still very much present at the airport was the Intourist guide with black limousine who drove me to a sky-scraper hotel where each room had its twin right-angled beds which doubled as sofas, its own small, well-equipped bathroom, and its picture window—exactly like every tourist hotel in every world capital. With one major difference: the telephone, which worked impeccably inside the hotel and for overseas calls, always seemed to miss connections within the city of Prague.

The Opening of the Conference

At the ancient town hall, which served as a dignified conference center, there arrived scientists of many disciplines from many many countries. And—whether from Brazil or Belgium, the Soviet Union or the United States, Sweden, Estonia, Poland or Great Britain—they all seemed to be doing research in one or another occult area. At the registration desk, flushed with excitement and pleasure, stood our chairman, Dr. Rejdak, offering the complete proceedings of the conference, already published in two volumes and five languages. (I learned it was becoming a tradition to publish the entire transactions of a conference before it had taken place.) For a brief time it was exciting to rummage through the thick volumes, finding articles (in Russian) by the Kirlians, Adamenko and Inyushin. But they, themselves, were nowhere to be seen. I sought out Dr. Rejdak who, still smiling, told me they would not be attending. Again that Soviet ploy of a gift not delivered. The absence of Soviet scientists left many of our American delegates feeling frustrated and foolish.

All the same, it was startling to hear the papers of those few Soviet scientists who did attend, for they were respected physicists and biochemists discussing, openly and in scientific terms, such ideas as levitation, dowsing, and PK.

This last was among the most popular topics. And the Czech inventor, Pavlita, was very much present to demonstrate his psychotronic generators. The demonstration was much the same as the one he had given Monty Ullman and me in his home—but with one big difference. In his home, he had disappeared into a back room for each new piece of equipment, leaving us to wonder if there were some chicanery. Here, on a large stage, he remained seated throughout. And in one stunning experiment (which I had not seen before), Pavlita started a small windmill rotating to the right by pressing his right hand to his right temple and then to the table on which the windmill sat, a good eight inches from his hand. Then he would reverse the movement of the windmill so that it rotated to the left simply by changing to his left hand. This looked very much like a voluntary shift of polarity (from positive to negative) through some kind of bioenergetic transfer.

But even this brilliant demonstration was eclipsed by a film from Russell Targ and Hal Puthoff of Stanford Research Institute, which showed controlled studies with the then-unknown Israeli psychic, Uri Geller. In one study, Geller demonstrated, much like Pavlita had, that at a distance, and without contact, he could deflect a compass needle first to the right and then to the left simply by moving his hands—or just his eyes, it seemed, at one point in the movie. Later in the day, a similar phenomenon was shown in a Russian film that featured Mme. Kulagina. In all three films, from three different countries, the same phenomenon of rotating objects from positive to negative through some unknown bioenergy which seemed to be influencing objects at a distance! Here, indeed, were demonstrations of "the interactions between people and the objects in their environment."

Healing

It was certainly not yet known whether the bioenergy of psychics like Geller and Kulagina is related to the bioenergy of healing. But in the panel on psychic healing, it was clear that this idea was being entertained by scientists of several countries who presented various native techniques of healing. Particularly impressive was the research reported by Brazil's Psychobiophysics Institute, for that group had been working for years, under the leadership of Professor Andrade—and unknown to me!—with Kirlian photography. In one of their presentations they showed an electrical photograph of a transfer of healing energy from healer to patient that looked very much like our own research.

I had not known of this group before and was delighted to exchange information with the Brazilian delegates, who told me that Andrade had successfully photographed the phantom leaf. This was wonderfully heartening news, for we in the lab, after two years, had still not come close.

Later that evening I was approached by a medical doctor from Vienna named Huber, who almost furtively asked if I would be willing to witness his healing technique. When I agreed, he took me into a deserted side corridor. (I believe these were precautions against medical colleagues seeing him, for he was still shy of admitting this strange talent.) Dr. Huber then asked if he might be permitted to demonstrate on my arm, which I offered him. He then held the palm of his hand about four inches above my arm and made passes in a way similar to Jack Gray's magnetic passes. Although I had never felt anything from Jack or any of the other healers who had worked in our lab, here in Prague, from Dr. Huber, I felt a sharp tingling/pricking sensation that was almost painful. I gasped and stared at Dr. Huber and nodded my head. He dropped his hand, and in awkward English said that he had always had this ability but could not understand it scientifically. I smiled and said I could empathize, for our lab, too, was having difficulty trying to define this healing energy—but we believed we had been able to photograph it. Dr. Huber was eager for more news of this and came next day to our panel on Kirlian photography.

That's Not Bioenergy! That's Just Bad Technology!

In that summer of '73 many Americans were doing research in Kirlian photography. But when they presented their papers, it became evident that most of them strongly disagreed with what our lab had reported! I listened, shocked, as one researcher after another announced that he (or she) had observed no changes in coronas due to emotion, or relaxation, or arousal. One physicist even dismissed Inyushin's theory of bioplasma (or patterned energy fields), claiming instead that with controlled atmospheres, the Kirlian effect could be shown to be due to gasses like nitrogen and carbon dioxide, which ionize on being emitted from the skin. Another researcher reported that the Kirlian coronas change because of the amount of pressure with which the finger touches the film—the heavier the pressure, the narrower the corona.

But by far the most devastating paper came from Stanford's physicist and crystallographer, William Tiller. Just the year before, Tiller had visited our lab after having seen Soviet research into Kirlian photography firsthand, which had impressed him enough to want to study it for himself. He had managed to get specific designs from the Soviets—something I had not been able to do—and had developed a sophisticated device with which he had been exploring the Kirlian effect from the point of view of physics. And his complex paper dealt, in rich detail, with several vital areas.

For one, he had studied the *colors* in Kirlian photography, which he claimed were due to the strength with which the electrons (from the electric charge) bombarded the three layers of the film emulsion. That is to say, the color blue appears in the photograph when the electron flow is not strong and penetrates only the top (blue) layer of film, while the red appears when the electrons are strongest and penetrate all the way through the film, to the metal plate, and bounce back to the third (red) layer, and the various shades of yellow, orange, lavender, or purple appear as interactions of one or more layers with the second (green) emulsion. Nowhere, I noticed, did Tiller explain why the color green never shows up in a Kirlian photograph.

This is, of course, a much simplified summary of Tiller's meticulous work. His chief point, with regard to colors, was that *they were not due to emotional arousal,* as we had claimed, but to how the electrons from the object being photographed strike the film. Could it be, I wondered, that the strength of electron flow was determined by the object's—or person's—energy level? I did not think to ask that question till much later, and even then the question was dismissed.

Tiller soon discovered that the placement, angle, and pressure of the finger pad on the film could create a wide variety of corona patterns. So, he concluded, rather than psychological or physiological or emotional variables being reflected in the pictures, the changes were more easily explained as mechanical ones, which had nothing to do with "bioenergy." And because fingers were so fickle, Tiller abandoned them for a metal stud of one constant size, angle, and pressure.

Using the metal stud, Tiller researched the differences that voltage, frequency, exposure time, and other variables might make, and he presented a great many Kirlian slides to show those effects.

His was a highly persuasive technical paper and the first one on Kirlian photography by a reputable American physicist. Because of Tiller's findings, serious scientists at the conference began to look askance at the Kirlian research, if not to dismiss it altogether.

As for me, I left the conference dazed and disturbed. For not only had there been Tiller's technical rebuttal, but in sharp contrast, there had been other papers claiming that the Kirlian emanations showed how spirits enter the body (through the gaps in the corona), and that through the colors of the "human aura," one can evaluate health and disease, and that "life readings" can be given, through the analysis of a finger-pad picture. All of which made Kirlian photography seem as silly and disreputable to me as Tiller's sophisticated technology probably made our research seem to others. Flying back to Los Angeles, I realized that our work in the lab—which we had repeated over and over again with consistent results—was being flatly contradicted.

Why?

9
Re-Search and Renewal

Being a Re-Examination, Through Which Comes a New Exploration into Bioenergy *Without Electricity*

TO LOOK AGAIN

Theree began a long period of re-search, in its original meaning of searching, again, through our findings. I was confident that our studies in the lab were basically sound and consistent. How, then, could Tiller and the others have found results so opposite to ours? Only slowly, as we traced our way back over the work, did we piece together odd pieces of data that helped us to understand.

For example, there had been over the years a series of events with graduate student Barry Taff (who was also the lab psychic). In the beginning of our Kirlian work, we were taking pictures of anyone who would volunteer, and Barry had volunteered. Repeatedly. And that was how we discovered, for the first time, the "disappearance" effect, for Barry's finger pads never photographed at all. Then later, when we began studying altered states of consciousness, we took advantage of the fact that Barry has the special gift of being able to go into trance at will. When he was in trance, we took Kirlian pictures and saw that his finger pads photographed with brilliant coronas! This was an experiment we repeated many times, with consistent results: Barry, in trance, took vivid pictures, but Barry, in his normal waking state, did not photograph at all.

Then, about a year before the Prague conference, Barry built his own Kirlian device and one day brought to the lab some photographs he had taken, which he thrust into my hands almost angrily.

"Look at these!" he had said. "They're *my* finger pads! Mine! When I'm wide awake."

I looked at the photographs and was stunned. For I saw very large, very fluffy coronas. Much larger than any we had taken on Ken's device.

"These are *your* fingerpads?

Barry nodded, vigorously.

"I always show up on my machine! In trance or not in trance. And my finger pads don't look any different from anyone else's. See?" He thrust more pictures at me.

It was true. All of his finger-pad pictures showed full, fluffy coronas. And each subject's pads looked very much like the others'. This was very different from what we had found with Ken's machine, where each person's finger *pad* was about as unique as his finger *print*.

"And look at these, in color." Barry gave me more pictures. Another surprise. These pictures were all of delicate yellow and violet hues, none in the reds and blues we had come to expect.

Immediate questions: was the film Barry used different? Developer? Color lab? Exposure time? All exactly what we had been using. Eventually we were left with the obvious difference—the electrical device. How was it different? Basically, Barry had built an instrument using a Tesla coil, similar to the Kirlians' device. But Tesla coils are generally hand-made, of turns of wire around a core, and the larger the number of turns, the greater the power. How powerful was Barry's device? He brought it to the lab so that we could measure its parameters. (This was not at all easy to do. In fact, back in '71, there was no one who could measure the Kirlian apparatus, not even electronics experts, who came armed with their oscilloscopes.) We did learn that Barry's voltage was considerably higher than Ken's, which may have been where the difference lay. For in the work that followed, we learned that too much electricity swamped the pictures through over-exposure. Barry took his machine back and kept it until its power caused the radios and TVs in his neighborhood to go berserk and the police came after him for violating the FCC code. Then Barry donated his device to the lab.

This incident was followed, a few months later (but again at least a year before Prague), when we were visited by Sheila Ostrander and Lynn Schroeder, who were in Los Angeles publicizing their now-successful *Psychic Discoveries Behind the Iron Curtain*. Sheila and Lynn had brought with them a Kirlian device, also based on a small Tesla coil, which they had encased in a slim valise. We were charmed with the idea of a device that could be hand-carried and plugged into a wall socket, so Ken built a similar one for the lab which we called the Portable. We soon saw that the Portable gave full, fluffy coronas for everyone, like Barry's machine. And it never showed the "red blotch of arousal." Then Ken began to manipulate the small dial on the coil, which regulated power and we saw that with *less* power, differences in corona patterns began to appear, as did the blotch. Again, too much electricity had swamped the pictures.

Question: was this what had happened with Tiller's sophisticated instrument? Was it essentially more like Barry's and the Portable, with so much power that it did not register differences? I began to see that if we had started our research with an instrument like the Portable, we would *not* have found changes due to the subject's emotions or physiology, because the power of the electricity would have blotted out all those differences into fluffy coronas that all looked the same.

Here was a major dilemma. Each researcher was building his own Kirlian unit and could only report the results from his own lab—which could easily be very different from the results of another lab! (This had happened before, in electrical research. In the first thirty years of electrophysiology, when each lab pioneered its own instruments to record EEG, or GSR, or EKG, there was great confusion in the literature over what was a real effect and what was simply bad technology causing phony blips (the artifacts) on the chart recorder.

What, in the Kirlian work, was a real bioenergetic effect, and what was simply a matter of electricity?

That's Not Bioenergy! That's Corona Discharge!

Just about every electronics expert we knew had told us, with a nice smile of Truth, that our Kirlian photographs were nothing but "corona discharge," a commonplace phenomenon often seen in lightning storms as a hazy blue halo around electrified objects. This notion of Kirlian photography as "nothing but corona discharge" had become so popular that at the New York conference in '72, our first paper was titled, "Bioplasma or Corona Discharge?" I had sent a copy of the article, with several of my own questions, to Inyushin and received a thoughtful letter in return, saying that the Soviet scientists believed they were studying bioplasma *through* corona discharge—meaning, I think, that the pattern of corona discharge gives information about the energy field around the object (such as, is there disease present? emotion? metal fatigue?). But few American scientists were willing to entertain that idea. And fewer still after Tiller's expertise had made it seem that just about every Kirlian effect could be explained as artifacts—or just bad technology.

This was worrisome. Because as everyone knew, Ken and I had both been electrical dunces at the start of the research. And Ken's first device, put together with courage and junk, was a garbage basket of wave forms, voltage, frequencies, etc., none of which could be adequately measured. I remember a well-known physicist from a think tank studying that first box of tangled spaghetti wires, then commenting with a grin that we were using a "shotgun approach"—which, like most shotgun affairs, he clearly considered illegitimate.

Different Instruments, Different Pictures: Before Prague

Before that Prague conference, we had learned—slowly—how different electrical parameters affected the Kirlian image. When, for example, Ken saw that the dial on the Portables could control voltage, he took pictures of a geranium leaf at different voltages and saw dramatic differences. Then he built a new instrument with a dial to control frequency (much like a dial on a radio which turns from the frequency of one radio station to another). By changing frequencies, we found one of our most startling effects, for we saw again and again that at one frequency, the image was clear and bright, then at a higher frequency, the image would blur and grow dimmer, and at a still higher frequency, the image disappeared altogether (again like changing the dial on a radio, from station to station). This cycle kept repeating as we went up the frequency scale (Fig. 9-1).

We stared hard at that new data, for it revealed the opposite of what the electronics experts had told us. They had said that the electricity going through the object creates the picture, which is nothing but corona discharge. Now we were seeing that the electricity going through the object would *sometimes* create a picture, but *sometimes not!* If Kirlian photography were nothing but corona discharge, then there should *always* be a picture, no matter what the frequency.

Something else was going on. Our guess: could we be dealing with a *resonance* effect? Just as hitting the right note can cause a glass to break, could hitting the right frequency cause a picture to appear?

Different Instruments: After Prague

Since different instruments have different parameters, and different parameters give different pictures, it seemed like a good idea to look at the devices used by other researchers. At Prague, some of

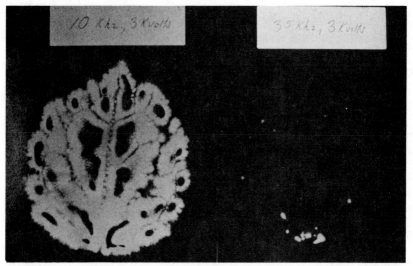

Fig. 9-1. *(Left)* Kirlian image of a leaf, brilliant at one frequency. *(Right)* Kirlian image of same leaf disappears at a different frequency.

the most exquisite photographs had been taken by Daniel Kientz, a student who had built his own instrument, on his own design, and had found effects similar (but more gloriously dramatic) than ours. So I asked Dan if he would build us one of his devices, and he did. When it was hand-delivered, we saw that his elegant, transistorized device took very different pictures than either the Portable or K.J.'s original. Of particular fascination were the very long filaments, or streamers, which emanated from the fingertips. This was to prove of immense value for our future studies in "interactions between people."

I also asked Henry Dakin, an electronics engineer from San Francisco who had helped create the Tiller machine, to build us a similar instrument. We found that the Dakin device again gave different pictures. Thus, we were seeing, ever more clearly, that the story of electrical photography was highly dependent on the instrument used to tell the story.

In fact, it was positively uncanny to photograph the same slice of carrot on two different machines, one right after the other, and to see that the Portable's version of the carrot was a blaze of lavenders, magenta, and orange, while the Dakin version was a murky red blob, without corona of any kind. Nor could we predict how any particular object would photograph on any particular machine. We were back to old-fashioned trial and error, with whopping surprises. My favorite study in this genre is of the same leaf, taken on three different instruments, looking like three different leaves (Fig. 9-2).

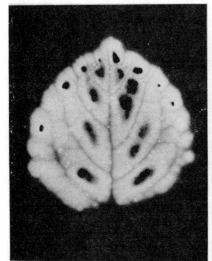
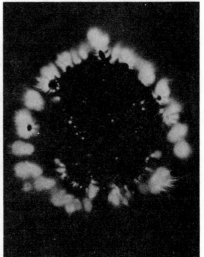

Fig. 9-2. One leaf, taken on three different instruments. Each conveys different information—which may one day be deciphered.

We were not nearly wise enough to unravel such problems, and went for advice to the experts, who studied our pictures but could not explain them. Probably the most frustrating of these incidents was when an East Coast research scientist from an international electronics firm visited the lab.

He was a pleasant man, that physicist, and after studying our pictures and equipment carefully, he asked if he might call the head of UCLA's Department of Electronics to join him. We were delighted. The two men proceeded to discuss the research and then proposed a simple test to find out what was being photographed in the Kirlian pictures. They believed that, whatever we were picking up, it was a known energy—none of that bioplasma nonsense!—

something within the electromagnetic spectrum. To prove their hypothesis, they proposed that we use filters to screen out all known wave lengths, from ultra-violet through infra-red. By so doing, they said, we should get no picture at all with the Kirlian technique. We were keen to see whether that were so and hunted down the necessary filters. They cooperated with the set-up, the pictures were taken, and in a very few minutes we saw the results—very much dimmer photographs they were, but they were definitely photographs. Our guests seemed pleased with the result.

"But you said—" I was angry, "—*there would be no picture at all!*"

"No picture at all," the physicist answered obscurely, "can be a relative thing."

And there the matter stayed, like a hot tamale in the stomach.

More Experiences with Experts

Even as were were continuing the re-search, the lab's fame/notoriety grew, and so did such visits. We became something of a good-natured joke to the other labs on the second floor, who were being intruded upon by people looking for the "Kirlian stuff." These included delegates from such prestigious places as NASA, Oak Ridge Atomic Energy Commission, Menninger Foundation, Rand Corporation, North American Rockwell, Langley-Porter Institute, and Hughes Research Laboratory. Each of these visitors would carefully explain that his was *not* official business, but simply a personal interest.

At the start we were flattered that such known and knowledgeable scientists would spend so much time in the lab asking meaningful and respectful questions. But it soon became clear that this was just another one-way communication, in which we were asked an inordinate number of questions, but when *we* would ask, as we invariably did, what they thought was being photographed, they would answer either not at all or with replies so complex that we got lost in the lingo. But one message was always perfectly clear: an unknown bioenergy was not to be considered. Period. Hours, and even days in the lab were spent in this profitless way, at the end of which the visitor would smile a dubious smile and say something like, "Thanks a lot, but no thanks."

So we decided to call a halt to the scientific freeloaders by granting appointments only to those willing to pay a consultant's fee. This ploy helped the financing, kept away the curiosity hounds, and sometimes provided amusement. One day an expert from the Jet Propulsion Lab called, asking to visit us to "see what we were doing." My mention of a fee caught him off guard.

"Oh? How much do you charge?"

"Two hundred dollars for an afternoon."

"No problem," he said, airily. "I'll get it from petty cash."

But we never heard from him again.

OLD, FAMILIAR FIGHTS

After Tiller, some of our most strenuous opposition to the Kirlian work began to come from—of all places!—the parapsychologists. Those very pioneers who had fought to make respectable such borderlands of science as telepathy and psychokinesis were now fighting to keep their own borders clean of such grungy stuff as Kirlian photography, acupuncture, and psychic healing (which, I blush to remember, would have been my own attitude just a few years earlier). Researchers who had presented papers at our ESP symposia were now reporting, in the journals, on the "unscientific nature" of our research. Sometimes this was blunt criticism and sometimes subtle—as with the kind soul who, to show us the errors of our work, sent an untitled, unpublished paper on the unsavory history of electrical photography.

That gift proved to be a pearl beyond price, though not at all in the way it was intended. We had, for years, tried to research the literature on electrical photography and had come up with close to nothing, except for the article given me by Adamenko, courtesy of the Moscow Public Library, about the "electrography" of the 1930s. But now, this unsolicited, unpublished article opened with a revelation: "The discovery of mysterious luminescent structures on photographic plates goes back almost one hundred years." And it goes on from there to give prolific, specific references, most of which we were later able to track down. It was the rarest of refreshments to learn that the battles we were now enjoying with Tiller *et al.* over bioenergy, bioplasma, and the Kirlian effect had already been fought (and fought better!), *in the nineteenth century,* under the names of "life force," "effluvia," and "electrical photography."

Those intrepid fighters of a previous century were, like us, searching for an unknown bioenergy. Their leader was a French medical doctor, Henri Baraduc, whose masterwork, long out of print, was *The Human Soul: Its Movements, Its Lights.* When, at last, we located a copy of Dr. Baraduc's book, we found it filled with electrical photographs of human fingers and hands that looked for all the world like our own Kirlian pictures, with the same kinds of coronas, bubbles, and blotches—which Baraduc christened "effluvia."

For many of the years that Baraduc and his group worked in

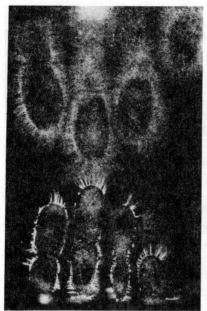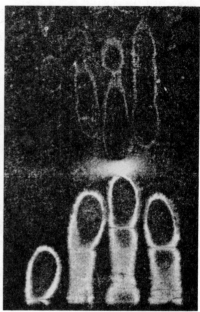

Fig. 9-3. Among the very first electrical photographs of hands, taken late in the nineteenth century by Polish doctor Iodko-Narkovitz. On the left, attraction; and on the right, repulsion.

Paris, we found out, a medical doctor in Poland, Iodko-Narkovitz, was experimenting with his own version of electrical photography. The two inventors were ignorant of each other's existence until, at last, they met and collaborated in Paris. I had learned about Iodko long before Baraduc, because at a conference in Monaco a group of Polish scientists presented me with a short biography of him, together with reproductions of his nineteenth-century electrical photographs showing how two hands sent lines of force *toward* each other—attraction—and two other hands sent lines of force *away* from each other—repulsion (Fig. 9-3). Proud were the Poles to show me Iodko's photographs, since I had just presented at the conference what I had thought were the first electrical photographs ever taken of attraction and repulsion between fingers. (It is discomfiting to learn that one has re-invented the wheel.)

That's Not Bioenergy! That's Heat!

I was also amused to read, in that same unpublished treasure, that the scientists of the nineteenth century were just as critical of an unknown "life force" as the scientists of today are of an unknown bioenergy. And in spite of the seventy-five years that separate them, their basic arguments have remained the same. A major opposing theory, then and now, was that the changes in the pictures were due to *heat!*

This was one of the first barbs tossed at us by the critics, early in the Kirlian research, when we came upon the red blotch which we believed was due to emotional arousal. But, we were told, the red blotch was simply the result of higher body heat caused by emotions like anger and sex, or physiology like exercise and sweat. To study that possibility, we had done strenuous sessions in which, after taking pictures at normal temperatures, we asked people to keep their arms, up to the shoulder, in water as hot as they could stand it for as long as they could stand it. We photographed their hot fingers, then asked them to plunge the other arm into icy water for as long as they could, and photographed their cold fingers. We found, with more than thirty people, that there was absolutely *no* relation between heat and/or cold and the photographs. The blotch would come with either, or with neither, or with both. So we dismissed the idea that the blotch was due to heat.

Now, in that fine unpublished paper, we learned that the same argument had been advanced against the Effluvists—whose critics, refreshingly, had backed up their arguments with experiments of their own devising. One deliciously macabre study (which was one of the few, sadly, for which we could not find the original source) was performed by a professional French photographer named Yvon, who somehow wangled his way into a dissecting room where he was able to obtain a hand freshly cut from a corpse (reminiscent of our dead man's hand, years earlier, which had unfortunately been contaminated with formaldehyde). Yvon's dead hand was uncontaminated and therefore better data. He took the dead hand and a living hand and proceeded to photograph each with his electrical device under several identical conditions. Thus, this nineteenth-century photographer was performing a controlled experiment in the best twentieth-century tradition. Yvon found that the living hand showed the "effluvia" while the dead hand did not. Then—and this is the crux of the study—Yvon *heated* the dead hand to 95° Fahrenheit and photographed it again. And the dead hand gave forth just as much effluvia as the living hand.

"Merely a matter of temperature," comments the unpublished article, which then suggests that heating a "dead" leaf would bring back its Kirlian image on film. By the time we read that suggestion, we knew from our research that a dead leaf, bathed in water or by the hot, dry Santa Ana winds, comes back to Kirlian life, but heat alone effects no such resurrection.

In spite of Yvon's ingenious work, the *heat* argument sprang to life again when the Effluvists claimed that the effluvia were not due to heat alone, but to heat *plus* the "magnetic fluid" of Mesmer—still another term for bioenergy. In reply, Dr. Menager of the Paris

Institut Metapsychique built a fake finger, out of hollow rubber, which he filled with water of various temperatures from 36° to 95° Fahrenheit and claimed that the photographs from the rubber fingers were "indistinguishable" from those of living fingers. By the time we read this research, we had done similar experiments with fake fingers, using a rubber surgical glove and filling its fingers with waters of various temperatures. We had always gotten brilliant, large coronas, with never a blotch or bubble or gap. Thus, in our opinion, the coronas of fake fingers were *too* perfect and therefore easily distinguishable from living ones.

FROM EFFLUVIA TO ORGONE

While we were still re-searching our work, and that of the Effluvists, there arrived still another invitation to still another conference, to be held in San Francisco. This one, like the one in Prague, was obligatory, for it was dedicated to Wilhelm Reich, the twentieth-century psychoanalyst whose search for an unknown bioenergy had led, ultimately, to his persecution and death. Reich believed he had discovered a universal life force, which he called "orgone." His description of orgone was, to me, very much like the "chi" of acupuncture, the "prana" of Yoga, the "bioplasma" of Inyushin, and the "effluvia" of Baraduc. (Not to mention fifty other names, in fifty other cultures.) What was unique to Reich was his claim that he could *harness* orgone energy and use it for healing.

Years of laboratory research had taught Reich (or so he thought) how to accumulate that orgone energy in special "orgone boxes" —which he began to use in his practice. This led to his arrest by the United States government on the charge of falsely advertising cures for illness through the use of those orgone boxes—which were empty! On the face of it, a scam. At least it must have seemed so during the trial, for Reich was found guilty, sentenced, and died in prison. One added insult: his books were burned. (Reich is the only American scientist with that distinction.)

So, for a very long time, Reich's books were illegal and impossible to find when we had wanted to study his orgone research. Now, twenty-five years after his death, he was to be honored in San Francisco. Several of us from the lab went to pay our respects— and were rewarded with new paths along which to continue our search.

San Francisco Reich

The audience at this conference was huge, and typical of the early '70s: enthusiasts of encounter groups, health foods, meditation, ecology, organic drugs, freedom of feeling. And they gave seemingly random ovations to the speakers recruited from around the world, none of whom presented recent orgone research. A typical paper, from a psychotherapist, gave lip service to Reich's "orgone" but went on to describe her own brand of sex therapy which seemed to have little to do with Reich. The lady received an ovation.

Later in the program, Eva Reich, M.D., daughter of Wilhelm Reich, was introduced and received a standing ovation before and after her talk. (I had not known Reich had a daughter.) She gave a demonstration of how to construct an "orgone shield," a healing aid for minor cuts, burns, and bruises. This is a simple device, its base an ordinary metal mixing bowl (the conductor) around which is wrapped a layer of cotton wool (the insulator), which is then covered with a layer of steel wool (the conductor). Eva explained it was this layering that causes the orgone to accumulate; the more layers, the more intense the energy. As I watched, I was struck by the similarity to a Kirlian device, which has a metal base (conductor), covered with glass (insulator), which can be repeated in layers. Was that of any significance...?

I kept gnawing on that idea during the next event, which was a panel scheduled to end at four o'clock, at which time I was to present. But the panel kept plowing on with no moderator to stop them, and it was five before the panel droned to a halt. Since there was to be an early-evening session with other scheduled papers, the audience was getting up to leave for a dinner break. The panel was still milling about on stage with no moderator, and, not knowing what else to do, I wandered to the stage where the moderator materialized, asking, "What'll we do?"

I found myself grabbing the microphone and yelling into the hubbub, asking the audience if they wanted to hear me briefly or to adjourn. Out of the disorder, a loud voice:

"Whatever you say, Thelma!"

I shouted back, "I'll present quickly for anyone who wants to stay, but we must have *quiet!*"

The shock of that last screamed word brought sudden silence to the auditorium and I was asked for the first slide. The lights went out and on the huge rear screen there shone a brilliant Kirlian image. This was greeted by an audible sigh of pleasure and people began to shuffle back to their seats. I rushed into a talk and another voice from the audience shouted, "Slow down, Thelma!"

Which I did. At the end, another mindless ovation. There is something disheartening about promiscuous applause and cheers, every bit as much as boos or indifference. Leaving the hall, that depression of "What the hell am I doing here?"

Meeting with Eva Reich

The answer came that night when John and I learned that Eva Reich had been impressed with our Kirlian work and wanted to meet us. We gathered in Henry Dakin's lab and Eva was encouraging about our research, which she thought might validate some of her father's theses.

"But—" She paused for emphasis, "—and this is of major importance—" She paused again and spoke each of the next words carefully, "—you must not use electricity to take your pictures."

"No electricity." I repeated the words stupidly. It was the same argument for which we had never found an answer.

"Correct. You see, Dr. Reich—" Eva always referred to her father as Dr. Reich, giving the German "ch" its full charisma "—Dr. Reich always insisted that electricity confounded the orgone effects."

We had been hearing exactly that argument of "confounding" from those few colleagues who were willing to consider the Kirlian effect.

"There's a huge problem here." I spoke aloud my confusion. "You see, it's the electricity that takes the pictures. How can we take pictures without it?"

"That's your problem."

True, but irritating. That night I went to bed, head buzzing with unanswered questions: Did we want to study orgone? What about non-electrical photography? How best to study bio-energy? What should be the main thrust of the research? I fell asleep, still with no answers. The next morning, on a San Francisco side street, I passed a coffee shop and saw Eva Reich at a window table. She noticed me at almost the same moment and beckoned me to join her. During breakfast, Eva talked of how her father had been led to his discovery of orgone. Early in his psychoanalytic practice he had found in his patients what he called "character armor"—unconscious tensions that locked in the patients' emotions. When such tensions were released, the patient would experience a liberating flood of emotions. (This seemed similar to my experiences of unconscious tensions which, when released back in Charlotte Selver's class, had given way to a flood of emotions.) Following the release, Reich's patients would frequently feel an unfurling of rich energy which Reich came to call "orgone" (derived from "orgasm," about which Reich wrote an entire book, long before Masters and Johnson).

As Eva talked, I felt that inner nagging grow stronger. It was vital to explore bioenergy without electricity... but *how?*

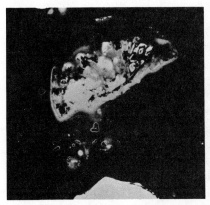 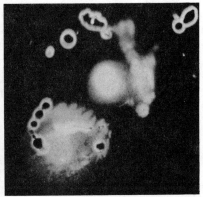

Fig. 9-4. *(Left)* Our first "non-electrical" photograph of a lemon slice, showing orgone energy, or a chemical reaction. *(Right)* Detail from the "lemon orgone" picture, showing the Bosch-like figures, with nuclei.

WE DISCOVER NON-ELECTRICAL PHOTOGRAPHY

After so many complex failures, the answer came simply. Take apart an ordinary, empty, triple film box, and in total darkness put one piece of color film on the bottom of the empty box. Then, directly on the film, put several small objects, like pieces of fruit, flower buds, etc., making sure they do not touch each other. Next, cover the objects with an "orgone blanket," layers of steel wool and cotton. Then close the box tightly with both lids so that the inside is light proof and leave it for several days. Then remove the film from the box and have it developed at your favorite color lab. Results? Startling.

There is an undeniable, undefinable, *Eureka!* with an unexpected discovery. I felt this more richly than at any time in my life when I first saw that particular image with its weird splatterings of Bosch-like images in colors like stained-glass windows (Fig. 9-4).

Animal Organs

This "orgone" picture, taken without electricity, was particularly pleasant because long before the Reich conference, we had tried non-electrical photography and failed. We were sent an article on recent Hungarian research in which film had been placed in contact with the cut surfaces of animal organs. This film, when developed, showed "minute details of the organs, *reproduced in the natural color of the tissues.*" (On black-and-white film!) Could this non-electrical photography be showing bioenergy? Intrigued, I had gone to a supermarket and bought chicken livers and hearts and tried to repeat the Hungarian experiment. But I got nothing but nondescript smudges and had abandoned the project as another false lead.

But now, with the orgone "fruit and flower fantasy," I went back to the supermarket for more livers and hearts. This time, a controlled study on color film: Orgone vs. Control organs—meaning that the two procedures were identical, except that there was no orgone blanket for the Control organs. Since we didn't know how long a time was needed to show the radiation (if radiation it was), we left them for five days, which was far too long. Not only did the organs smell to high heaven when we opened the boxes, but they had eaten clean through the emulsion in spots. And yet, both the Orgone and Control organs had photographed—not in their natural colors, but in brilliant blues, reds, yellows, greens, and purples. Of far, far greater interest, though, was that *only the Orgone pictures showed myriad red and yellow bubbles where nothing at all had been in contact with the film.* We studied and studied those bubbles, which were of intricate sizes and shapes, each containing a nucleus, blue inside yellow or black inside red/orange. And we noticed time and time again how the bubbles would be merging with—or separating from?—each other, looking for all the world like a reproductive process. Whether uniting or hatching, the major question was: what *were* they?

Could it be that these orgone bubbles were showing a *transfer* of bioenergy between the animal organs? A bioenergy which was being made visible through the orgone layering? This suddenly made sense of Reich's claim of accumulating orgone, since none of the bubbles appeared on the Control films, which had had no orgone layering. We showed these "orgone bubbles" to several colleagues, who were loath to accept an orgone energy and offered other ideas.

That's Not Bioenergy! That's Smell Molecules!

A research physicist who was a regular Monday volunteer in the lab studied the orgone bubbles carefully and said, "About those enucleated forms that appear at a distance from the animal matter—" He tended to be wordy.

"You mean the orgone bubbles?"

He grinned. "Okay. The orgone bubbles. Well, it's just possible those orgone bubbles are smell molecules."

"What?" I just stared.

"Surely you're aware that the smells of onions, perfumes,

skunks, saturate the atmosphere?" He was inclined to be didactic. I nodded. "Well, those smells, any smells, travel via molecules of matter. In your experiments, using the closed triple box with the orgone blanket, there's nowhere for the smell molecules to go—except to fall back, perhaps, on the film emulsion."

This was dazzling. "Honestly? Do you think we may be getting a picture of *smells?*"

"It's possible."

"Has anyone ever gotten a picture of a smell before?"

"Not that I'm aware of."

"How could we test for it?"

He shrugged. His domain was theoretical physics, and he was not into experimentation. Eventually the lab hit on a nice test, in which we compared strong smells versus little or no smells (perfumes vs. water; roses vs. daisies; onions vs. jicama). And time after time, we found that materials with powerful smells gave off no more bubbles than those without smell. As we were puzzling over these results, a student found an article, published in 1928, relevant to the smell studies.

The "Human Aura" versus the "Odorous Envelop"

In 1928 American physicist Hugo Gernsback took to task an English medical doctor, Walter Kilner, for his claim that one could see the human "aura" with a special screen of his invention. Kilner stated that the "aura" was invisible without the use of his screen because it lay in the ultra-violet range. But Gernsback pointed out that Kilner could never *photograph* the "aura" through his screen, even though film is very sensitive to the ultra-violet range. So, Gernsback suggested, what Kilner might be seeing through his screen was *not* the "aura," but the "odorous envelop" which surrounds the human body.

> Take a piece of scented soap, or perfume, or an onion. You will have no difficulty in smelling the odor of these substances from a distance . . . [because smell travels] via fine particles floating in the air.

Gernsback went on to guess that if the smell molecules could be made visible, one might see a misty "aura" around soap—the same hypothesis advanced by our physicist, fifty years later! Gernsback's final, rhetorical question: "Has Dr. Kilner made odors visible?" We believe we can now answer his question: we found no misty "auras" around soap, or onions, or any other smelly substances.

But of course the big question remained: what *were* those bubbles in the orgone pictures? There was another, more common suggestion.

That's Not Bioenergy! That's Chemistry!

The suggestion of a chemical reaction arose reasonably, because our fruits and flowers and animal organs had been in direct contact with the film emulsion. So now, instead of electricity, we had chemistry confounding the results. Long years before, the Effluvists had been attacked on the same grounds. (It seems that scientific history, like every history, repeats itself.) After being criticized for using electricity to take their pictures, the Effluvists had counter-attacked (like us) by trying non-electrical, contact photography—with considerable success. There was, for example, the work of French Commandant Darget who, by placing his hands directly on photographic plates, created pictures that looked very much like our Kirlian pictures of fingers, complete with coronas, bubbles, and blotches—all without electricity. But the critics came back with the argument that this was a *chemical* interaction between Darget's fingers and the emulsion. Darget then changed his technique and did not touch the emulsion on the plates at all, but placed his fingers only on the *glass* side of the plates. He obtained the same effects. Then he placed his fingers only in the *developing fluid,* and obtained the effluvia. As a final refinement, he simply made magnetic passes above the plates— and again obtained the effluvia.

This last experiment with magnetic passes reminded me of an early visitor to the lab—before we had even thought of the possibility of Kirlian photography.

"PSYCHIC PHOTOGRAPHY" FROM MEXICO. A man from Mexico had come to see us because of his talent for "psychic photography," which he demonstrated by asking us all to concentrate on an image (a star, a cross, a flower) while he waved his hands above the film that had been placed in the developer. Each piece of film came out with strong, swirling "fogging" patterns— similar to those Olga Worrall produced for us years later. But since this was our first foray into photography, we saw nothing of interest in the fogged film, and since none of the swirling patterns looked like the images we had concentrated on (no stars, no crosses, no flowers) we dismissed the whole idea of psychic photography. When our Mexican visitor left, we found that none of us could get any fogging on film at all, no matter how much we concentrated on an object or how much we waved our hands over the developer.

But at that time we were not studying bioenergy. Looking back, it is easy to see that the necessary ingredient for the fogging, swirling patterns may be a strong bioenergy in someone like the man from Mexico, or Olga Worrall, or almost a century earlier, Commandant Darget.

That's Not Bioenergy! That's Bad Photography!

We had, of course, shown Olga Worrall's "ectoplasm" and Bernie Grad's "slanting rain" to several experts, including experts in photography, who had dismissed those images as nothing but poor film processing. Similar effects occur, they said, with inadequate baths or old, stale developer or uneven distribution of developer, etc. and are called "reticulation," "fogging," and other names. Chastened, we had returned to the lab and put away the non-electrical photographs. But then, out of curiosity, we had tried to get those effects—the slanting rain, or ectoplasm, or fogging—by deliberately whirling the film around in baths with too much or too little developer. The film emerged flawlessly clean.

So it was charming to find, in that same unpublished paper on electrical photography, that the nineteenth-century critics had taken to task a distinguished Parisian radiographer, M. Ch. Brandt, for his claims of non-electrical effluvia. Replying to the very same arguments of faulty film processing and developer, M. Brandt had answered crisply, "The liquid in the bath may be moved about in every direction without affecting the results, showing the image did not result from any deposit or unequal action of the developer."

Thank you, M. Ch. Brandt, for exposing—once more!—how tenacious a scientific bias can be. (The world is flat, man cannot fly, there is no such thing as bacteria, or hypnosis, or bioenergy.)

A Silly Millimeter of Glass

That same treasure of an unpublished paper gave us more research on an unknown bioenergy, totally new to us, done more than seventy-five years ago by British scientist William Russell, whose several papers were published in the distinguished Proceedings of the Royal Academy of Science. Russell's non-electrical photography included many "self-portraits" of wood, obtained by the simple process of putting the wood on film and leaving it there long enough for it to take its own picture. (In later years we were to do our own research with "bioluminescent self-portraits" with the help of a twentieth-century botanist.)

Russell's critics, as might be expected, had brought the inevitable charge that these "self-portraits" were simply a chemical reaction between the wood and the emulsion. To answer that charge, Russell *separated* the wood from the photographic plate by three-quarters of an inch—and achieved the same clear pictures of the wood, *even though the wood never touched the film*. No chemical reaction there.

After this triumph, Russell went on to discover that if he put a very thin piece of glass between the wood and photographic plate, he could not get any picture at all. So he mused—air can carry the picture, but a millimeter of glass stops it—and he arrived at the sage conclusion that since the glass stopped the picture, the energy could not be radioactive. And, like the other Effluvists, he proposed an unknown bioenergy, which cannot penetrate glass as radioactivity does.

This finding was crucial to our own research. We had also tried to rebut the chemistry theory with our orgone pictures by placing a thin piece of glass or plastic between film and objects—and, like Russell, had found no pictures of any kind. We had stopped there, nonplussed.

(Naturally, after reading about Russell's non-contact photography, we tried that, without success. But the fact remained that Russell had obtained the pictures, without contact—perhaps because the film emulsions of those days permitted it.)

RE-EVALUATION

Studying those splendid scientists of a previous century made us humble, for they had surpassed us in ingenuity and insight with their non-electrical techniques. (We are still struggling in that mystifying field.)

All the same, it is fair to say that we have been able to contribute some original research to the pool of knowledge in electrical photography. For one thing, we learned how to make electrical motion pictures—which the Effluvists never did. This is no boast, of course, for how could they have? Motion pictures had not been invented then.

10
Some Original
Explorations

**Special Projects in Kirlian Photography,
Involving Emotional Interactions
Between People, "Family
Portraits," and Biological Studies—
Winding Up at the Movies**

NEW KIRLIAN

All the while we worked with non-electrical photography, we kept on with the Kirlian research, which branched out in unexpected directions as new volunteers joined the lab. There was a steady influx of Ph.D.s and undergraduates, government experts and psychical researchers, housewives and M.D.s—often working side by side, incongruously but well. Sometimes projects were brought to the lab—as with Hans Engel, M.D., who brought in his version of psychic healing—and sometimes a project seemed to evolve of itself, as with this next exploration, which just seemed to happen one night.

EMOTIONAL INTERACTIONS BETWEEN PEOPLE

It is odd, but I cannot remember whose idea it first was, to take two persons' finger pads simultaneously in one picture. The first night we tried it, Ken and I saw that our coronas did not meet each other but looked almost as if they had struck an invisible barrier. This gave us the idea of trying to get our coronas to *merge* with each other, in the manner of magnetic fields showing attraction. We spent some time building empathy between ourselves and then trying to direct that feeling into our fingertips. But the photographs showed only moderate success in the merging. However, when we

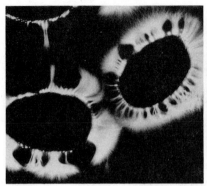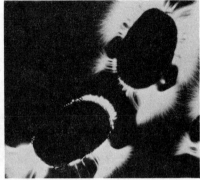

Fig. 10-1. *(Left)* Two people's finger pads showing attraction. *(Right)* Same two people showing repulsion (the "haircut effect").

worked up a strong feeling of antipathy (repulsion) we saw a dramatic change in the coronas, which Ken christened the "haircut," for the emanations cut off sharply from each other. It was psychologically interesting that we could show dislike more easily than liking. Could we learn to show empathy? We tried again and again, and by the time the evening was over, the emanations from our fingertips were interweaving with each other (Fig. 10-1).

As a psychologist, I realized that these emotional interactions might be of some professional interest. So, with anyone who would volunteer (and many people did), we explored this new technique of placing two people's index fingers next to, but not quite touching each other, then having the couple feel a strong emotion, and then taking the picture of the two fingertips simultaneously. Right from the start, we saw that certain couples shifted remarkably in their corona patterns as they went from love to hate to anger to sex, but other couples showed little or no change. Only gradually did we realize why. Our best results came consistently from actors or group therapists or therapy patients—in other words, for the Kirlian effect to reflect emotions, the emotions had to be *felt* rather than *thought* or *pretended*.

We also saw, on color film, that strong emotions like anger and sex produced billiant crimsons and reds—a phenomenon reflected in our language with expressions like "He became red with anger" or "She turned crimson with passion," etc. The more relaxed, gentle emotions like peace, rapport, harmony, generally showed in shades of blue. Whether this was due to the strength of the electrons hitting the layers of emulsion, as Tiller had maintained, we could not say. But it was pleasant to know that Kodak had so designed its film emulsion to match the English language.

We found another interesting corroboration of the language: we

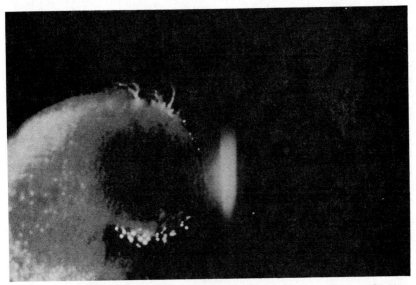

Fig. 10-2. Interaction between two people angry at each other. We see a barrier between them, and one person's "disappearance."

often speak of there being an "invisible barrier between people" and, in some Kirlian pictures, that invisible barrier became visible (Fig. 10-2). Another example of bioenergy telling us what our language already knows?

Family Portraits

Our studies in human interactions took a fascinating twist, again without our planning it, when a family of father, mother, and six-year-old son came into the lab. It happened that John Hubacher was the only one there that day, and he got to wondering how the family would photograph together. So he grouped the three index fingers close together, but not touching, and took their picture. The next day, with shy, quiet pleasure, John showed me the result (Fig. 10-3). We could clearly see how the father's corona billows out to merge with the mother but is cut off from the son, and how the son tends more toward mother than father (which is exactly how Freud would have predicted it would be at the height of a six-year-old's Oedipal conflict).

Such family portraits might be of considerable importance to the behavioral sciences, provided we could prove this was a real phenomenon and not just a fluke. So we sent out a call for families, and our best lady volunteer, Frances (ex-airline stewardess, former UCLA campus queen and resourceful researcher), took charge of the study, which grew into an ever-expanding notebook she called her "Family Album."

It was Frances who discovered a new "disappearance" phenomenon when a family of four—father, mother, son, daughter—produced several pictures in which the son's image was totally absent (Fig. 10-4). As was common lab procedure then, Frances was developing the film immediately so that the family could see their pictures. It was not long before the sixteen-year-old son saw that he wasn't there and demanded to know *why!* (From that day, it became standard procedure not to develop the film until the subjects had left.) Frances thought swiftly and took the son into the booth, alone with her. And there, either by himself or together with Frances, the son's finger pad showed up brilliantly. Clearly, something made his corona brightly visible with Frances but invisible with his family. (Why? The obvious guess was, of course, the beautiful lady.)

This disappearance phenomenon was to occur many, many times with families. One family, consisting of father, mother, and a tyrannical, adopted, nine-year-old daughter showed up on film

Fig. 10-3. Our first "family portrait," showing father, mother, and six-year-old son. Father and Mother are merging, but are cut off from the son (who shows up least).

each and every time with only the daughter's corona. And when I did a session with personal friends—father, mother, daughter—only the mother appeared on film. And, since I had broken the lab rule so that my friends could see themselves on film, they insisted on trying to change the results. No matter what they did, no matter how many times we tried, it was only the mother's corona that appeared. She left protesting she was *not* a vampire.

Although we have never been able to explain these disappearances convincingly, we do not subscribe to the vampire idea. Among the several suggestions we tried to test, the one that seemed most likely was that the most dominant person's corona was the one to appear.

Strong Eye Contact

The dominance hypothesis grew in favor when we began studying strong eye contact between two people. This started because of newly received articles from Soviet scientist Inyushin, who was researching the "radiation" emitted from the eyes, which he was able to record on "cryogenic" film (which we took to mean very cold film). This had stimulated us to explore the effects of eye contact—as in hypnosis, for instance—which evolved into the simple task of two people, each with index finger on film, staring at

Fig. 10-4. Another "family portrait" of four persons. It is the sixteen-year-old son who has disappeared.

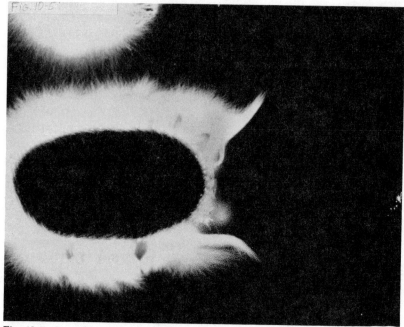

Fig. 10-5. One of our most reliable effects, the "disappearance" of one person's fingertip during strong eye contact.

each other until they had established strong eye contact, at which point we would take a Kirlian picture. Time after time after time, with hundreds of subjects, we saw that only *one* of the two finger pads showed up on the film (Fig. 10-5).

Was one person dominating the other?

We tried to find out by testing many husbands and wives, interviewing them first, to see which of the couple was the dominant one. Oddly, they often did not agree on which of them was dominant, and the hypothesis remained in limbo.

Then one day there wandered into the lab one of our curious "crazies," an affectionate label for those off-the-beam members of the lunatic fringe who are attracted to psychical research. This lady, in a long dress, medallion, and earrings, was a self-proclaimed witch. Generally John or Frances or I would have had her out of the lab in a twinkling, but here, I thought, was an opportunity to study the dominance hypothesis, for I was convinced I could dominate her in eye contact. The witch was delighted to participate in the Kirlian study, so we went into the booth, where we first took several baseline pictures, alone and together, without eye contact. It was clear that both of us were photographing with full, strong coronas. Then, the eye contact.

We did not develop the second round of pictures until after the witch left. As expected, we found only one finger pad on film. But it was not mine. It was hers.

Family Therapist

These interaction studies, particularly among family members, began to attract the attention of psychiatrists doing family therapy. Occasionally a therapist would bring a family in for a Kirlian session. Among the most interesting of these was a family of four—father, mother, son, daughter—in which the daughter was the special patient. She was a brilliant, twenty-one-year-old undergraduate, with a straight-A average, but she weighed only sixty-eight pounds. For she was suffering from anorexia nervosa, meaning she would not or could not eat. During the session, it was arranged that Frances would take pictures when the psychiatrist nodded to her. Skillfully, he brought the conversation around to problem areas. When he arrived at food and eating, he nodded to Frances and she took the picture. There, for the first time in the series, can be seen a large gap (no communication) between mother and daughter—a visual representation of the problem.

What About Bioenergy and Emotions?

Such explorations into family dynamics and emotional interactions between people are—so far as we have been able to learn—unique in the annals of electrical photography. And the results we achieved were contradictory to what electronics experts had told us *ad nauseam*: that it was the electricity going through the object that took the picture, which was simply a picture of corona discharge. Now we were seeing time and time again—repeatedly and reliably, which is one criterion for a scientific effect—how the corona discharge changed, and even disappeared altogether, with changes in emotions between people. That is *not* supposed to happen, according to electrical theory. And that was heartening...particularly so when we were asked in 1974 to present papers at both APAs (the American Psychiatric Association and the American Psychological Association), which were well received. (It almost looked as though our research might become accepted!)

BIOLOGY AND BOTANY

None of us expected to do research in botany or biology, but that too came to pass starting in 1972, when we were told that the senior curator of the Los Angeles Museum of Natural History wanted to learn about our Kirlian work with plants. Welcome news! From the start we had been mystified by those pearly bubbles inside and outside the leaves which no one—not even Soviet biologist Inyushin—could explain. So we prepared a special slide show for the senior curator, to be accompanied by a barrage of questions.

Dr. William Emboden arrived right on time, a surprisingly slim and erect young man, elegantly dressed, with aquiline features topped by a shock of red hair combed down to his eyebrows ("I hate foreheads!" he said once and never elaborated.) At that first meeting, he was reticent, almost cool, and businesslike, so without preamble, I started the slide projector and my prepared talk. Dr. Emboden interrupted on the very first slide to ask how we explained the bubbles in the leaves and the corona. I sputtered that we were hoping *he* would tell us, and did he think they could be related to something in the leaf's anatomy or physiology?

Dr. Emboden studied that slide, and a few others, and then answered, "No."

"Then what could they be?"

He re-examined each slide carefully, taking his good time, and finally said, "I haven't the least idea."

This was just about our first experience with an acknowledged expert who said, pointblank, that he just didn't know. We warmed to him and he to us. For Bill had come to the lab, he told us later, prepared to be handed some occult jingo about auras and energy flows, at which point he would have walked out, never to return. Instead, John and Frances and I pummeled him with questions about plant physiology and a possible "bioenergy," about which he, too, had been thinking.

Plant Cancers

In fact, that first day Bill talked, in many-syllabled words, about a possible relation between the brightness of a plant's corona and its metabolism. For example, plants with cancer have a very high rate of metabolism. And, Bill guessed, if what was being photographed were linked to metabolism (energy processes, if you like), then plants with tumors should give a much larger, more brilliant corona than normal plants. When he hit on that idea at our first meeting, Bill jumped to his feet, took Frances by the arm, and headed her out the door, straight to the Botanical Gardens, to hunt for plants with cancer.

So began our research in the world of bizarre plants and plant pathology, which was to continue for a rewarding three years, during which Bill served as a volunteer (classification: post-doctoral scholar).

In no time the lab was overrun with plants bearing evil-looking growths. And Bill's idea proved correct: cancerous plants repeatedly photographed with much more vivid coronas than normal ones, suggesting that the metabolism (or bioenergy) of the plants played a part in the Kirlian image.

Plant Sex

And so did their sex organs. Bill brought in the "sexy stuff"—the male stamens and the female ovaries of flowers—and we found that the male stamen always photographed in blue, while the female ovary photographed gold. (Bill was enchanted and all for writing a book to be titled, *The Golden Ovary*.) These colors were of particular interest because William Tiller had put down the Kirlian colors, in his presentation at Prague, as an artifact due to the layers of film emulsion. But here they seemed to be due to a sexual difference, a polarity, perhaps: female $(-)$ = gold; male $(+)$ = blue.

Seed Power

One afternoon, Bill said with wonder in his voice that one of the most mysterious and powerful things in the world was the dry seed. I started to answer flippantly, but Bill stopped me by placing a seed in my hand.

"Think about it," he said.

I shook my head, for I did not understand. "It's little, and lifeless..."

Bill nodded but added that within that puny, seemingly lifeless thing was the entire knowledge of its species. And given the four elements of earth, water, fire (the sun) and air, it could with incalculable force push through the toughest of materials, like cement, to show its leaves and flowers. That force within the seed, Bill continued, moves in opposite directions, at the same time, down into the ground and up into the air from some invisible center. Take the seed apart, dissect it, and examine it through an electron microscope—but that mysterious center cannot be found, for it has no anatomical structure. What is it, that growing, dynamic force? I caught Bill's excitement, for he was speaking of that dynamic force exactly as we would speak of that elusive bioenergy.

I was suddenly reminded of a study we had done a full year before Bill joined us. That study had been prompted by a letter from a research chemist at a national seed company, asking if the Kirlian technique could be used as a non-destructive test for seed fertility. I answered that we had done non-destructive testing of metals for NASA but had not tried it with living materials. The chemist shot

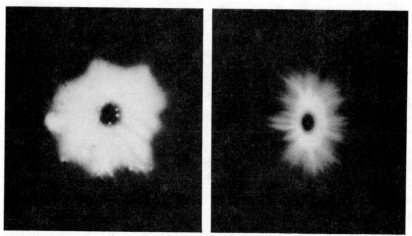

Fig. 10-6. (*Left*) A soybean from sample B, with a brilliant double corona. (*Right*) A soybean from sample E, chemically killed.

back a letter, suggesting a double-blind study: photograph five samples of soybean seeds, varying from healthy to dead, the code of which would be known only to him. In the lab we would know the samples simply as A, B, C, D, E.

When the shipment of soybeans arrived, the five sample packets looked identical, which meant that the study might truly be "blind." (More often than scientists are willing to admit, "blind" studies aren't blind at all, because there is some detail, unforeseen by the designer of the study, which becomes an immediate give-away to the people actually doing the experiment.) John Hubacher volunteered for the dreadful task of finding a way to photograph the tiny, rounded beans in total darkness. And by the time he had worked out a viable technique, he was sure the "blind" was blind no more, for the sample B beans gave brilliant pictures, with large, double coronas, while the sample E beans showed up as the runts of the litter, hardly photographing at all (Fig. 10-6). The remaining A, C, and D were run of the mill, not distinguishable one from the other.

In spite of feeling he had already cracked the code, John still had to plunge into the tedious task of photographing five hundred in-dividual soybeans, fifty from each sample, first in black and white and then in color. It took him ten days to finish, but when he did, we were startled to see that, while samples B and E were still re-spectively bright and dim, the differences were not nearly so dramatic. Could the ten-day interval have been responsible?

We sent our report, together with the photographs, to the chemist and received the gratifying news that our star, sample B, was the company's best soybean, that sample E had been chemically killed (meaning the seeds would no longer germinate), and that the others had been indifferently treated. We were cheering in the lab that day, with visions of the research having a practical, fundable application. But no further inquiries came from the chemist, and there the study languished.

Until Bill spoke that day of the mystery of the dry seed. Undergraduate Joe Gannon was listening. Joe had come to the lab hoping to do a special "199"—a course in Independent research for credit, where the student designs and executes an original experiment under faculty supervision. Such students were welcome, for they were generally inventive and industrious, and Joe was no exception. He wondered aloud if the soybeans from John's study would still germinate after having been "electrocuted." This was very good wondering, particularly since the original purpose of the study (somehow forgotten in the excitement of correctly discriminating the samples) was to find out if the Kirlian technique would be a non-destructive test of seed fertility.

Seed Germination

So I wrote the chemist suggesting another study of the soybeans, this time going further, to see if the seeds would germinate and grow normally after being photographed by blasts of electricity. The chemist promptly sent a second batch of samples (coded differently, of course). And this time Joe Gannon did the photography, obtaining results very much like John's work. Gratifying.

Now to see if the twice-blasted seeds would germinate. Bill Emboden showed us how to wrap both the Experimental beans and Control beans (which had never been photographed) in moist newspaper. And we waited a few days, wondering. Would those blasts of electricity that had taken the Kirlian pictures have killed the bioenergy, or life force, that makes seeds grow? Or would the electricity have caused a mutation of some kind? Or would they be normal? Four days' germination showed that both Experimental and Control seeds had sprouted, and we took Kirlian pictures of their roots and shoots. Then Bill took them to plant in soil and observe their growth. In good time, we found that those twice-blasted soybeans produced healthy plants, with every bit as much fertility as the Control beans.

And there was an added bonus. In every instance (both Control and Experimental), the root tips, as they sprouted from the seed coat, showed in the Kirlian pictures as a brilliant red/pink instead of the seedcoat blue. And as the root tips grew longer, that brilliant red/pink followed down to the tip, visually indicating where the most active growth was taking place. This was exciting for Bill, and for us, when he explained that this was another bit of evidence that an *energy* was being photographed—particularly since the movement of the red color down to the tip seemed to be following the energy process, which had little to do with the layering of the film emulsion.

"Out-of-the-Body" Cactus

With Bill's help, we also began photographing leaves under chloroform. (The celebrated Indian botanist Chandra Bhose had anesthetised bushes and trees before transplanting them, claiming that vegetation survived far better under chloroform, just as people do in operations.) We saw that the leaves under anesthesia certainly looked very different. The bubbles which characteristically show inside the leaf now, under the chloroform, showed up *outside* the leaf, in the corona. (An out-of-the-body effect?)

That question was brought under careful study by a volunteer housewife, Vicki, who was intent on getting the "phantom leaf." She latched on to the use of chloroform, cutting off a leaf section under the drug and then taking its picture. And it worked, about forty percent of the time, which increased our batting average for the production of phantoms. Then, a new twist.

There was a cactus which, during its life at the lab, had developed some new growths which looked like small appendages. One day Vicki wondered if the cactus, under chloroform, would give a phantom of an amputated limb. (This might help answer the frequent question of whether a "phantom limb"—which people often describe as being painful, even though the limb is no longer there—can be photographed.) The day Vicki began this research she was joined by undergraduate Tracy Garfield, who was volunteering her first day in the lab. This was lucky on a couple of counts. First, because two people were needed for the study, if only to remove with tweezers the slender but painful cactus needles that pierced the flesh on contact (and contact was made frequently in the total darkness of the booth). Also, Tracy had hoped to see a phantom picture but had never expected to be around when one was made.

It happened that on the very first photograph of cactus without its appendage, there emerged so magnificent a phantom it looked as if the appendage was still there. (I personally could not accept it was a phantom and ran through each stage of the experiment myself—needles, tweezers, and all—to emerge with a phantom appendage almost as splendid.)

So Tracy joined Vicki, and together they came up with a new

chloroform effect—the cactus that goes "out-of-the-body" (see Fig. 12-1). Again and again we were to find that blob-like image, attached by a "cord" to the parent body. And in the color pictures, that blob was a brilliant red, in contrast to the blue body. Could we be photographing the *energy body* of the cactus, separated under anesthesia?

HANS ENGEL, M.D., PSYCHIC HEALER

During this prolific period (1973 to 1976), there were ongoing research projects in the lab each day of the week: movies on Monday nights, biology with Bill on Tuesdays, Jack Gray and magnetic passes on Wednesdays, emotional interactions on Thursdays, and undergraduate projects on Fridays and weekends. Meanwhile, I juggled classes, seminars, students, conferences, testing, and the research as best I could. Even so, from time to time there would appear that special, meaningful new study that could not be denied.

One of the finest of these started with a letter from a respected physician of UCLA's clinical faculty in the Medical School, who was also chief of staff at a prominent hospital and a leading member of the Los Angeles Academy of Family Practice. Altogether a man of impeccable credentials. Yet Dr. Hans Engel's story was exceeding strange.

It seems Hans first became aware that he had "healing hands" on his honeymoon, some thirty years ago, when his bride complained of a headache and Hans responded sympathetically by putting his hand to her forehead. He felt an area of intense cold under his hand and asked his wife if the pain were in that spot. It was. After a time Hans felt the cold disappearing, and at almost the same moment his wife said that her headache was gone. This coincidence was so striking that the next time his bride suffered a pain, Hans offered the same "treatment"—and felt the same cold, which disappeared at the same time as the pain, usually. For many, many years Hans offered this healing treatment, but only to his wife, never his patients.

Then, Hans developed a virulent cancer (lymphosarcoma), diagnosed from X-rays taken at his hospital, where he was advised he had about six months to live. Hans decided to continue his practice as usual, for as long as he could—all the while watching his body develop tumors the size of golf balls. During this period he wrote an article for a medical journal describing how it felt to know that in a few months he would be dead. But then, inexplicably, his golf ball tumors began to shrink until they disappeared and he was cancer-free. This phenomenon is called "spontaneous remission" in medicine, and there is as yet no explanation of how or why it occurs. After this gift of recovery, Hans decided to research, in as scholarly a way as possible, the healing talent he had discovered with his wife. We welcomed him joyfully.

For several years, Hans devoted every Thursday morning to the lab, treating a wide variety of patients sent him by doctors, usually as a last resort after medication, surgery, and even acupuncture and hypnosis had failed. In addition to our Kirlian pictures, taken before and after treatment (much more good data!), Hans gathered his own fastidious data, which revealed that his major successes were with patients suffering intolerable, intractable pain. And his statistics showed that roughly fifteen percent of his clients did not respond *at all*; another fifteen percent had complete remission and recovery; while the remaining seventy percent varied from slight to marked improvement.

None of the patients paid a fee, and all volunteered for the Kirlian photography, which added volumes of evidence for that special red/orange "healing energy" (which had now been obtained by labs in England, Brazil, Czechoslovakia, Austria, and the Soviet Union, as well as by several labs in the United States). One of Hans' most remarkable cases was a lady suffering from a chronic case of "tic douloureux," in which a facial nerve goes berserk, sending out incessant and nearly intolerable spasms of pain. This patient had suffered over an eight-year period and had tried every possible therapy, with no relief. Somehow, after just a week with Hans' "hand healing," her pain disappeared (and has not returned as of this writing, some four years later).

The Heat and Cold of Healing Energy

What was it that stopped the pain? Hans was baffled, just as we were. For his entire treatment is a simple movement of his hand around the body, at a distance of a couple of inches, looking for the cold spots which tell him where the problem lies. When he finds a cold spot, he holds his hand over it, or sometimes on it, until the cold goes away. During this treatment, time after time after time a patient would exclaim that Hans' hand felt too hot for comfort. This was such an odd state of affairs—the patient feeling heat, Hans feeling cold—that we took on a special research project, using sophisticated biofeedback instruments to study the temperature differences in Hans and the patient. And we were never able to find any change in temperature at all in either the patient, where he felt the heat, or in Hans, where he felt the cold.

Here seemed to lie another major, unfathomable clue: people feeling heat and cold, but a heat and cold which our instruments could not measure. Was it possible there is a *subjective* heat and cold that has nothing to do with temperature as we are able to measure it with thermometers and thermistors? And if so, could this heat/cold be a special attribute of that elusive bioenergy which also escapes our modern technological instruments?

Hans's Reward

Psychic healing by a medical doctor is, naturally, big news and Hans' gift was widely reported in the media. Which did not seem to please the university authorities, for Hans was brought before committees for his "unusual research." He felt compelled to offer his resignation, which, sad to say, was accepted. Thus, he is no longer on UCLA's clinical faculty. But his research into unorthodox healing continues, as well as his private practice, which remains, as always, orthodox.

BIOENERGY: THE PK OF URI GELLER

Probably no psychic in history arrived with the fanfare of Uri Geller, who showed on TV programs around the world how he could bend heavy metal keys, nails, etc., with a gentle stroke of his finger, and how broken clocks and watches somehow repaired themselves in the living rooms of his TV audiences while he was on the air. Both extraordinary feats of psychokinesis...*if* the feats were genuine. But how could they be? Most logical scientists labelled Uri and his PK as especially cute tricks by an unusually skillful magician.

So has it ever been with the famous psychics of history: Eusapia Palladino, D.D. Home, Rudi Schneider, Eileen Garrett, Edgar Cayce have all been branded and dismissed by most scientists as frauds and charlatans. Yet most of these psychics offered their services in the laboratory to those few scientists who wished to study them, only to find those few scientists raked over the coals for letting themselves be duped by clever tricksters. In fact, since the era of Harry Houdini, it has been *de rigueur* to have a stage magician in the lab to observe and expose the ploys of seance mediums and their messages. And make no mistake: most psychics have a bag of tricks, very good tricks sometimes (described with neat details in the book, *Psychic Mafia*, written as a confession by a clever, fake psychic).

Scientific Studies with Uri Geller

Uri Geller, to a far greater extent than most psychics, has worked for scientists in labs all over the world, providing documented research. I saw one particularly impressive film of his work with research physicists Russell Targ and Hal Puthoff of Stanford Research Institute, which was shown at the Psychotronics Conference in Prague in 1973. Geller had been studied under rigorously controlled conditions with a prominent magician on hand to detect the frauds (which he was unable to do). In fact, so rigorous had Targ and Puthoff been that Geller's most famous effect—the bending of metals—was not shown in the film because, as Puthoff emphasized at the conference, there had never been sufficient controls during the metal-bending to make it convincing.

What they did film, among other psychic demonstrations, was a PK study in which a magnetometer was so mounted inside a bell jar that Targ and Puthoff, pounding and jumping up and down on the floor, could not disturb the needle by a hair's breadth. Yet in the film, when Geller moved his hands around the jar—much as Jack Gray or Hans Engel would in making magnetic passes—the needle deflected widely and in opposite directions (+ and −). When I saw that, I thought of our Kirlian pictures of attraction and repulsion (+ and −) and longed to know if Geller would show those patterns in Kirlian photographs. I was also keen to learn if his PK would photograph, which would be a formidable example of the bioenergy we were searching for. But there was slim hope of his visiting the lab then, for he was on a whirlwind tour of many countries.

But two years later, out of the blue, came word that Uri Geller would like to come to our lab on his next visit to Los Angeles! Brave new opportunity—for in the interim I had learned about a Kirlian study with Geller, done by Henry Dakin and Kirlian researcher Jim Hickman, both of whom had visited Geller's hotel room in San Francisco with their Kirlian apparatus. They had first taken a picture of Geller's finger in its normal state, at a slight distance from Henry's metal watch band, which they also photographed on the same piece of film. Then they had asked Geller to "send energy" to the watch and had taken another picture (Fig. 10-7). The "energy picture" clearly shows a "spurt" coming from Geller's finger pad. Also, the watch band photographed with far more brilliance than in the baseline picture.

Would we be able to get an effect like that? We made our plans, and hoped. For Geller was notorious for his fear of electrical instruments, for his temperament—and for not keeping appointments.

Uri Geller in the Lab

Somehow, whenever a celebrity is scheduled to make an appearance, in spite of all attempts at secrecy the news spreads like an epidemic. And so it was with Geller's lab visit. We were so be-

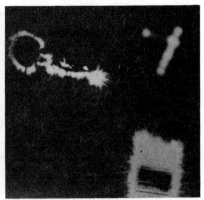

Fig. 10-7. *(Left)* Uri Geller's finger in a state of rest near Dakin's watch band. *(Right)* Uri's finger "sending energy" to the watch. *(Pictures courtesy of Jim Hickman and Henry Dakin.)*

sieged with requests from friends and colleagues that our lab was packed with people long before Geller was to arrive. As the hour for his visit approached, with no word from Geller, I murmured to my daughter Pauli (home on a rare visit from Harvard), "He probably won't show up." At exactly that moment the phone rang. This was no ESP effect, because the phone had been ringing off its hook all morning. All the same, this time it was Geller's associate, saying they were lost and in a nearby drugstore.

"Stay right where you are!" I was relieved they had called, for trying to find the lab in the NPI maze, from the drugstore, might have required skills even Uri Geller did not have. "Don't try to find us. I'll send two girls to fetch you." That was a ploy. Geller was famous for girl-watching, and girls for watching him. Pauli volunteered to be one of the girls.

We could relax, now, with the knowledge that Geller was en route. John and Barry and I checked yet again the metals and broken watches we had assembled. At length the door swung open and all the talking stopped as everyone focused on the handsome, dark, lithe young man with the quiet smile.

GELLER AT WORK. The first hours in the lab with a psychic are by far the most difficult. The psychic is on the defensive against the skeptical, sometimes hostile researchers; and the researchers are distrustful, even with a magician there as a guard against trickery; and generally there are false starts, apologies, and an uneasy time for all. Since Geller had offered to be with us just this one day, we had planned as easy an entry into experiments as we could, based on the knowledge that he had bent nails and keys in labs all over the world. As a first and least intimidating task, we had provided cutlery for bending, to be followed by metals of various tensile strengths, each encased in plastic or glass by a cooperative Physics Department. As an alternate, non-threatening task, lab workers had brought in assorted clocks and watches which they guaranteed had not functioned for two years or more. Should Geller have success at either or both of these tasks, perhaps then he could be coaxed into the isolation booths for a go at the photography.

So here we were, face to face with Uri, as he asked to be called. After a few pleasantries, I pointed to the metals on the table, but Uri frowned.

"That's old! I do not want to bend things."

I was caught off guard. "What would you like to do?"

"You have Kirlian photography, yes? I have never done it."

The lab chortled approval, and I said we'd be happy to do a study like the one Henry Dakin did in San Francisco.

"Who? What?" It was Uri's turn to be taken off guard.

"You remember? That experiment with your finger, and Henry's watch band?"

This drew a blank with Uri. Happily, I was prepared and flipped on the slide projector, which already contained the two photographs of his finger which Jim Hickman had sent us. Geller studied the slides with the pleasure of a child. He had never seen them, he said. He now remembered the experiment, but no one had ever told him the results. (This is a common disappointment for many subjects, who are lost to follow-up.) Later Jim told me that the film had not been processed until he and Henry returned to their lab—both to avoid chicanery and to develop them properly. By then, Geller was off in another country.

Uri seemed dazzled by that "spurt" of—what? bioenergy?— which he could see on the film, for it might mean that Kirlian photography could make visible his PK ability. A big smile. "Let's go to work!"

I opened the door to the booth.

A big frown. "But, T'elma! Can we see, right away, is there something on the film?" He did not want another study with unknown results.

"Sure. If you don't mind black-and-white pictures. Color takes twenty-four hours to process."

"Then we do black and white! I want to see."

And he walked into the booth.

MANY TRIALS. We allowed only a select few inside the booth: John Hubacher, whose job it was to process the film; Ruth, a lab volunteer who had brought two of her own traveling clocks into the booth, neither of which (she swore!) had worked in three years; Hans Engel, whose healing research had made him curious about bioenergy and PK; and Douglas Price-Williams, psychologist/ anthropologist and the only colleague in the NPI with an interest in parapsychology.

Uri stood next to me at the Kirlian machine and was clearly nervous (fearful?) of it. He spoke of having been almost electrocuted as a child when he was playing with his mother's electric sewing machine, which had led to a lifelong distrust of things electrical. When at length he put his finger on the film, close to one of the traveling clocks, I took a deep breath—and pressed the button. Uri felt nothing and began to relax. John processed that first photograph immediately so that Uri could see his finger pad, which looked like any other relaxed finger pad, with a full corona, next to the large round metallic corona of the traveling clock.

Now for the Main Event. I asked Uri to "send energy into the clock" and he asked everyone in the booth to shout, *Work!* in unison with him. We shouted *Work!* until the booth fairly rang. And then Uri nodded to me and I pressed the button, thinking to myself that just the reverberation of sound waves in the booth should change the picture. I was wrong. It looked almost exactly like the first picture.

We tried several more times, everyone shouting *Work!* each time. With no results at all on film. At a loss, I suggested rather lamely that we try the other traveling clock. Ruth lifted up the one we had been using, brought it to her ear, and said in a bemused way,

"It's working."

Shock of silence in the booth.

Uri grabbed the clock from Ruth and held it to his ear and, like a child who has just found his Christmas present, he laughed.

"It works, ya!" He held it to my ear. It was ticking loudly. I stared at Uri as the clock passed from ear to ear. This was what I had seen on TV and heard about and not believed. Now it had happened in the booth.

But that was just the beginning.

Ruth picked up the other traveling clock, which no one had touched, and found that it was ticking, too. More exclamations. And then I remembered that there were six more broken clocks and watches outside the booth. So we trooped out to examine them and discovered that four out of the six were now working. No one in the outer lab had touched them, so swore Barry, who had remained with the observers to guard the equipment.

The lab began to buzz with pleasure. But only briefly, for Uri was impatient. After all, he had seen countless watches start, but he had seen only one Kirlian spurt from his finger pad, and that one just hours before on the slide projector. He wanted more "spurts." As did I. So back we trotted into the booth, where I decided to abandon the clocks for a key. Suppose it were to bend on film, what would that show? For the next forty-five minutes Uri was at his concentrated best. Trial after trial after trial. But nothing showed on the thirty-odd pieces of film John developed except the key and the finger pad, both normal. Tension was mounting now with Uri, too.

"Is this expensive, this film?" He turned to me anxiously.

"No." It wouldn't have mattered if it were. This was a rare opportunity.

"It is okay, we try maybe one hundred times? One success is worth one hundred failures, yes?"

"Definitely yes."

It was many trials later that John murmured in his off-center way, "It's here."

"What?"

John showed me the negative (Fig. 10-8). It was just a blob, above the finger and below the key, but a blob where nothing should have been. Uri cut short our excitement because he wanted to do

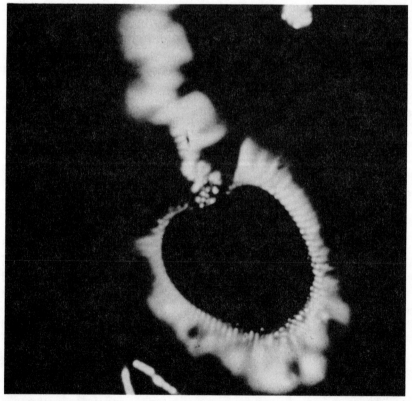

Fig. 10-8. Uri Geller's finger, taken in our lab, shows the same kind of "energy spurt."

more experiments. After many more trials, he produced three blobs in all.

But what wonderful, welcome sights they were! Three separate images of a possible PK energy, or bioenergy, which had appeared when Uri was trying to demonstrate his metal-bending PK. Uri was so pleased that he volunteered to return the next night to try for color images—and on that occasion we got three more spurts, in brilliant reds and blues.

It had been an exhilarating two days.

Aftermath

In the quieter weeks that followed, we stared hard at the fact that those fabulous Geller pictures, with those spurts of "bioenergy," had been taken in a dim red light (or in total darkness for the color ones) in which sleight-of-hand would have been duck soup. Could those spurts have been faked?

We tried to answer that question by devising all the tricks we could think of, and in time we produced very good imitations either by placing a human hair under the finger tip, or a piece of a paper clip, or a rubber band. And even as we worked to fake the effect, I realized how much I had railed against those critics of the Kirlian effect who had shown how easy it was to fake a Green Thumb, or Brown Thumb, or healing energy—even a phantom leaf, which we had not yet been able to get.

The point is: it's easy to fake almost anything. But a fake ghost, or a fake seance, or a fake UFO, or a fake banana doesn't for one second mean that real ones don't exist. No, faking the Geller effects was no way to study the Geller phenomena. Rather, was there anything Geller had done in the lab that we felt could *not* have been faked?

THE WATCH WORKS

Friends around the world—in Colombia, France, Switzerland, Austria, Brazil, Japan, and Mexico—had told me of their personal experiences with broken toasters, blenders, watches, etc., that had started up while Geller was appearing on TV. But no anecdote ever has the impact of something "impossible" that happens to you, yourself.

Which it had, to me, when Pauli and I had watched Uri on TV (the day after he had been to the lab). I brought to the TV set an antique gold watch that had not worked in nineteen years. I wound it, shook it, listened—nothing. I gave it to Pauli to hold. When Uri asked the audience to shout *Work,* we did, feeling foolish. Then Pauli held the watch to her ear, shook her head, and gave the watch to me.

"It's a beautiful watch," Pauli said. "May I have it for my birthday?"

"It's yours."

"Could you have it fixed? I'd like it more if it kept time."

"Sure."

I was holding the watch to my ear and thought I heard something. I shook it and listened again. Uri was now off the air. And the watch was ticking. Steadily. Loudly. What is more, the second hand was now moving around its little circle. Steadily.

"It's going." My voice sounded flat.

"Oh, sure."

I held the watch to Pauli's ear. She looked puzzled. "How could that happen?" Her Harvard training.

I couldn't answer. Still can't. But I do know the watch continued to function and kept good time for five weeks.

I began to wonder if this particular magic, or bioenergy, was a possibility for study? A new experiment took shape when I was able to buy a videotape of Uri Geller from a local TV station.

Fourteen Experiments in Search of the Geller Effect

All together, we did fourteen studies, on various campuses, like the one which follows—and all fourteen followed this pattern. The first was with the parapsychology class, at UCLA, where the students were willing—beyond all bounds!—to bring us their broken radios, electric blankets, tooth brushes, stereos, and even a TV set in addition to eighty-five clocks and watches. These were all lugged to the lab to make sure there was nothing in the lot that worked. We left them all quietly (complete bed rest) for two weeks, just in case, as we had been warned, spontaneous remission were to occur. It did not. Then, an afternoon was set aside to check each and every instrument. This included winding, shaking, thumping, jarring, and any other mumbo-jumbo we could think of to make them go. If they did begin to work, they would of course be barred from the study.

We had already gone through forty-five of the eighty-five clocks and watches, none of which had been made to work, when John Hubacher strolled in, saw what we were doing, picked up a watch from the pile that had already been tested, shook it, held it to his ear, and said,

"This one's working."

"Don't be absurd—" I stopped because John was holding it to my ear and I could hear it ticking, clearly.

"John—!" I tried to speak casually. "Would you check that pile? If you find any more that work, let me see them."

"Sure." When John was finished, seventeen of those forty-five watches were ticking steadily.

This was difficult to digest. John had started seventeen watches that had already been tested and found not working. (John, so far as we had seen over the years, had no PK ability. But after this feat, we christened him URI II.) I took all seventeen watches home with me and I wound them each day and, of the seventeen, fourteen kept accurate time right up to the night of the experiment some ten days later.

And on that night, I called on stage several students whose watches had been "healed" by John, and each issued a gasp of disbelief when they heard their watches ticking. Some of them reported they had taken their watches to jewelers who had said the watches were not worth the repair bill. As these tableaux took place, I found myself wondering what I would be thinking, were I in the audience. It was simply not believable that a watch could be repaired by someone holding it and shaking it, when the owner says the watch had not worked for six years and the jeweler had said to forget it.

The next part of the program produced more wonders. As the teaching assistants returned all the non-repaired items to their owners, I outlined the rules of the game. And as I was explaining about the Geller videotape, one after another excited student called out that his watch had started up. This was totally unexpected. Why had they started suddenly, when they had not worked before? This led to a general hoopla in the audience, so that there was a highly charged atmosphere (bioenergy?) when the Geller videotape started. By the time it had finished, the class was in an uproar, for person after person stood up, holding out his "healed" watch to be checked. In addition to the seventeen watches John had started, another twenty-three instruments had begun to function, among them the broken TV set.

What Happened?

This was a question well worth pursuing, for it related to the new field of "psychotronics," which had been defined at the first international conference in Prague in 1973 as "the study of all interactions between man and objects, both animate and inanimate," and which—though not specifically named—might be due to a bioenergy. Here was a first-rate example. And we pursued it, thirteen more times, on various campuses. Successfully. On the average, slightly more than thirty percent of all the "broken" watches and appliances started to work, and along the way, we unearthed a few possible clues.

INTERACTIONS BETWEEN INSTRUMENT AND OWNER.
Time after time a few watches had started in the lab, and had kept good time until returned to their owners. Then, sometimes within minutes or even seconds, those watches stopped. The owners, most of them, admitted to a lifelong problem with watches. And in three different instances, in front of a class, I personally gave a ticking watch back to its owner, only to have it stop as soon as the owner held it to his ear! In fact, on one occasion the owner gave the watch back to me, saying it was not working. When I held it to my ear, I could hear it ticking and said so, handing it back—and again the owner held it to her ear, said it was not going, and returned it to me. This time, when I heard it ticking, I kept holding the watch and put it to her ear—now the ticking continued, and she heard it. This whole sequence was then repeated for a student in the audience who volunteered to listen to the ticking and non-ticking as the watch changed hands. And the student, mystified, confirmed what went on.

I was mystified, too. Had I acquired the Geller gift—like John? How many others had it? The students again and again volunteered that they could start a TV set by touching it—or, the reverse, that when they approached, the TV set would fade, blur, or go blank. The editor of this manuscript, who deplored this data on Geller and wanted it cut, admitted that her TV set develops problems, no matter into what apartment she goes.

WATCHES THAT RUN TOO FAST OR TOO SLOW.
We learned, by asking each class, that there are watch-wearers who have special problems. For certain people, whatever watch they buy soon runs up to fifteen minutes a day too fast; for others, watches slow down each day. This phenomenon applies to all watches worn *on the wrist.* Some of these watch-wearers found that pocket watches worked well for them; it was only the *wrist* watches that sped up or slowed down. (I recognized this phenomenon because for years Barry Taff, the lab psychic, had complained that every watch he had ever owned gained ten minutes each day—even a birthday Accutron, which he had taken for repair several times, only to have the watch repair man swear that the watch kept perfect time until Barry started to wear it.)

There was also a small group of people, at every class, who had stopped wearing watches altogether because each new watch would stop, totally, within months.

Here is a phenomenon never reported, to my knowledge, in the literature of psychotronics, much less in physiology or physics, where it might more properly belong.

Man ⇄ Machine

In the field of electronics, the influence of man on machine has been admitted, but usually only unofficially. Just as Kodak won't permit certain persons to process film because they fog it, so certain persons are not hired by some firms because they cause static on radio, blur TV pictures (like my editor), or cause telephones to ring for no apparent reason.

Parapsychology has found it commonplace that poltergeists raise havoc with electricity—lights inexplicably go on and off, without cause and telephones ring when no one is on the line (or, as in one case we investigated for eighteen months with the cooperation of the telephone company, the phones when answered would give the weather report, which no one had dialed). It is also well attested that psychics like Uri or Barry of our own lab can create chaos in TV and radio transmission. And, in haunted houses and some seances, tape recorders which have functioned well up until the time to play them back reveal blank tape or static (a special kind of Watergate phenomenon).

My own favorite memory of this man/machine problem concerns the day when an agent from a prominent federal agency came to the lab to see our research. I started the slide projector, which made a strange noise and stopped. Something had broken. The Fed laughed and said ruefully, "I did that. I'm sorry." When I asked him to explain, he said that he was never permitted on field trips because equipment was always breaking down when he was around. When he confessed that the plants he put into the ground all died, I asked if he would be willing to try our Brown Thumb experiment, but he refused.

KIRLIAN MOVIES

Probably our most productive research into bioenergy came when we learned how to make Kirlian movies—a goal long cherished, but long in arriving. So often, when we would chance on a special effect—like the healing energy—someone would murmur how great it would be to have that on film, in *motion*, to play over and over, the better to study what is happening. There had been several tries at movie-making, from Ken Johnson and William Tiller and others, but with no success. Which is where we were, until the winter of '73. After one particularly frustrating session, John Hubacher muttered—yet again!—about how much movies could help. I grunted and he went on saying maybe a transparent electrode was the answer. I asked what that was and he explained it was a piece of glass coated thinly with metal which could be electrified. I listened with half an ear as John told how we could put finger pads on the glass electrode, electrify it, and then see the finger pads light up to give the Kirlian effect, dynamically, over time. As we left the lab, John asked if he could get a transparent electrode and try for the movies. I said sure, and forgot about it.

A few days later, John brought to the lab the transparent electrode—and a delicate-looking young man with lank blonde hair whom John had found in UCLA's Department of Cinema.

Clark Dugger, Student Cinematographer

Clark was anything but prepossessing on first meeting. Shy, meek, seemingly ineffectual. (What an absurd first impression!) But he did say he was interested in trying to make movies of the Kirlian effect and that he had access to all kinds of movie equipment which he could bring to the lab, provided he had our permission to do a research project.

Wow...!

We sat Clark down and showed him the only Kirlian movie any of us had ever seen, made amateurishly on eight-millimeter film by the Kirlians in their lab. We had played this five-minute silent film numerous times, never understanding how it was made. It showed the dynamically changing coronas around leaves, with those ever-present, mysterious bubbles, sometimes moving out of the leaf and off into space and sometimes moving toward the leaf and going inside it! Those bubble dances were in marked contrast to the movies of metal objects like a coin, or safety pin, which simply glowed steadily without producing bubbles.

Clark kept nodding as he watched, so afterwards I asked if he knew how the film was made. He said he could make some guesses and started talking about lenses and apertures and film speeds and ASAs—technical jargon, meaningless to me. But Clark did seem eager to work nights with John in the lab and that was full of meaning. I told them to go ahead, on their own, having learned to give students free rein with no authority around to inhibit or intimidate. Students, left to themselves, can sometimes work wonders.

This was one of those times. Within two weeks, John said in his sheepish way, "We got movies." I could not believe any such swift result until Clark set up an eight-millimeter projector and ran black-and-white footage showing leaves and finger pads bouncy with bubbles and coronas and coins that steadily glowed, just as in the Kirlian film. Clark kept apologizing for the amateur quality of the film, even after it ended, so I told him to keep quiet, keep working, and let me know when I could join them.

First Flops, First Hit

It wasn't long before movie-making became a weekly evening event. In the beginning it was very rough for there were no guideposts and it was trial and error all the way. Being a remarkably creative young man, Clark experimented with all kinds of films, camera speeds, and lenses—and made whopping mistakes. He shot one entire, excellent night's work on healing with infra-red film—which came back from the lab with absolutely nothing on it. But another experiment with color film, shot at a very slow six frames per second and "pushed" at the lab (a technical word meaning to increase brilliance), gave us the first color Kirlian movies in the United States.

The movie-making evolved slowly, partly because all the equipment and crew had to be packed into the isolation booth, where one false move could send a powerful electrical shock through one or more of us. Once the equipment had been set up, John would put a leaf on the electrode. All the lights had to go out then, because only in total darkness could we record on film the faint luminescence that the leaves or fingers sent out when the electricity was turned on. First, though, we would simply watch the corona discharge in which the bubbles and streamers did their sparkling dances for as long as the electricity was on. When an effect seemed worth recording, Clark would turn on the movie camera, which faced the transparent electrode.

As we slowly learned the *how* of filmmaking, we began to record in moving pictures the effects we had found in still photography. Some of those effects were even more powerful in the movies, and a few effects appeared on film, that we had never seen before. Naturally, we experimented with our various healers—Jack Gray, Olga Worrall, Hans Engel—and we saw again and again, vividly, the increased luminescence that came to the patient *after* treatment. We also saw that the intensity would vary—as in the still photography—from night to night and patient to patient and, inevitably, we found those times when no changes at all could be seen.

Then there was one special event. When John had the flu and Hans Engel was trying to heal him, we saw—as Hans' hand approached John—a stream of "effluvia" (vapor? gas? water?

energy?) pouring from John's thumb onto the transparent electrode, there to be recorded on film. (One might have expected this from Hans, but from John?) We had no idea what we were seeing on the electrode on the TV monitor, and later on film. It happened again and again that night, but then never again, no matter how much John tried to recapture the flu.

Interactions between people were a particular fascination in the movies, for we could see with our eyes that mysterious "disappearing act" when two people were in strong eye contact or in strong argument with each other. During one angry exchange (simulated, but effective) between two men, we saw—literally—sparks flying between the fingers. Just as our language has it, "Sparks flew between them."

Another kind of "flying sparks" came in a kissing study, for which we had more than one hundred volunteer couples. Each person would keep his index finger on the transparent electrode before, during, and after the kiss. Sometimes there was no change at all; sometimes it was only the man, or the woman, whose corona grew brighter. But the best performance by far was from one young couple so dynamic that during the kiss a large red "bubble" sprang between the fingers and exploded into a spark—which shocked them out of the kiss. They were game enough to try it again, and it happened again. (More than a year later, they wrote us to say it had happened still once more, at a psychic fair which they had attended in the Midwest.)

Interactions like these became treasured pieces of film, for they seemed to be showing an exchange of a bioenergy that looked a lot like "just electricity."

Another brilliant effect we could get again and again in the movies was the *imbalance* that acupuncture describes. A person with a sprained ring finger showed clearly how much larger that corona was than the corona from the normal ring finger of her other hand. And we could watch and see how treatment with an acupuncture needle brought the two fingers back to a balance of equal-sized coronas.

Even more intriguing, we saw, demonstrated on film, an acupuncture principle we had not even known existed! As so often happens we were looking, not for what happened, but for a healing of a patient's chronically aching arm. It was Dr. Kroening who needled the lady, that night, on a point close to the wrist called Heart 7. As usual, we photographed the wrist before the therapy and then again after it. In the Kirlian movies we saw that *after* the needling, the brilliant luminescence on her wrist had dimmed considerably (even though the pain had not lessened very much). This dimming of the corona was unusual, since after acupuncture treatment it usually became brighter. When Dr. Kroening saw this effect he was intrigued, because the point that had been needled, Heart 7, is known classically as a "sedation point," meaning that stimulation of the point proves tranquilizing to the patient. In fact, stimulation of Heart 7 is often used to induce sleep in patients with insomnia.

Having discovered that dimming of the corona with a sedation point, the next step was to organize a double-blind study in which two points would be needled, one a "sedation" and one a "tonification" (meaning that needle therapy on such a point would energize, rather than tranquilize). We saw, vividly, that the tonification point increased the luminescence of the toes on the right foot, while the sedation point almost extinguished the twinkling toes of the left foot.

Here was a visible demonstration of "tonification" and "sedation" points, perhaps for the very first time, more than five thousand years after the principle had been stated. How had the Chinese found it out? A wonderful puzzle.

Then suddenly, all of this wonder and puzzlement was overshadowed when, after four years of failure, we managed to capture and put on film the "phantom leaf."

11
The Mystery of
the Phantom Leaf

Which Involves the Whole
Idea of an "Energy Body," with All
the Implications Thereof

THE ENERGY BODY

From the start my chief fascination with the Kirlian effect had been the "phantom leaf." Both Adamenko and Inyushin in Russia had told me that when a small section of a leaf is cut off, it is possible—rarely—to get a Kirlian picture which shows the entire leaf, including the part that had been cut away. This phenomenon was deeply meaningful for the Soviet scientists, as it was for me. For if there could be photographed this second "energy body" of the leaf, *still attached to the physical body* (but invisible to our eyes), then it would be scientific proof of that ancient concept: that all living things have an energy body which is supposed to duplicate the physical body exactly and extend slightly beyond. This second body cannot be seen, the theory goes, because it is made of a fine energy substance, like the "chi" of acupuncture, or the "bioplasma" of Inyushin, or any of the other names given that bioenergy by so many world cultures. And, just as the energy has its special name, so does the energy body. It has been called the "ka" in Ancient Egypt, the "desire body" in Tibet, the "dopfel-ganger" in Germany, the "verdoger" in Scandinavia, and the "utai" in Japan, etc.

According to esoteric teaching, this energy body separates from, but remains attached by a silver cord to, the physical body during sleep, anesthesia, meditation, or hypnosis—and quits the body totally at death. In recent years this idea has been made more acceptable to the Western world through the researches of psychiatrist Elizabeth Kubler-Ross and Dr. Raymond Moody, both of whom—independently of each other—had worked with, or studied, that increasing number of people who have been declared medically "dead" but who, through the miracles of our technology, have been brought back to life. These briefly "dead" people report extraordinary experiences in which they felt themselves separate from their miserably painful, sick bodies. Many experienced a sensation of rising into the air, feeling a wondrous release, as they saw beneath them the physical bodies they had left behind. Then, sometimes, they found themselves hurtling through space and time into a new dimension of light and peace so exquisite that they felt only regret to come back.

Rich material, surely. But after all, nothing but anecdotes.

Solid laboratory evidence of this invisible energy body has continued to elude science in the same way that the transformation of base metals into gold eluded the alchemists. (Ironically, gold can be readily made from the cheaper metals today, but the cost is too high to make the work profitable.)

What solid laboratory evidence could Kirlian photography provide? It had been interesting, and even exciting, to photograph the coronas and bubbles and blotches of leaves and fingers and to speculate that these were aspects of the energy body. But to *see*, on film, the actual shapes and details of the leaf sections that had been cut away would give much more convincing evidence of this presumed second energy body. Suppose, one day, we could repeatedly and reliably capture that phantom—of what value would such pictures be?

Certainly none of the practical value that X-ray has for medicine, or thermography for cancer diagnosis. This is purely conjecture, but it might be that studying the energy body could show that the acupuncture theory—of an energy flowing in and out of the physical body through acupuncture points and along meridians—is, actually, defining the "anatomy" of that energy body. Or, as some research already indicates, that magnetic passes affect the energy body in special ways so that it absorbs a healing energy, or alters it somehow to create a trance state. Or that anesthesia, meditation, sleep, and hypnosis can be literally *shown* to separate the energy body from the physical one. And by far the most mind-tingling possibility—it might show how the energy body leaves the physical body at death to go on to other dimensions of reality.

These were the lures held out from the very first day that Ken Johnson made a workable Kirlian tool. And almost every day of those first two years we had sought the phantom leaf and had failed to find it.

K.J.'S FIRST PHANTOM

Months after Ken had left the lab for a paying job, he came in with his very first phantom. A success which only later did he tell us was achieved by squashing the entire leaf on film, *then* cutting off a section, and *then* taking the picture.

That information was bad news. For such a "phantom" could have been merely the result of moisture or gasses or residue from the leaf that had been squashed into the film emulsion. When I said this to Ken, he disagreed and pointed out that for months he had tried the squashing technique with no success at all. (In all fairness, John and I tried that technique time after time—without getting the phantom.)

All the same, from that moment on, the lab had strict rules about how to hunt for the phantom:

1. All leaves must be cut *before* they are placed on film.
2. Glass slides placed over the leaf (to keep the leaf flat) must be washed with alcohol before each trial, to eliminate any possible residue from an earlier trial.
3. To be called a true phantom, the photograph must show the specific *shape* of the section cut away.

This last rule was to answer the criticism that the "phantom" was nothing but gas or moisture escaping from the cut end of the leaf. For gasses and liquids, according to physics, do *not* hold any shape, but mold into the shape of their container (like water in a glass). Therefore, if a photograph of a phantom were to show the actual shape and pattern of the leaf as it had been before it was cut, then it could not be called a gas or liquid.

With these rules in force, the lab produced nothing but failure upon failure for more than a year—with the possible exceptions of some "near-misses" by John Hubacher, who must have taken more than a thousand pictures of cut leaves, varying his technique, the species of leaf, the instrument, and every other variable he could think of. On rare occasions he produced an intriguing picture (Fig. 11-1), but none of us was really satisfied—until the day we saw a phantom come alive on the transparent electrode. And later, when we were able to photograph them in moving pictures.

THE PHANTOM OF THE MOVIES

One afternoon, when only John and Frances were in the lab, a film producer came in to see if Kirlian photography might be used in a documentary he was making on plant life. John and Frances spent hours with him, showing the "dying leaf," the Green Thumb/

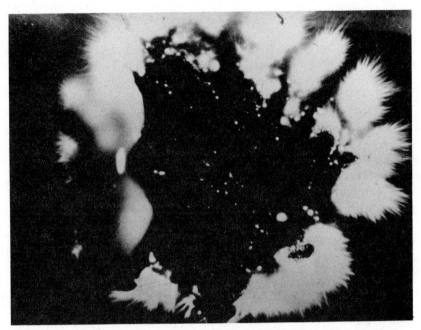

Fig. 11-1. A "near-miss" phantom leaf by John Hubacher.

Brown Thumb, sick and healthy leaves, tumors and seedlings, etc.—but the producer seemed bored with the still photographs.

So John, ever eager to help, hooked up the transparent electrode to show how we made movies. He put a scalloped geranium leaf on the glass, speared it with a ground wire, and electrified the glass. The leaf sent out its dancing blue bubbles, but still the producer seemed unimpressed. On impulse, John grandly took the leaf from the electrode, picked up a scissors, and with a flourish snipped a few scallops from the leaf.

"Now—" John had said, "—this is how we search for the phantom leaf."

And he put the cut leaf back on the glass electrode and touched its stem with the ground wire. Immediately the leaf lit up, *complete with the scalloped edges that had been cut away*. There, for all of them to see, was the sparkling phantom which continued to sparkle while John held the wire to the stem.

The producer called his photographer to hurry into the booth! Get the phantom on film! The photographer hurried, saw the phantom, but was too late in setting up to get its picture. According to John he muttered, "If that happens again, I'm getting out of here." Naturally John did not expect it to happen again, but he touched the leaf with the wire once more, and there was the phantom once again. This time the photographer was able to make several still photographs which he said he could put together into a strip of "motion pictures," a copy of which he promised to send but never did.

As soon as they left, John and Frances telephoned me at home with the news of our first phantom. Of course I did not believe them, but Frances insisted that she had seen the phantom blinking on and off like an electric sign. That convinced me. There had been no description of anything like that in any paper, and it was such an improbable idea that it would be hard to invent it. A blinking phantom! John promised to show me one the next day—which made us all laugh.

But the next day, John had the electrode and the leaves all set to go. I watched as he cut a geranium leaf, just as I had watched hundreds of times before. Then he fixed it to the glass and touched its stem with the wire. The leaf lit up to show the sharp edge of its cut side and nothing else. I was not really unhappy, because I had not expected to see a phantom. John tried several more leaves, with no success. But then, when he touched the wire to a freshly cut leaf...

"My God..."

We all stared at the brilliance of this phantom geranium leaf, showing the scallops of the section that had been cut away as if they were intact. It glowed steadily (not blinking on and off) for about thirty seconds.

I hardly knew how to cope with this event. After so much controversy about the Kirlian effect, so much criticism that it was nothing but an electrical artifact, or moisture, or gasses, or heat, or pressure...so much doubt, truthfully, in myself. Now in one brilliant half-minute, it was all resolved. We were seeing something we had almost despaired of seeing: the exact shape of the fluted edges of the geranium leaf—which had been cut away before it was placed on the electrode.

We stared at each other.

What had we done right? What had we done differently? Why had it never happened before? Would it ever happen again?

It did. And at rare, exhilarating times we were able to record them in the movies and on videotape.

THE ONE THAT GOT AWAY

By far the best phantom any of us ever saw was also our most devastating. It had been a night of long, dreary failures with leaf interactions on movie film, and Clark did not want to quit without one good piece of film. So he suggested a last go for a phantom, and we agreed. He checked his camera and said, wryly, "It had better be a fast phantom. There's not much film left on the reel." I nodded. It was late. We were all tired and frustrated. And it had been weeks since we had gotten a phantom.

John chose a needle-point ivy leaf and cut away a large part of its pointed, central shaft. Then he attached it to the electrode, and touched the wire to its stem. The leaf lit up brilliantly, showing exactly its cut-off shape and nothing else. Not a sign of a phantom. Clark asked, "Shall I run it?" I nodded. Clark started the camera.

After a moment, like a liquid fire tracing the edges of the pointed shaft that was no longer there—there leaped out a complete and precise image of the whole leaf, which stayed, unwavering, for almost a minute.

No one spoke. John turned off the power. Clark murmured, awestruck, "Did you see that—?" No one answered. I think we all knew the gorgeous show we had watched began *after* the film had run its course. Clark said, "Let's hope." But it was no surprise when the film came back from the lab, showing in the last feet of the reel the blunt end of the cut-off ivy leaf and nothing else.

We did get others on film. And with each new phantom, there was excited speculation. What were we looking at? Was it the energy body? What else could it be? Would we ever get skillful enough, knowledgeable enough, to produce it when we wanted it, at least forty or fifty percent of the time, instead of the ten or fifteen percent we were struggling with? Here was the hub of the problem. For without repeatable, reliable results—the keynote of scientific success—we could not begin to play with the *qualities* of the phantom.

So we kept struggling.

CLARK'S FINEST

And out of those efforts, Clark produced a thirty-minute documentary, made up of the best of our Kirlian work, which he hoped would fulfill his requirements for the Master's degree in cinematography. This meant he wrote a script and photographed in the conventional way the lab, its research associates at work, its projects—all intercut with the actual Kirlian movies. He also directed, dressed the sets, did the lights, edited, dubbed the sound effects, made the titles, arranged the musical score—and came up with a film, "Explorations in Kirlian Photography," which has been shown at conferences and universities around the world, with excellent comments from both scientists and the lay audiences.

But when Clark showed the finished film to his academic committee, they refused to accept it, commenting that he had not done a "creative project." Stunned, I asked Clark what they meant. After all, he had created the only technique of Kirlian movie-making in the United States at that time. He explained that such "creativity" was not the issue. It was necessary for him to invent and film a "story."

Academia, oh academia.

12
Devastating Criticism and a Romanian Coup

Concerning Discoveries in Unexpected Places, with Unexpected Phases

MORE NEW STUFF

Throughout 1975 and into 1976 we plowed ahead, finding further small clues on the flow of bioenergy in human interactions, acupuncture therapy, eye contact, healing, plant pathology, and, every once in a lovely while, a new phantom leaf. Rich, busy work, which was abruptly turned upside-down by two major Kirlian happenings. First the bad, then the good.

SCIENCE AND KIRLIAN PHOTOGRAPHY

There had been a host of articles and books published on Kirlian photography by '75, with our work generously quoted not only in the popular press but in respected journals like that of the *New York Academy of Sciences,* the *Smithsonian,* and *Psycho-energetic Systems.* And we were in constant demand to present at national and international conferences, both here and abroad. But in spite of the intense interest—almost a furor—no grants had been given to anyone doing research in the field.

Then, in 1975, an interdisciplinary group of scientists at a major American university received a large federal grant to study the Kirlian effect; and in '76 those scientists published in our most distinguished journal, *Science,* an explosive report which lit up the media all over the country with headlines like: KIRLIAN PHOTOGRAPHY

ALL WET and COLD WATER THROWN ON KIRLIAN PHOTOGRAPHY. The gist being that the scientists of Drexel University had proved the Kirlian effect was "nothing but moisture."

That's Not Bioenergy! That's Moisture!

This argument had surfaced early in our research when "gasses," "vapors," and water were thought to conduct electricity onto the film, thus creating photographs of leaves. Eventually, as the leaves became dry, the electricity could not be conducted through them and no photographs could be taken. Thus, the "dying leaf effect" (leaves slowly taking less and less of a Kirlian image, until no picture at all could be found) became a function of plain, old-fashioned electricity. This argument had more or less died away for lack of evidence and also because so many other dry things had been photographed.

But now, in this new *Science* article, the moisture argument was re-born. Not with leaves, but with fingers, and the argument took an opposite point of view. This group of researchers had latched onto the idea of using fake fingers as well as real ones (like the work of nineteenth-century Menager, and our lab). And those researchers had noticed, right away, that the coronas of dry fingers looked very much like the coronas of fake fingers, and that *wetting* either the dry finger or the fake finger gave a much weaker picture and sometimes no picture at all. In other words, they found that the *presence* of moisture brought on the "disappearing act."

So had we, with moist fingers. But moist leaves had created brilliant photographs. We had also experimented with freshly cut slices of apple—rich in moisture—and they photographed brilliantly; but those same apple slices, gone dry, did not photograph at all. To recapitulate: dry fingers and wet apples photograph brilliantly, whereas dry apples and wet fingers don't photograph at all. We decided that people are not like apples (perhaps an obvious conclusion). But we did not conclude that moisture in Kirlian photography was a major variable. And that was the hub of the problem. For the *Science* article did state succinctly, "Most of the variations in the images of the coronas of a living subject . . . can be accounted for by the presence of moisture on or within the subject's surface."

Period.

As we studied this erudite article in *Science*, we could hear the bell tolling. For here was the hard data to refute our "nonsense." It did not matter that we could—and did—refute that hard data with other hard data. What mattered was that we were on the "bioenergy" lunatic fringe, while the Drexel group had the high sanction of a large federal grant and a prestigious publication. Kirlian photography had been tested in the crucible, and had gone up in steam.

BUCHAREST AND ELECTRICAL PHOTOGRAPHY

Even as we were reeling with the impact of the *Science* crisis, there came another major piece of news, to the effect that still another version of electrical photography—this one called electronography—was being touted in still another Soviet satellite country. This news came, oddly, via a phone call marked ASAP from a Beverly Hills physician, Dr. Sapse. Usually such calls were a request for psychic healing on a particularly difficult case. This call had nothing to do with a patient but concerned Dr. Sapse himself. He told me on the phone that he had just returned from Romania, where he had had electrical photographs taken of himself—from which a Bucharest physician had made an accurate diagnosis!

This was really big news, and an appointment was swiftly made and promptly kept. Dr. Sapse arrived at the lab with a small attaché case and a worried smile. It seems that over the years he had made many trips to Bucharest to study the gerontological research of a Romanian doctor who, now in her eighties, was winning international fame for her anti-aging therapy. On his most recent visit, Dr. Sapse had met a group of scientists doing research not only in electrical photography, but acupuncture! (We all snapped to attention at that bit of information.) Since Dr. Sapse knew nothing of either discipline, the Romanian scientists offered to demonstrate with Dr. Sapse himself.

At this point in his story, Dr. Sapse stared through the window with unbelieving, almost frightened eyes.

"I cannot truly explain what happened—" he began and stopped.

"Did they take pictures of your finger pads?"

His look of near-fear changed to one of near-scorn.

"Finger pads? Good lord, no. My whole torso, from neck to groin."

It was my turn to stare out of the window, unbelieving. I had never heard, anywhere, from anyone, about full-body pictures with any kind of electrical photography. "That's hard to accept," I murmured, and Dr. Sapse looked at me with surprise.

"But you are supposed to be an expert in electrical photography!"

I laughed. To be called an "expert" it is necessary to have at least two articles published in major journals, and to have at least fifty

TV and radio appearances in one's *curriculum vitae*. By those criteria, I had qualified as an expert in telepathy, hypnosis, acupuncture, Kirlian photography—all the while knowing my wealth of ignorance. I explained as much to Dr. Sapse, who smiled and continued to narrate what sounded like a spy movie from the fifties.

The Romanian scientists had arranged that he be picked up at his hotel and driven to the government chemical complex where—as with most federal agencies—cards had to be stamped, IDs issued, fingerprints taken, intercoms activated, elevators unlocked and so on. At length, Dr. Sapse found himself in an elegant laboratory where he was to be initiated into the workings of the elaborate electronics with which the group was studying acupuncture and "electronography," the special name given to the apparatus by its inventor. I asked for the spelling of this inventor's name: it was Ioan Florin Dumitrescu. His credentials included not only doctor of medicine, but specialist in electrophysiology, as well as other graduate degrees.

Electronography

In order to take a picture, Dr. Dumitrescu explained, Dr. Sapse would have to disrobe and lie stomach-down on a couch, in the center of which had been inserted what looked like a large, flat piece of glass. This, he was told, was part of the instrument which would take an electronograph of Dr. Sapse's nude torso. X-ray film was then placed on the plate, and Dr. Sapse lay down—not without some anxiety, particularly when a rubber strap was clapped around his ankle. This, he guessed hopefully, was not an entrapment but a grounding device (he was right). Then Dr. Dumitrescu pressed a button for the briefest moment, which was the whole photographic process, for then Dr. Sapse was unstrapped and told to dress.

When the film was developed it was put on view, and Dr. Sapse saw that it looked nothing like an X-ray picture, nor like any photograph he had ever seen. After studying the film carefully, Dr. Dumitrescu suggested that perhaps Dr. Sapse had suffered a colitis, from which he was now recovered, but was presently suffering a gall bladder problem. This information transfixed Dr. Sapse, because both diagnoses were correct but unknown to anyone except his own doctor in California.

"How had he made the diagnosis?" I blurted the question.

Dr. Sapse paused, then took from his attaché case a large piece of X-ray film, which he placed flat on the table. Although on X-ray film, this was obviously not an X-ray picture, for it did not show the interior bones or organs. It showed, rather, the typical Kirlian corona discharge around the edges of the torso, with very little interior information, except for the obvious crease of the belly button, and the general area of the groin. The only other distinguishing marks seemed to be three odd, pimplish vortices with nuclei.

I stared at the picture and could only repeat the question, "But how did Dr. Dumitrescu make the diagnosis?"

"He said it was—" Dr. Sapse paused, looking bemused and a trifle ashamed by this next piece of news, "—it was because of those three...acupuncture points."

"What—?!!" John and I stared at each other, and back at Dr. Sapse, who became apologetic. "I know it sounds crazy—" he began.

"Oh, no, not to us! Please, tell us exactly what he said about those acupuncture points."

"I will tell you what he said, but I do not know what he meant. I can only give you his words, I hope correctly."

"Please."

"With this electronography, he said, when someone is sick, then these pimples—these acupuncture points—come on the photograph. Not where the illness is. This is not where the gall bladder is, of course. But where the acupuncture points indicate that the illness is."

"Wait, please!" I wanted as precise data as I could get. Our own years of acupuncture research had shown us, time and again, the flow of energy along an acupuncture meridian. And I knew there was a gall bladder meridian which runs through the torso. John and I checked our acupuncture chart. Yes, the pimplish spots looked as if they might be on the gall bladder meridian.

"Could you explain a bit more about the diagnosis? Are you saying—"

"I am saying *nothing!*" Dr. Sapse was alarmed.

"Right." I withdrew the phrase, realizing that Dr. Sapse was a gerontologist and not geared for the unorthodox in medicine. "Is Dr. Dumitrescu saying that the acupuncture points show up in the pictures *only* when there is illness present?"

Dr. Sapse nodded, and looked even more befuddled when John exclaimed, with a happy laugh, "That's the best news yet!"

I explained to Dr. Sapse that John had been working for years trying to photograph acupuncture points, but had never been sure that they *were* acupuncture points because they would come and go. But now Dr. Sapse was saying that the points come and go with illness and health, and—

"Please." Dr. Sapse interrupted again. "Don't try to explain it to me...not yet. You see, I haven't told you the most strange part."

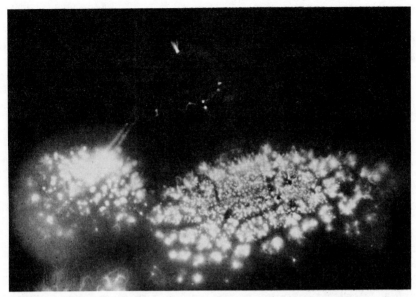

Fig. 12-1. Using chloroform, we were able to get Kirlian photographs like this, showing a cactus (the main body) with what looks like an "energy body" dissociating.

Dr. Sapse paused and pulled from his attaché case several diagrams and articles (in Romanian, of course) and many photographs with captions, which he translated for us. We listened, and learned that Dumitrescu had discovered a technique for taking electrical photographs through a microscope and had pictures of exquisitely detailed cell structures to prove it. But by far the most curious photograph—and the one that disturbed Dr. Sapse the most—was that of a rat taken after its death, showing a shadowy second image, which looked like our "phantom" or "out-of-body" effects. We pounced on that picture, and Dr. Sapse's face again took on that bemused, almost ashamed look.

"I asked about that picture, too. And Dr. Dumitrescu said—if you can believe this, and I guess you can—he said, 'Who knows what that is? Maybe the soul of the dead rat.' That's what he said."

"Marvelous!" John and I looked at each other and laughed.

Dr. Sapse looked away, apparently embarrassed. But he turned back when we offered to show him our research, and the similarity of the rat's "soul" and our "out-of-body" leaves and cactus (Fig. 12-1). He was interested, which encouraged me to say how much we would like to exchange information with Dr. Dumitrescu. Happily, this was easy to arrange, because Dr. Sapse was returning to Bucharest for another conference and would be pleased to bring Dumitrescu anything we cared to send. Within ten days, Dr. Sapse was en route, carrying the bulk of our articles, our best slides, and our newest work—Clark's movie, "Explorations in Kirlian Photography," which showed in motion pictures our acupuncture research and the phantom leaf effect.

We learned a few months later from Dr. Sapse that these all had been delivered. After which, for more than a year, silence. Which, from a Soviet satellite, we had come to expect.

ANOTHER COUNTRY, ANOTHER CONFERENCE

Then, early in '77, an invitation in the mail, just like any other invitation to an international conference (this one on acupuncture), with enclosures for hotel reservations, schedule of events, tentative speakers and papers, etc. But on another day, in a separate letter signed by Ioan Florin Dumitrescu (was it a personal invitation? Hard to tell because the English was so Romanian), I was asked to attend the conference because of "outstanding research contribution." A survey of the agenda revealed many papers on energy fields, electrical photography, and acupuncture from several Soviet countries. An opportunity not to be missed. There was *no* funding available for travel to Bucharest, of course, particularly since the *Science* exposé of Kirlian photography in '76. But I was still permitted to present papers at international conferences, even on energy fields and acupuncture. Jolly West was keeping his word on academic freedom.

So I wrote prompt acceptance and plunged into a new paper on the recent movie research into acupuncture.

A few months later, at home late one night, I turned to a TV newscast and saw the city of Bucharest, devastated by the worst earthquake of its history, with films showing corpse after corpse being pulled from the rubble that had been the center of the city. For the next two weeks, I tried telephoning Dr. Dumitrescu daily. Although the Bucharest telephones were working, Dumitrescu was unreachable, even with repeated messages that he return my call. To go to Bucharest or not to go? Teeter-totter, as time raced on. Until, just three days before flight time, a letter arrived with the news that the conference was to be held as scheduled, but at a different hotel, the Resort Parc, in the suburbs of the city. More appealing, and cheaper!

BUCHAREST

That inevitable black limousine and Intourist guide were waiting at the bucolic airport to drive me through narrow country roads, massed on both sides with pink and red roses (were they growing wild? The Intourist guide did not understand the question). We drove in near-silence, never coming near the city, and at last pulled up at the rural but very large Resort Parc Hotel. In the lobby, the International Acupuncture Conference was elegantly displayed on posters designed around that glorious abstract bird in flight, by Brancusi, the celebrated Romanian artist.

As the Intourist guide led me straight to the reception desk, I thought I caught sight of Dr. Dumitrescu at the entrance door, looking much more attractive than the pompous-looking photographs I had seen. He seemed to recognize me, too, in one sharp, interconnecting glance, but then I was at the hotel desk for the formalities of registration. During which, a touch, lightly, on my elbow—and there was Dr. Dumitrescu, smiling and polite but speaking—?!—something we came to call Romanian English, not at all comprehensible. Was he saying there was to be a meeting? that night? and would I join them, and what time? I hazarded, "Eight o'clock?" and repeated the number and day in French, the second language of Romania. Dr. Dumitrescu smiled, nodded, and left. Then the Intourist guide led me to the elevators and up to a bright, pleasant room with private bath.

There was time to unpack and have an early dinner. I glanced through the conference calendar, where I saw there was to be an evening "film gala"—at which our "Explorations in Kirlian Photography" was being offered! (That was the first inkling that our film had ever arrived in Bucharest.) Then, I was astonished to see, our film was to be followed by a Romanian one on electronography—which meant Dumitrescu had learned how to do electrical cinematography! Maybe, at tonight's meeting, we could exchange ideas on film techniques...

But first, an early dinner. At six o'clock I presented myself in the enormous formal dining room of the hotel—which was totally empty. At length a puzzled young waiter arrived, and I somehow got across the idea that I'd like dinner. He gaped at me. "Dinner—? Now?"

I nodded my head up and down, while he shook his from side to side. Then without warning, he left, and I sat at a table, quite alone. After some time I was brought a nicely broiled chicken and potatoes, which I devoured. As I walked back across the lobby to return to my room, a man's voice burst in my ear, "Darleenk!"

And I was engulfed by Czech parapsychologist Dr. Zdenek Rejdak, the organizer of the First International Psychotronics Conference at Prague, and the Second International Psychotronics Conference at Monaco, both of which I had attended. I was to attend the Third International Psychotronics Conference in Tokyo, in three weeks time, as Dr. Rejdak of course knew. I had always found him to be a polite and formal man, but now he was embracing me publicly, and with too much enthusiasm, too loudly, telling me how the Tokyo conference was coming together brilliantly, with the Proceedings already published—he had the two volumes in his hand—with many more papers than this Bucharest Acupuncture Conference. As he chattered, it became clear he had been sitting, unattended, in the lobby. Which meant that he would not be joining our eight o'clock meeting, which meant that he was not in the Inner Circle. But I did not want to probe into the politics that surrounded these affairs, so I excused myself and went to my room.

Moon over Bucharest

Promptly at eight, standing in front of the elevator out of which I walked, was Dr. Dumitrescu and colleagues—an older man, introduced (I think) as head of the chemical industry; a younger man, Paul, clinical psychologist; and a Santa Claus of an Italian man, white-haired, pot-bellied, with a hohoho laugh, who spoke Italian/French and was primarily, I learned, a parapsychologist. We were an odd group, talking at each other in different tongues as we walked out of the hotel to a small car where the driver/translator explained to me that we would be taking a brief tour of Bucharest before dinner.

Dinner! (Was there any way to hurry up my digestion?)

The night's full moon lit up the boulevards of Bucharest. Although the earthquake had been only three weeks earlier, the city looked intact, for the rubble had all been cleared so that the empty holes between the buildings that had been left standing could be mistaken, in the dark blue light, for parking lots. We arrived, too soon, at an outdoor restaurant on a lake. Its pavilion was lit by torches and candlelight, and was scattered with tables surrounding a dance floor. An orchestra played alternately—but always loudly—Romanian jazz and American rock. The night, in spite of the golden moon, was damp and cold, and I was grateful for my heavy coat.

Almost immediately, as we sipped a prune-based liquor, we began to call each other by our first names. I was T'elma, and Dr. Dumitrescu was Flor'een, and we struggled with the language barrier to get to the core of each other's research. Florin told of his enchantment when he first saw Clark's film, discovering that someone in the world was doing the same sort of acupuncture research that he was doing, and finding similar results! We stared at each other, almost goony with the wonder of finding the energy fields of acupuncture through electrical photography almost at the same time, yet nine thousand miles apart!

"Your cine—" Florin was twice lost for words, both in language and in expression. "Is like...inspire! I say, Paul..." The young psychologist next to me nodded. "...Paul, we make cine! These researches!"

"Did you use a light intensifier?" Florin, of course, looked puzzled and I tried again. "I mean, the light from fingers, it is very little. How did you make the light bigger? So it can show on film?" He still looked puzzled. And I remembered I had sent him Clark's articles, which explained his technique of light intensification and "pushing" in the lab for brightness. I mentioned that, and Florin's face grew clear with understanding and excitement.

He told—to my awe—how he had collaborated with the Romanian film industry and developed a technique of using regular film, regular speed, with regular cameras, which could record the emanations clearly from not only the fingers and hands, but from the whole torso! This was something no one anywhere had yet been able to do. How? What technology, what instruments?! But here, language became an insuperable problem, and we lost contact. So I plunged into Florin's work with diagnosis. The president of the chemical industry who was with us told me that Florin had recently completed a huge project, taking electronographs of the entire labor force of Romania's chemical works, which numbers thousands of people. This research had a twofold goal: to learn if electronography could detect cancer earlier than standard medical tests, and to see if electronography could be used as a diagnostic tool. The answer, on both counts, after several years of work, was a definite *yes*.

And with that infectious excitement which seems part of the creative scientist, Florin and Paul, medical doctor and clinical psychologist, told how they had slowly, slowly learned to read the hieroglyphics of electrical photographs which led them—against all of their logic and all of their training—to acupuncture charts. And they began to see, to their astonishment, that the appearance in the electronographs of special acupuncture points foretold a special illness. They came to recognize the pattern of points for ulcers, and for arthritis, and for problems related to heart, colon, gall bladder, intestines. Equally remarkable was the fact, slowly learned, that after the illness had been treated and cured with medication or surgery or acupuncture, *then the acupuncture points no longer appeared in the pictures*. Here was still another triumph for 5,000-year-old acupuncture theory, for Florin and Paul had learned how to interpret their electronographs by studying ancient acupuncture charts.

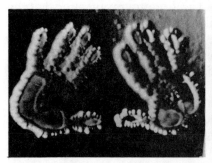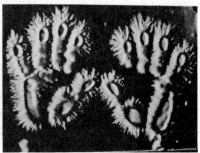

Fig. 12-2. *(Left)* Electronographs, processed through a computer, of an Indian swami's hands in a normal state. *(Right)* Same hands "sending energy." *(Pictures courtesy of Dr. Ioan Florin Dumitrescu.)*

Again we stared at each other, awed by the mystery of invisible acupuncture points showing up visibly through electrical photography. And that gave rise to a question which I was almost afraid to ask, but knew I must.

"Does anyone else in Romania—" I stopped; it was not an easy question, "—does any other group of scientists in your country believe in your acupuncture points?"

A loud, telling laugh. Clearly, the schism between orthodox and unorthodox science was alive and well in Romania. Out of the laughter, Paul began to talk hesitantly of how deeply committed he was to the concepts not only of bioenergy, but of the different states of consciousness, for he had been studying yoga with a swami from India who was now living in Bucharest. This swami—like Swami Rama in the United States—had come into their laboratory to demonstrate his command over the flow of bioenergy.

"Did you get electronographs?!"

Another loud laugh, but now the laughter was of success. Florin said that the pictures of the yogi's transfer of bioenergy would be shown at the conference, and that he would give me duplicates to take home with me (Fig. 12-2). We talked much more of meditation and spiritual disciplines—against the blare of "Rock Around the Clock"—while being served a rich dessert of Romanian pancakes with ground hazel nuts and syrup and espresso coffee on the terrace overlooking a lake sparkling with fiery moonlight.

Paul struggled to explain his awe at finding that meditative states could produce patterns of mind where one believes one can communicate over distances, and that one can leave one's body, and that one can ascend through ceilings and fly through the air. All of these—telepathy, out-of-body experiences, and levitation—are fields of parapsychological study, but all of these, too, are the ancient teachings of yoga, Buddhism, and Zen. I was to hear again and again from scientists at this conference how they were not only doing research in bioenergy and acupuncture and altered states of consciousness, but were also training in one or another spiritual discipline.

I spoke of how a similar trend could clearly be seen with scientists in the United States, where these ideas were forming into special clusters. Like parapsychology and holistic health, involving unorthodox therapies like acupuncture, herbs, bioenergetics, psychic healing, and research into the possibility of life after death and other dimensions of reality. We began to wonder if there might be a world-wide movement, a *Zeitgeist*, an evolution into a different realm of mind and spirit.

This rapport was invaded, sharply, by the Italian Santa Claus, who wanted to shift from the spiritual to the political aspects of parapsychology. Since he spoke in an Italian/French, which did not jibe well with my American/French, I lost track of the talk and instead studied Florin and Paul. Here were two avant-garde scientists who may have discovered a medical technique as valuable as the X-ray by following the dictates of a 5,000-year-old medical anomaly, acupuncture. Moreover, this ancient anomaly was presently coming in for serious study, as evidenced by the medical doctors from twenty-nine countries who were in Bucharest for this conference. Here, perhaps, was another part of the *Zeitgeist*. . . .

But there were more practical problems with which to deal. And, driving back between the rose-covered road banks (the roses *did* grow wild, I was told), I said several times that I hoped to buy one of Florin's electronograph units for our lab at UCLA. Each time I was told that the instruments would be exhibited at the Conference. At length, and with some exasperation, I said that to see instruments at an exhibition might be interesting, but not nearly so persuasive as working with them in a laboratory. No response, from anyone. I began to feel that frustration with which I had become too familiar in Moscow and Alma-Ata and Prague years before. Although there was clearly much research going on, it was clearly government policy to reveal as little as possible.

First Day of the Conference

It was cold and raining heavily the next morning (and stayed that way through the week). Since there was nothing on the agenda until the opening reception at six in the evening, and little opportunity to explore beyond the hotel lobby, which was now congested with new arrivals, I spent most of the day studying the published Proceedings of the conference which had not yet begun. Actually, I had come to admire this quirk of pre-publication, for most of the papers are published in English—the international language of science—and are much more easily read than listened to, particularly if the speaker has a strong accent or if the paper is given instant translation, which is often misleading if not downright wrong.

There were papers from twenty-nine countries, ranging from South Africa to Japan, with several from the Soviet Union and its satellite countries. Of particular interest to me were those papers that dealt with energy fields around the body and attempts to measure those fields, for this was still another try at merging ancient theory with modern technology. When I went foraging for lunch, I met one of the authors of those papers, a young, red-bearded Hungarian physicist who told me that he had studied just about everything our lab had published because it was so pertinent to his research, which dealt with measuring the amount of carbon dioxide emitted at the "electrodermal points." (That term, first coined at Bethesda's Acupuncture Conference, was now being generally adopted in place of "acupuncture points," which are still not conceded to exist by orthodox science.) The idea behind the Hungarian's search for carbon dioxide was to show that those points—electrodermal or acupuncture—were a source of energy flow, even if that energy were labelled an exchange of a respiratory gas. (Ancient yogic texts clearly say that we *breathe* through the pores of our skin, taking in oxygen and emitting carbon dioxide.)

When I asked the red-headed physicist how he took his measures, he plunged kindly into a lecture on theoretical physics, but I was soon hopelessly lost and told him so. He took my ignorance as a matter of course, for he too had changed fields, from classical physics to esoteric physiology—an area still unacknowledged in most universities. (Changing careers has become commonplace for young scientists today, for there is an ever-widening stream for them to flow into—like holography, astrophysics, and space biology. How can one keep up?)

TWO OLD ACQUAINTANCES. There arrived together, that opening day, two special friends whom I had known separately. One was Dr. Huber, the Viennese physician in private practice whom I had first met in Prague, when he had led me, shyly, into a lonely corridor to show me his "healing energy." Dr. Huber was the first medical doctor I had met who dared to admit, even in private, that he might be a psychic healer. Now, just four years later, he was in Bucharest to deliver a paper on his success in curing a variety of illnesses with the "laying on of hands." He was also anxious to tell me about a large grant he had received from the Austrian government to research a special yogic breathing technique in the training of athletes. Together with Dr. Huber arrived Andreas Resch, Ph.D., whom I had met in the early '70s at an ESP symposium in San

Francisco. At that time he was a young Catholic priest, gentle and courteous with alert brown eyes (it was whispered to me at the time that he was teaching parapsychology to the clergy at the Vatican!). Over the years, Dr. Resch had expanded his field of expertise and was currently editing a journal on scientific parapsychology while at the University of Vienna.

Both men were pleased to see me, for they had read the recent *Science* article on how the Kirlian effect could be explained as moisture, and wished to lend their support to my research. In fact, Dr. Huber said, pointblank, that he knew that moisture could not explain the pictures of that "healing energy" he was now getting, on film, with his own apparatus in his own laboratory in Vienna. Fine news.

THE RECEPTION. It was clear that this was a big conference in Bucharest, for the opening reception in the Art Deco Grand Ballroom boasted a superb spread of Romanian hors d'oeuvres, sparkling glasses of different wines and beers, and Colombian coffee, freshly brewed!—all served by a flawless staff. When I walked in, there were already about two hundred people in the room, drinking, laughing, talking, just as at any cocktail party—at which I am generally ill at ease. I hung back until that smell of Colombian coffee struck me—and in the same moment a waiter was at my side with a steaming cup. I sipped it with deep pleasure, trying without success to identify the guests, almost all of whom were young men (probably students)—an item which makes *scientific* social gatherings much more attractive for me than the other varieties.

In time, first one and then another of these young men approached me, shyly, to talk of ESP and Kirlian photography. They began to introduce older men, and finally a path was made for a retired medical doctor, perhaps in his seventies, who, in spite of failing health, had come to the reception to present me his papers on psychical research, published in French in the *Journal Metapsychique*. These were, he said, theoretical papers about the energy fields and energy body which now seemed validated by our Kirlian work, particularly by the phantom leaf effect, which he said with mounting excitement was "the key!" He was so moved that his whole body began to shake uncontrollably and he turned aside. The young student who had presented him told me that the gentleman's lifelong interest had been psychical research. I asked if any of the young generation had a similar interest—and the student waved his hand toward the large group now surrounding us. Everyone laughed.

Then, as if on cue, through the group stepped Florin and Paul, who were bringing a request from the Romanian delegation that a

Round Table on current parapsychological research be arranged if possible. I was delighted to accept, but even as I did, I wondered if the Round Table would ever be formed. It was not. For it has ever been so, in the Soviet countries; much private interest from scientists, but no public statements. (This is, of course, also true in the United States, in the sense that visitors to the lab from federal agencies always insist their interest is a personal curiosity and nothing more.)

Preliminaries

Never before in Romanian history, I was assured by every Romanian I met, had there been so distinguished an International Conference with so many eminent visitors. And every preparation had been made. There were exhibition rooms displaying new devices in acupuncture research, including the red-headed Hungarian's device for measuring carbon dioxide. But dominating over all were the many sophisticated electronic devices of Florin Dumitrescu, with interfaces to TV monitors, computers, spectral analyzers, and so on—but nowhere was there an electrical hookup so that one could see the machines at work.

Such a thing would be unheard of in the United States, where every scientific conference includes rooms and rooms displaying the most recent inventions, all of which are hawked and operated constantly to attract customers. Manufacturers, after all, want to sell what they make. But here, although there were handsome brochures which told (in that impossible Romanian English!) of the remarkable feats by Dumitrescu's machines, there were no demonstrations, no schematics, no specifications, no prices quoted. And no one taking orders. I was told to write for more information and prices to a special address. (I did. Never a reply.)

With none of Dumitrescu's devices at work, I was left with the dreary suspicion that, imposing as it looked, it might be nothing more than an expensive mock-up. But this was too important to dismiss with suspicions, so I managed to corner Florin for a moment and all but demand a demonstration. He listened, bit at his moustache, but said nothing.

Meanwhile, I had a different kind of problem to solve. Just before leaving for Bucharest I was told that the Soviet countries used a video system which cannot play our videotapes (the number of lines do not match—a technical thing, like the European 50-cycle electricity versus our 60-cycle, which makes our appliances unusable abroad). I did not know how to solve that problem, but with our videotape in hand, I sought the media man. He smiled and nodded and tried to take the videotape, but I held on tight, trying to explain the problem. He did not speak English, but smiled and nodded and wrested the tape from me and vanished, leaving me with the uneasy feeling that I might never see it again.

There was no need to worry, for Florin's staff had done a fine job. They had not only found, but adapted an American TV set. And they had also gathered a fine collection of slide projectors and movie projectors of all millimeter sizes, and electric pointers, and rheostats, and the best contraptions I had ever seen for simultaneous translations, via ear plugs and eight channels, for the delegates to listen in the language of their choice. Technology had kept abreast in this small country, more notorious for Count Dracula and Transylvania (which legend was reaping a rich tourist traffic).

The Outer Conference

Most papers at a conventional conference are presented in a time-honored, time-consuming pattern, since conventional research deals mainly with one or another detail of a settled method (such as: Does a placebo give best results with migraine or backache or stomach pain? Do artists or business people do better at ESP with card-guessing? What degree of electric shock gives best results in avoidance conditioning with smokers?) Such papers begin with an *Introduction*, which tells why the study is done; the *Procedure*, which names instruments, measures, and technique of use—such a complex mess these days that only silent study can make the meaning clear; then *Results*, giving a statistical analysis that only a statistician can make and/or make sense of; and finally the *Discussion*, which is exactly that, ending with a traditional phrase like, "Further research is needed."

But a conference like this one on acupuncture is a very different affair. For no one is yet an authority, nor has a pattern been established for research. So any kind of experiment can be tried, with no one to cry, "Poor science!" Thus, at Bucharest, every sort of paper was heard. At one extreme, we heard evidence to support the recent Western guess that the anesthetic effect of acupuncture needling is the work of "gates" in the nervous system, acting like brakes to stop pain impulses before they reach the brain. At the other extreme, a speaker proposed that acupuncture therapy influences not the physical, but the energy body, in which all pain sensations lie. And in between, there were papers to endorse the reality of acupuncture (electrodermal) points, since they can be measured electrically—very much as we had done with Zion, using Ken's acuometer, or as Adamenko had done with his tobiscope, or as the Germans and Japanese were doing with instruments of their own inventions. There was even a paper which reportèd that acupuncture points had been measured on corpses and were found to have different electrical characteristics than other areas of the dead body.

Then there were many clinical papers, showing how acupuncture treatments can give relief for a gamut of medical problems from arthritis to asthma to childbirth to frigidity; while other papers claimed that acupuncture gave no better therapeutic results than hypnosis or aspirin or a placebo. And there was also a group of papers that dealt with acupuncture in combination with nutrition (Africa), unorthodox medicine (Soviet Union), and animals (Italy).

But the outstanding contributions, for me, were the many papers from Dumitrescu's group, ranging from clinical research to anthropology to medical diagnosis—all illustrated with his electronography, which used different techniques. One technique fed the electronographs into a computer, which then gave a printout that looked like a relief map, showing the heights and depths of the corona discharge, useful for measuring changes in the fields. Another technique employed a TV monitor on which one could watch the energy patterns as they were emitted around the body. And still another technique applied electronography to microscope studies. But his finest work by far was the technique of making medical diagnoses—appendicitis, gall bladder, colon infection, lung disease—all from the appearance, on the electronograph, of the "electrodermal points" in special areas.

Dumitrescu stressed his rare finding that acupuncture points show up in his pictures when there is pathology but are not visible when the pathology disappears. The most impressive of these photographs showed a torso with a series of acupuncture points in a near-straight line, conforming remarkably to a meridian shown on the ancient acupuncture charts (Fig. 12-3). This was as if the far galaxies of the universe had all been accurately located on a map by an ancient people who had never looked through a telescope.

Dazzling.

And there was more to come.

Film Gala

That night we watched a film made by an Italian doctor, obviously an amateur photographer, who had spent his own money to document his research into acupuncture. A familiar story. This was Dr. Rossi, a tall, blonde, blue-eyed surgeon from Milan, one of the handsomest of men. His movie (of which he had only one copy) had been shot in cinema-verité style during actual surgery. The print was literally falling apart from overuse, with torn sprockets,

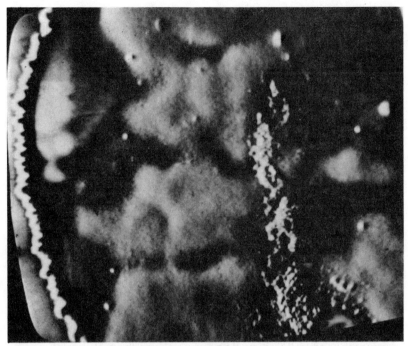

Fig. 12-3. An electronograph of the human torso, showing a series of acupuncture points in a straight line, which conforms to the stomach meridian of ancient acupuncture charts. *(Pictures courtesy of Dr. Ioan Florin Dumitrescu.)*

scratches, and numerous splicings. But enough remained intact so that one could see convincingly how a mule, given acupuncture needling as its only anesthetic, was totally still—and seemingly without pain—during the excision of a large tumor. This operation was followed by a similar excision of a tumor from a man, with the same success. The film also showed a Caesarian section under acupuncture with a woman and then with a dog. (One wonders if there might have been some social comment here, along with the medical one.) A remarkable film. For it was showing, dynamically, that somehow slim metal needles stuck into points of the body *can stop all the pain of major surgery.* (A bioenergetic phenomenon?)

I watched the Caesarian sections with special interest, because for years I had been showing students a film of painfree Caesarian section in which the only anesthesia was hypnosis. In medical circles, the suggestion had been made that acupuncture might be a form of hypnosis, but how to hypnotize a dog for a Caesarian section with acupuncture needles? A better notion might be that both hypnosis and needling affect the *energy body,* which is what the esoteric teachings of many cultures specifically say.

Our film, "Explorations in Kirlian Photography," became a victim of mechanical mishap right off, even though, in contrast with Dr. Rossi's beat-up print, I had brought a fresh one to the meeting. There developed in the sound system a rhythm of now you hear it, now you don't—with the sound fading so much that the audience became restive and vocal. I charged up on stage (somewhat dramatically, I'm afraid), took the microphone, and in English asked that the film be stopped and started again, without sound, so that I could narrate it. Florin then came on stage to repeat my request in Romanian. The film was stopped, the house lights came on, and the film was rewound while Florin spoke to the audience. Then, at a signal from the projection booth, Florin smiled at me and left the stage. Lights down, film on again, and I narrated for a few minutes—until I began to hear my voice, twice. Somehow, someone had repaired the sound system and my film narration was being clearly heard. So once again the film was stopped, rewound, and I returned to my seat, flushed with discomfort—how could anyone in the audience know what the film was about after so many false starts?

Apparently the audience did understand, because at the end there came that standing ovation, which has become standard in the last few decades for dancers, politicians, movie stars, sportsmen, rock figures, and scientists. Somehow this ovation was less odious than most, probably because Florin called me on stage to accept a bouquet of flowers, just like a ballerina.

Finally, the long-promised, longed-for Dumitrescu film, made with the facilities of the Romanian film industry in a splendidly professional way. The movie began with lightning in the sky and vast electrical storms, then whirled through other majestic electrical effects in nature (described in English by the narrator as the effects of energies which are electrical, but may be something more). This display culminated in images of the discharges from the body made visible through electronography—which, when enlarged on the screen, looked very much like the lightning storms in the sky. The dramatic imagery of the film's opening emphasized the *sameness* of the discharges, from macrocosm to microcosm, from visible to invisible. A neat, sharp comment. Then the film took us to Florin's laboratory, where we saw a full torso (of a beautiful nude—this was a bit of Romanian show biz, it seemed) first, as the physical body was placed on the transparent electrode, and then as it was seen with its flares of corona discharge emitted from all parts of the body. A living body of fire, in a sense, and as that living body breathed and moved, one could see the interplay of movement reflected in the dynamic scintillations around her body.

From there, we were shown on Dumitrescu's several instruments eruptions from acupuncture points, looking not unlike volcanic eruptions. (In the lab, we had seen signs of such outpourings, as when John had the flu and "stuff" poured from his thumb, but these were very rare.) The film moved far too quickly for me to absorb all that was shown, and far too soon it was over. Another standing ovation, for Dumitrescu, in which I happily joined. Ioan Florin Dumitrescu, in Bucharest, Romania, had surpassed in technology the research efforts in the Soviet Union and in the United States and had shown that electrical discharges from the body can be brilliantly seen, in motion pictures, and that such emanations can be used to explore living systems in sickness and in health.

I longed to see the movie again. It certainly seemed to confirm things we had observed on our own transparent electrode, but the film required seeing several times to absorb it fully. Even more than that, though, I wanted so much to manipulate those instruments with my own hands, and to see with my own eyes. ...

The Inner Conference

The last afternoon session was reserved for clinical studies—of special interest to those acupuncture practitioners who wanted to argue which points were best suited to which illnesses. These details of acupuncture therapy were, for someone like Zion, rich in meaning; but for someone like me, interested in the bioenergy of the acupuncture system, they would serve only to confuse.

So I stood at a booth, drinking another cup of that fine Colombian coffee, wondering how best to spend the last afternoon, when suddenly one of Dumitrescu's staff appeared at my side. It was clear from his almost furtive look that it was best not to ask questions, but simply to join him. I nodded, and we strolled to the far end of the hall, disappearing through a doorway into an annex of the Resort Parc Hotel where I had not yet been. But we did not linger there. Instead, I was led at a swift pace past a small reception desk and up three flights of stairs. As we rounded the last flight, I was surprised—and somewhat relieved—to see Drs. Resch and Huber being led up the stairs, too. We greeted each other in subdued voices, for somehow this seemed an illicit maneuver.

This sense of intrigue was enhanced when our guides stopped in front of a hotel door, which looked exactly like all the other hotel doors in the corridor, and one of them knocked sharply, but quietly, twice. The door was first opened just a crack, then wider to permit us inside, after which it was closed swiftly behind us. Inside the room were assembled on the bed, floor, tables, and in the bathroom, all of the apparatus needed to show us how to make an electronograph. What is more, Florin himself was there, to show us his

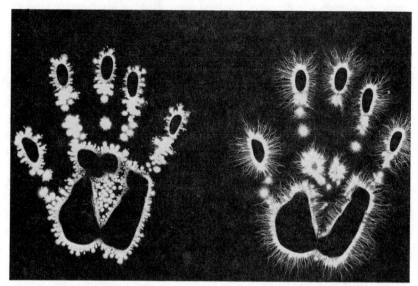

Fig. 12-4. My hands, taken by Dumitrescu, in Bucharest. *(Left)* Negative polarity. *(Right)* Positive polarity.

technique. Which meant that he was not chairing the afternoon's meeting, as he had done throughout the conference. How had he managed to wangle all that equipment—power sources, developing lab, instruments—*and* himself, into this hotel room? However accomplished, it was a daring maneuver, just for Drs. Huber, Resch, and me. Here was a gift, a rare gift, which no one in any Soviet country had offered to any colleague that I knew. My admiration for Florin zoomed.

And continued to zoom, when he began to operate the equipment. For it was clear that he had mastered a series of complex steps so that they were done almost by rote. In our lab, for example, we had experimented with changing polarities and had seen how the positive gave lightning-like flares and the negative a soft, diffuse pattern. These are the classic "Lichtenburg figures," known for two hundred years and reproduced by the Effluvists. But Florin had evolved this technique to the point where a flick of a switch would change the image from positive to negative in a millionth of a second, as can be seen in the two electronographs of my one hand (Fig. 12-4). What is more, it was routine for Florin to photograph two hands, simultaneously, on one piece of film, with that exposure time of one millionth of a second. This was beyond anything we had conceived of doing; Ken Johnson had sweated over a way of taking Olga Worrall's hand picture on a piece of eight-by-ten film, and we had danced a jig when it turned out well. Dr. Dumitrescu's group had been photographing two hands, simultaneously, for years.

Even as we saw these wonders, I felt a nagging frustration, for we were still not seeing any acupuncture points in the pictures, which could then serve for diagnosis. And that, after all, was Florin's chief, valuable contribution to medicine. Just as I was thinking this, Dr. Resch expressed his own frustration to Florin, who chewed briefly on his moustache—and asked a student to strip for the torso picture. Then Florin turned to us and said ruefully that there might not be any acupuncture points—and therefore no diagnosis—if the student were healthy, for the points only appear with pathology. As the student took off his shirt, Dr. Resch stopped him and asked Florin if he might be photographed instead. Florin smiled and nodded.

Now Dr. Resch disrobed and lay, stomach down, along the rectangular plate which had been covered with X-ray film. Then one of his legs was lifted from the floor and a bracelet attached to his ankle. This, I now knew, was a ground wire, precaution against electric shock. When Dr. Resch's body was aligned on the film, Florin pressed the button. Nothing seemed to happen—no sparks, no faint blue corona glow—but in that twinkling of a moment, the photograph had been made and Dr. Resch was dressing. Florin promptly took the film into the bathroom to process it personally. The procedure had been just as described by Dr. Sapse and just as we had seen it in Dumitrescu's film. When Florin returned in a very few minutes with the developed film, our excitement grew, for we could see that the torso picture looked very much like the others we had seen in Florin's presentations. We all became still as we watched Florin study the photograph to make his diagnosis.

In the silence, I asked, "Andreas, are you healthy?"

"Yes, I think." He answered in his gentle, serious way.

"Oh dear, too bad..."

Gentle laughter.

Dr. Huber asked hopefully, "Maybe just a little sick?"

More gentle laughter.

Then silence. Everyone stared at Florin who, after a few moments, pointed to some very faint specks on the film.

"You see? It is a little. Not important. Maybe stomach."

"My stomach?" Dr. Resch repeated. "No. I am well."

"But no worry. Please." Florin went on. "Maybe Romanian food. Or wine. Upset. Or maybe ulcer. You have incipient duodenal ulcer, maybe?"

"I have not this history." Dr. Resch frowned. And then he did exactly what I would have done. "Would you permit me this photograph? I will go to the university hospital, and I will have X-ray and examination, to see if there is duodenal ulcer."

Florin rolled up the film and gave it to Andreas, repeating that he could be wrong and it could be nothing more than an upset stomach due to the food or wine. Then he gave me my hand pictures, and with that the demonstration was over. In the same clandestine way we had been taken to the rendezvous, we were taken back to the conference, where Drs. Resch and Huber and I had an excited, whispered conclave. Would there or would there not be a duodenal ulcer—and how could they let me know the results? That was when we discovered that we three were to meet again in Tokyo for the Third International Psychotronics Conference in three weeks' time. Andreas would know then whether there was any merit to the diagnosis—though he personally felt that there would not be.

Another Clandestine Meeting

On the last morning of the conference, as I was waiting at the coffee counter for the morning session to begin, I was approached by a young Romanian doctor whom I had met earlier. Now he looked intense and agitated and asked if we could speak privately. I murmured there was not much time and he said not much time was needed. Then he led me, not quite forcibly, along the same corridor I had been led the day before for the electronography demonstration. But now the doctor steered me into a corner of the hotel lobby and asked, in nervous English:

"You have American money?"

I was not all that surprised. On just about every European visit, this had been a request from even the most eminent of scientists. In those earlier days everyone was in search of American dollars (a state of affairs which seems to have come to a whimpering end).

As it happened, I had very little American cash.

"But you have twenty-five dollars?"

He was so desperate I asked why, and he explained that he had been given an examination in acupuncture theory and practice the previous evening by a Chinese-American doctor, who had told him that he had passed and could receive a diploma as a licensed acupuncturist—for which he must pay twenty-five dollars, in American money.

Cold water shock. Here was surely one of the oldest scams in the world—the diploma-from-nowhere-for-cash—but it was being played by an American M.D. on a Romanian M.D.—for a miserable $25! The Romanian M.D. went on about how valuable such a diploma would be in his practice, which was surely true, for the Romanians—like so many Europeans—have a deep fondness for titles, degrees, and diplomas. (At the end of this Bucharest conference, each delegate was awarded a diploma, and several received two for "important contributions.")

Wondering frantically if it was the right thing to do, I began to open my purse, but the doctor stopped me, saying the transaction would be better done in the Chinese-American doctor's hotel room. Would I please go, to witness the "graduation"? I went, because I was curious to see the man who played the con game and how he played it. He played it rather dully.

Not dull the sequel—which came the next day, when there was a commotion at the reception desk of the hotel involving the Chinese-American doctor-of-the-diploma, who was arguing that he had been charged twice for one night's lodging. The clerk did not agree, and the acrimony was growing strong, for the doctor's luggage was being held and he had to catch a plane. When the doctor saw me, he came over to complain about what was being done to him. I was curious.

"How much money do they want from you?"

"Twenty-five dollars!" He answered indignantly. I stared at him as he walked back to the reception desk. He did not for one moment, I am convinced, see any kind of justice, esoteric or otherwise, in his being done out of that particular number of dollars.

Au Revoir

At the formal dinner which ends most conferences, I was awarded the place of honor on the dais, between Dr. Rejdak and Dr. Dumitrescu. Once more I learned that we three also would meet again at Tokyo in three weeks' time—after which, Florin was going on a lecture tour of the Republic of China to discuss his research. Once more, Florin promised to send a print of his film for laboratory study.

So we ate and drank, feeling an added exuberance at parting, for we were soon to meet again. It had been a soaring time in Bucharest—to find research so much like ours, yet so far transcending it.

There was no inkling, none at all, that Bucharest was, for me, the end of the road.

13
Lab's End

Which Comes Not
with a Bang, but Not with
a Whimper, Either

ONCE MORE INTO THE BREACH

In spite of Dr. Rejdak's thick, two-volume pre-publication of the Proceedings, the 1977 Third International Psychotronics Conference in Tokyo was a dud. Intimations of this arrived early, when I looked for someone with whom to make the trip. Where there had been about two hundred American delegates at the first conference in Prague in 1973, and about one hundred at the 1975 event in Monaco, I could not find one colleague who was planning a trip to the Tokyo conference. All the same, I wanted very much to attend—not only to see Dumitrescu again, and Drs. Resch and Huber, but also to report the new research out of our lab, which had taken on a new dimension. Again we owed much to the contributions of volunteers, one being a graduate student from UCLA's Media Department, Kazuo Chiba, who for his Master's thesis in TV had created a half-hour program out of our Kirlian research titled "Patterns of Energy"—which this time was not only approved by his faculty committee but won second prize at a national TV contest. (Was academia growing more accepting?) Kazuo's work was made possible only through a marvelous gift to the lab (from a firm called "Impossible Electronics") of an expensive, low-light video camera, with which we were able to record the dimmest of Kirlian emanations that could not be seen any other way. This opened new kinds of bioenergetic research, which included some curious non-electrical, bioluminescent "self-portraits," and a new look at the secret energy in seeds.

Energy Centers in Seeds

Still curious to explore the hidden life energy in the dry seed, Bill Emboden came to the lab one day, seeds in hand, when Ken Johnson happened to be visiting the lab, and experimenting with a new technique on the video camera. This technique involved spearing a leaf's stem with an acupuncture needle, which was attached by a wire to a special Kirlian device, whose voltage could be increased or decreased by a twirl of the dial. The leaf, suspended in mid-air, lit up its Kirlian flares in 3D, which is what we were recording on the videotape. Bill wondered aloud if any kind of flare pattern would show up from his seeds, and Ken promptly speared a large pinto bean and suspended it. At first, with the low voltage, there was nothing at all to be seen. But as Ken turned the dial slowly, raising the voltage, sparks started to stream steadily from a special point—which, Bill announced in a stunned, quiet voice, was the point from which the *roots* would emerge during germination.

Then, as Ken continued to increase the voltage, there was a second steady sparking from a different point of the bean, which Bill said was where the *shoots* would emerge. Ken did not stop, but increased the voltage still more—and a third center of sparking began. We pounced on Bill to know what that third point could be, but he did not know. We watched this fireworks display from the three centers of the bean on the video monitor, until Ken started to lower the voltage and, one by one, in reverse sequence, the sparking centers went out. This orderly sequence was impressive, particularly when it occurred with each bean we tried that afternoon. It was as if we had latched on to a law of energy emission related to growth: from root, to shoot, to...?

And so we included this data as part of the "Patterns of Energy."

Magnetic Passes over Leaves

Through Ken's new technique of spearing leaves in midair, combined with Bill Emboden's fine curiosity, we latched on to another effect, through the video camera, which might otherwise have eluded us, an effect which seems very much related to our earlier work with Jack Gray's magnetic passes. One day, as we were recording on tape the flares from a leaf, aglow with bubbles, Bill reached out his hand—and as he approached the leaf, we could see on the video monitor that the leaf began to glow much more

Fig. 13-1. A "self-portrait" of bioluminescent mushrooms, taken *without electricity.*

brightly. Ken and I yelled to Bill to keep his hand there, and the leaf continued to glow brilliantly. Then we asked Bill to take his hand away slowly, and the leaf dimmed down. We played this again and again—hand close, bright leaf; hand away, dimmed leaf—while we recorded it for the videotape. And as we watched, it seemed as if we were seeing an energy flow from hand to leaf which might be related to the energy in the kind of magnetic passes which Jack Gray had first shown us.

Bug Bioluminescence

Another finding emerged from Bill's restless probing for an explanation of the Kirlian effect. Bill hit on the fact that certain "bioluminescent" plants and bugs glow so strongly, with some sort of bioenergy, that they can literally take their own pictures. He brought slides of such "self-portraits" to the lab—one particular beauty being of bioluminescent Japanese mushrooms, photographed at a Japanese university through the simple process of putting some film near the mushrooms, which over time took their own ghostly pictures without electricity (Fig. 13-1). (Naturally, I was reminded of William Russell's "self-portraits" of wood, photographed in similar fashion.)

Bill's idea was a simple and exciting one: that the Kirlian tech-

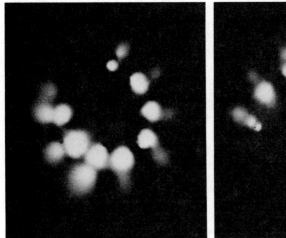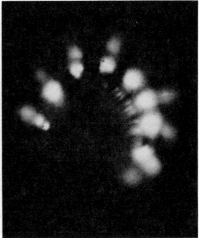

Fig. 13-2. *(Left)* Self-portrait of a bioluminescent zarhippus. *(Right)* Same zarhippus in a Kirlian image (the photographs give essentially the same coronas).

nique, in essence, just heightens the natural bioluminescence (or bioenergy)—if we consider *light* to be energy made visible—that exists in all life forms. In other words, those mushrooms (as well as other plants and animals and people) may be constantly radiating an energy which cannot be seen under ordinary conditions. But under special conditions, that radiation might be photographed. X-ray shows what is inside people, not ordinarily seen with the eye; infra-red film shows what is concealed from the eye by total darkness; and perhaps Kirlian photography shows what is being emanated around an object—again not visible to the eye.

Here was a keen notion, but how test it? Bill's idea was to find something bioluminescent, get it to take its own picture, and then take its Kirlian picture to see if the two kinds of photographs were similar. Wonderful plan, with only one drawback. We had to wait until a bioluminescent something could be found, since those bioluminescent mushrooms don't grow in California.

Months later, Bill arrived with a prize desert insect, the zarhippus, which glows in the dark. This is an insignificant bug to look at, a scant inch in length but generally curled into a smaller, half-moon shape. This particular zarhippus was stubborn and refused to glow in the dark for us. How could it take its own picture if it didn't glow? Ken solved the problem scientifically—by picking it up and squeezing it. The zarhippus promptly lit up and Ken put it on film, where in just a few seconds it recorded its image. We had it take several self-portraits without electricity—and then we took several Kirlian photographs (Fig. 13-2). The comparison is interesting, for brilliant circles of yellow appear in both the self-portrait and the Kirlian image, as does a similar corona around the insect. However, the corona *colors* are different: in the self-portrait an emerald green, in the Kirlian its typical royal blue.

Could it be that Bill's hunch was right? That the Kirlian images are simply *heightening* the bioluminescence which exists, perhaps invisibly, around almost every object in nature?

This intriguing research was also included in the paper I prepared for the Tokyo conference.

TOKYO TRAVESTY

Just before leaving, alone, for the Orient, I received a call from an old parapsychology friend, Russell Targ, who with Hal Puthoff at Stanford Research Institute had done that fine film of their research with Uri Geller, shown at Prague. Russ had made a last-minute decision to go to Tokyo and was looking for a traveling companion. I was happy to accept. And an odd couple we made, Russ being twelve inches taller and six inches thinner than me, wearing glasses twice as thick. But we shared a sense of the absurd, which eased the miseries that were to come.

Both of us had already attended many conferences in many capitals of the world, but Tokyo was the first, for both of us, at which almost no one appeared. On registration day, Dr. Rejdak was there, of course, beaming his welcome as chairman. And later in the day, I was elated to meet Drs. Resch and Huber—and to learn from Dr. Resch that he was, indeed, the victim of an incipient duodenal ulcer. This unpleasant news delighted us all, for it was exactly what Dr. Dumitrescu had diagnosed from the electronograph we had seen taken in the Bucharest hotel room. This was first-rate validation for the Dumitrescu technique. We told Dr. Rejdak, and he, too, was excited by the news.

But by the day's end, Dr. Rejdak was showing severe strain. For it had become clear that the conference would be poorly attended—there proved to be only about fifty delegates in all—putting it in bad financial straits. For the Japanese capitalist who had promised to finance the Conference had reneged, which meant the conference was bankrupt before it began. Which fact gave birth to travesty, for in the tackiest of last minute maneuvers, our large conference hall was turned into a TV studio for a major Japanese network, which picked up the tab for the conference with the understanding that the conference would "cooperate." This meant a steady stream of psychics and scientists in and out of the improvised studio—the psychics to perform their "tricks" for the audience, the scientists to explain and/or expose the feats of the psychics. Meanwhile the business of the conference was shoved into a small back room—where from time to time the door would burst open and an assistant TV director would ask the chairman for one or another scientist to appear on the program.

Someone viewing this scene with an objective eye might have seen this as an allegory of our times: Make way, science, for you are fodder for the media!

But I was angry. Oddly, Russ seemed amused and I asked, irritably, what was with him?

"You might learn something just watching the show."

"Like what?"

"When I was a kid—" he grinned, "—I studied to be a magician. And y'know, I got so good, it scared the hell out of me."

"I don't get you."

"Well, it got so I knew the answer before I did the trick. Time after time."

I stared at him. "You mean, you were doing ESP instead of magic?"

He nodded. "Blew my mind. So I started asking other magicians. And they said it happened to them, too. Magicians...?"

We laughed, for we both had been warned, so many times, that psychic stuff was nothing but a magic trick. And so I went down to the TV studio, for as Russ reminded me, the more tricks I knew, the better researcher I could be.

A Child "Psychic"

I entered the hall just as a winsome girl of nine or ten was having her eyes covered with a heavy blindfold, which had already been tested by members of the TV audience who agreed that nothing at all could be seen through it. When the blindfold was secured, the girl made one small gesture, as if to settle the blindfold more securely. That one small gesture was the giveaway to an old trick; she was allowing herself just enough room to see clearly (a tiny slit is all that's necessary).

So, on TV camera, the child performed ESP wonders, describing with clear and fine detail the hair color, features, clothes, and shoes of the members of the audience who would stand up for her. The audience roundly applauded her talent. Then, when the TV announcer asked for comments from the scientists, I stepped forward with a large placard and asked that the experiment be done again with the placard in front of the girl's eyes instead of the blindfold. This request was pleasantly refused, on the grounds that the girl was able to see because her vision was in her nostrils....

And the audience roundly applauded in defense of the child.

Sic semper, suckers.

The Rise of "Holistic Medicine"

The majority of research reports at the conference dealt with unorthodox medicine or holistic health, as it was coming to be called. This was suddenly the most popular area of psychotronics research. Where, just five years before, Dr. Huber of Vienna had taken me around a corner to show his healing hands, now he presented a movie which showed the recovery of a six-year-old child from a terminal illness through his "laying on of hands."

A Brazilian delegate, Jarbas Marinho, presented a topic most unconventional in Western medicine. He suggested that what we label "schizophrenia" might be, in many cases, spirit possession. At least in Brazil, medical doctors in good standing with the Brazilian Medical Association will seek help for their untreatable "schizophrenics" by asking the Spiritist Federation (which consists of more than ten million members) to perform an exorcism, which is often successful in healing the patient. Marinho, an engineer, had himself participated in such exorcisms.

Another paper, from an African delegate, spoke similarly of schizophrenia and possession in discussing research with fetish priests (no longer called witch doctors). Dr. Ayisi of the University of Ghana, a research psychologist studying the healing techniques of these fetish priests, had spent several weeks with us at UCLA, studying the Kirlian technique. In fact, Dr. Ayisi had shocked a psychology seminar by telling of one particular healing ritual, a "reverse voodoo," for which he used the example of a patient suffering a broken leg. It is thought unseemly for the priest to touch the patient, so instead, the patient's family brings a chicken, and the priest carefully breaks the chicken's leg in a place corresponding to the patient's break. The priest then treats the chicken with ointments and herbs, and when the chicken's leg is healed, the patient's leg is healed. Here, if you like, is a striking instance of the "transfer of bioenergy" from chicken to man—or sympathetic magic. This paper was greeted, as was Marinho's, with silent skepticism, except from the Brazilian delegation, who had seen similar healings in voodoo-like ceremonies all over South America.

Admittedly, it is not easy for us in the West to accept these data, for there is nothing in our culture to support such ideas. Yet, the very next year, I received calls from Canada from both a patient and her psychiatrist, asking about techniques of exorcism. And that highly respected Canadian psychiatrist admitted that none of the accepted psychotherapies or drugs had been effective in relieving his patient from what she believed—and he was now willing to consider—might be "spirit possession."

Dumitrescu's Paper

Away from Bucharest and the security it offered him, Florin Dumi-trescu seemed less dynamic, less assured. To most of the conference members he was just another delegate giving another abstruse paper—in fact, for most, it was an unintelligible paper. For, although he presented the same material as in Bucharest, its meaning was lost because of that impossible Romanian English in which he spoke, and his glorious electronographs—without a basic understanding of his research in acupuncture and medical diagnosis—were as meaningless to the Tokyo audience as an X-ray or thermograph would be to the layman. I kept telling delegates I spoke with that their confusion would be relieved with the showing of Florin's film, which was narrated in excellent English. But at this Tokyo conference—can one conceive of such a happening in the land of Sony and Sanyo?—there was no movie projector to be had, and Florin's film was never shown.

We spent our free hours together—Florin and his associate, the Viennese doctors, Russ and I—exploring Tokyo from the depths of its superclean subways to the heights of the New Otani Hotel's cocktail lounge from which one can see a panorama of electric signs lighting up a more dazzling sky than New York's Time Square. All the while, as often as I could, I reminded Florin of his promise to send me a print of his film and one of his instruments. And each time he would nibble at his moustache and nod his head. But the film never came, and neither did the instrument. And Florin's research is still unknown in most of the world.

Stalemate.

It seems that science is *not* the free exchange that once it was, or claimed to be. And it is not just countries keeping secrets from countries; one lab at UCLA keeps secrets from other labs, for there exists competition. Even in academia.

Foreshadowing

Like Dumitrescu's film, our "Patterns of Energy" almost missed its showing, for lack of a video player. Hackles raised, I stormed the Japanese delegates and Dr. Rejdak until, on the last day, a video was found. But even as the tape was being played, more TV people charged into the meeting, asking for more scientists. Our group looked at each other stonily, and Russ shook his head. Further protests were, clearly, pointless. The disintegration had gone too far.

Certainly I had been a porcupine quill through most of this Tokyo debacle, by refusing to participate in the TV circus (except for the nostril vision vulgarity) and by protesting repeatedly the lack of a film projector and video player and above all the constant interruption of presentations. So I shouldn't have been surprised when, at the final business meeting, the chairman announced that only members whose dues had been paid could remain. No one left, and the chairman repeated his statement. Still no one left. Then:

"Dr. Thelma Moss!"

"Yes?"

"You are not a paid-up member. It is here written." A page of typed paper was waved from the dais.

And I saw that I was being driven from the temple. I was free to stay and fight, of course (I had paid my dues, or so I believed), or I could go.

I found myself getting up and leaving.

No one stopped me.

This, I realize now, was a foreshadowing of things to come.

BACK IN THE GOOD OLD NPI

Back to the same teaching duties, the same research schedule in the lab, the same load of invitations to lecture and to participate in conferences. At first. But within that year of 1977/78, the auditoriums that had once overflowed with crowds of participants began to empty. Where one meeting with Olga Worrall and Uri Geller as headliners had attracted thousands, with hundreds turned away, a year later, a similar program with more stars and much more publicity attracted less than half a house. And shortly after that, programs were being cancelled for lack of interest. This was the Tokyo phenomenon, on a wider scale. Meaning the bubble had burst.

Just as so many others had burst, in my twenty years with psychology. In graduate school, the first bubbles had been sensitivity training, then behavior modification, then—my song—LSD for psychotherapy, which, in no time, became the hippie trip and was then banished by law. In the wash of the psychedelics had come, overlapping each other, Rolfing, encounter groups, Gestalt, psychosynthesis. And then came the sex explosion, which seemed to start (to the horror of clinical psychology) with nude marathons, then sex surrogates, group sex, and the gay liberations (what had been a psychiatric illness became an alternative lifestyle). All culminating in "How To" sex movies, shown at national psychology conferences: How to use a vibrator, How to masturbate, How to perform oral sex—none of which was treated as pornography, but as science. Meanwhile, there were other bubbles, for other bubbleheads, particularly those seeking instant Satori. One could choose Mind Control, or Dianetics, or est, or Kundalini Yoga, or

Hari Krishna or TM. Mantrams, as someone said, for tantrums. By the year 1978 most of these had been supplanted or incorporated into holistic health, which offered therapy through herbs or hypnosis, through needles or the laying on of hands, through thought, or energy—and even these burst into "aura cleansings" and "chakra readings" and "chanting for health," etc. etc. etc.

How explain the tides of movements? Creation, preservation, destruction. Omnipresent, revolving wheel of the universe, a more basic law, perhaps, than the normal bell curve. And our UCLA lab was no exception; it had been almost miraculously created and preserved for more than a decade, and now had come the time for its destruction.

The Seven-Year Itch

Actually, it had been a longer time in coming than the usual academic ritual, which has built a seven-runged ladder to climb, from Assistant Professor, Level One through Assistant Professor, Level Four, one step to be taken every other year—until, in the seventh year, it is mandatory to make a quantum jump to Associate Professor. In other words, by the end of the seventh year, you're either "up or out." For Associate Professor brings tenure, which means that you have the university for life, or vice versa.

During my years at the NPI, those biennial promotions had arrived as a matter of course—until the seventh-year quantum jump which, to no one's surprise, I did not make. What *was* a surprise was a meeting with Jolly West who, after saying once more that he did not agree with what I did, but would defend to the death, etc., offered me a change in job from Assistant Professor to Assistant Research Psychologist. This was an unexpected bounty. Which, in my naivete, I thought meant I could devote more time to research.

Wrong.

"Research psychologist?" my psychology boss had said bluntly. "That's a change in title. Only. You're to continue your teaching duties."

"But I don't understand—"

"You didn't make it. You should be out. Instead, Jolly kept you on. You've been rewarded for failure."

"I don't see it that way."

"How do you see it?"

"I think I've been punished for success."

He blinked. He knew that my *curriculum vitae* had more publications and references than any other NPI psychologist's. All the same, I *was* the odd one out. And always had been. Even as a teacher.

Different Levels of Consciousness

During the late sixties, when flower children roamed the campus spreading riot and rebellion, I had been called in for special assignment by the psychology department's vice chairman—the very same fellow who had pushed statistics (balls or cells?) on our first-year graduate class. Mort had gone on to prosper in the field of Learning Theory, and was asking me in his shy and kind way if I would teach an undergraduate course, on any subject at all.

"Come on, Mort!—Parapsychology?"

"Anything you want." He meant it. "But you have to go the academic route. Syllabus, grades, the whole thing. Make it legitimate, and you can teach it."

"I like it!"

"Hope so." He smiled. "Because there's no money in it. None."

"But you expect I'll do it anyhow." He nodded, and I laughed. "Why me?"

"Because it's time to expand the curriculum."

"Before the hippies burn down the new psych building."

"Something like that."

We grinned into each other's eyes. And Mort went on to talk of syllabi and texts and grades and computers. That was the trivia. The big question was, what did I want to teach?

Not parapsychology. It was time, it seemed to me, to go beyond the phenomena toward the mysteries of the spirit. From the *mechanics*, as they say in science, to the *process* of emotional and spiritual evolution. So, in the syllabus I put together, men from many centuries—from Patanjali to Ram Dass—were linked into the one fabric of different levels of consciousness: dreams, hypnosis, visions, drugs, meditation, fantasies, hallucinations. I was concerned about how the students might react to ideas like freedom from desire, or freedom from the physical body to roam as energy through time and space. I discovered some of them were way ahead of me speaking glibly about Kundalini and out-of-body experiences. Where they did need help, and asked for it over and over again, was with their own creativity.

And gradually an idea for an experiment in creativity took shape. The students would take a midterm exam, for which they could not study. If anyone resented the idea or felt he could not do it, he could instead write a paper on his objections or the problems with it. (Out of ninety-six students, four did that.) An air of excitement filled the classroom that day the students sat for an exam they hadn't studied for. But when they were asked to let go all rational thinking and let their pens do the writing—a murmur of confusion.

"Okay..." I started, "...you've probably never done an exam like this before—" I was drowned out for a minute by a roar of laughter. "Let me offer some ideas. A good way to break out of a habit into a flow is to write one word—your name, for instance—over and over and over until the pen flows of itself. No criticisms, no erasures, just flow with it. And watch what is written. If the flow stops, wait for it to start again, and if it doesn't then hand in what you've done and leave."

Within moments the room was very, very still. After five minutes, two students got up quietly and left. Then another. And another. But when the bell rang at the end of the hour, all the rest of the students were still in their seats, writing. Some twenty minutes later, the last young man brought me his paper. He looked dazed, and said softly:

"That was incredible...I was writing poetry...for the first time in my life...."

Which was what the exam had been about.

Reading those papers was the most profound experience of my teaching career. They ranged from rhymed to blank verse, to forgotten childhood memories, to fantasies of previous lives, to just a name repeated over and over again as someone struggled to break loose—and on the last pages, did.

That exam became the key to their understanding the course, for now a "different level of consciousness" had been a lived event.

In some universities—and UCLA is one of them—it has become a practice for students to grade the teachers. I rated high with the students, who commented again and again how fine it was *not* to be required to memorize and regurgitate by rote. And at the annual psychology faculty meeting (to which I was not invited) my name—like Abou Ben Adem's—led all the rest. In high ratings.

And I was never again invited to teach an undergraduate course.

Another Ending

It had been different in the lab. Year had followed year, with no one trying to take over the space, in spite of the severe space shortage. But soon after Tokyo came a call from the space commissar, a whimsical Irish psychiatrist named Mike, who sent out memos like:

> SUBJECT: Money to spend. Your requests will be put in a pot and picked out by an unbiased, blindfolded green vervet.

On the phone Mike said that the lab next to mine had become vacant (which I knew; it was half the size of our small lab), and wouldn't I find it refreshing to move there, so he could move into my lab? The words were whimsical, but the message wasn't, and I sought out Mike in his office to protest. It wasn't easy finding Mike's office because—even though he was a full professor—his space turned out to be a walled-off section of an ex-hospital ward. The handwriting on the makeshift wall was easy to read: Your gig at the lab is over. Strange, it had been so long in coming and when it finally happened, it somehow seemed anticlimactic.

Illuminating, packing away the work of a decade, which had overflowed the drawers and shelves up into the ceiling itself, for John had somehow loosened the modular sections of false ceiling to stuff the very space above our heads with relics of past performance. Up there, hundreds upon hundreds of slides from the emotional telepathy studies, all jumbled together now, mute testimony that we had abandoned the ESP studies. And far back in the ceiling, gadgetry we had used to induce hypnotic trance back when "trance" was a taboo cult word. We had had no success then with those black-and-white geometric discs which were supposed to transfix when revolved at a brisk rate. Now we tried again, revolving them, and failed again. And as the discs were dropped into the garbage bin I told of the time in Bogota when a Peruvian Indian, without a word or gesture, but merely with his eyes, had felled a Ph.D. anthropologist to the floor like a rag doll.

"What *is* hypnosis?" someone asked. And after all these years of studying it, and teaching it, there is still no answer.

We came down from the ceiling then, and from behind the isolation booth someone pulled out reams and reams of EEG paper on which we had tried to get evidence of the telepathic dream. We looked once more at those squiggles we had recorded, when all night long we had tried to find the start of a dream through REM marks (Rapid Eye Movements, which signal the beginning of a dream). Suddenly the EEG expert had marked REM on the chart, when the rest of us could see no change in the squiggles.

"It takes practice," the expert had said kindly.

We never got the practice, but we did learn that reading the squiggles is more an art than a science, similar to the reading of an X-ray or a Rorschach or the corona patterns in Kirlian photography. All ambiguous data, in which the skill of the interpreter is the crucial variable. This had come as a surprise, as did the fact that the famous EEG Alpha Rhythm (eight to eleven cycles which are supposed to indicate relaxation) can only be deciphered via computer. Almost non-existent is a pure Alpha Rhythm, except from the head of a Zen master in meditation.

Into the bin, the EEG papers.

Then, from the recesses of the filing cabinet, a forgotten set of Chinese acupuncture needles, still sharp, and valuable now that Ken had found a new use for them in the video recordings.

Fig. 13-3. *(Left)* Olga Worrall's hand in a state of rest. *(Right)* Olga's hand sending energy. Perhaps our most famous Kirlian pictures.

Screams of delight when someone discovered a long-hidden brown paper bag stuffed with every variety of drugs, legal and illegal, a relic from the days when we were searching for their Kirlian effects.

At last we settled down to the main work: sorting through the stacks and stacks and stacks of Kirlian negatives, slides, and prints. These included countless "phantom" failures, all carefully dated and labelled, all useless, all dumped into the garbage. As well as superfluous family portraits, and repetitious human interactions. In the clearing away, we occasionally came upon a forgotten treasure, like pictures of the dead man's hand, long mourned as lost, or a bonanza of soybean germination pictures, or a complete set of Kirlian photographs, over time, on one of Jack Gray's best healings. That was Joe, who had been shot in the neck and left with a paralyzed arm which, the doctors said, would never move again. When Joe first came to the lab, he was wearing a sling-like contraption to support the useless arm. Jack had worked with him many weeks, with no observable results. But then a gradual improvement—and after a year, Joe came in triumphantly to report the fulfilment of his ambition; he had gone fishing, using the arm for trout casting.

There was a long and futile search for the original eight-by-ten color negatives of Olga Worrall's hand, before and during healing. The slides made from those negatives had graced the covers of books and magazines around the world (Fig. 13-3). But we never, ever found those negatives, not even in that last dismantling.

We did, though, compile notebook after notebook of Kirlian data; prints, negatives, slides, all according to category. We had twenty books of healing studies, eight books of Emboden's biology, six books of family portraits, four of human interactions, along with volumes on phantoms, acupuncture, Green Thumb/Brown Thumb, psychics, metals, chloroform and other anesthetics.

Here was the lab's chief product. But what did it mean?

On the Meaning of Life

Somewhere along the way a German journalist had spent a full, meticulous day in the lab, watching, asking questions, even participating in a few studies. And always, always taking notes. At the end of the day, after reviewing his material, he said formally,

"I wish to thank you. It has been most instructive. And I have for you only one more question."

"Please."

"Why are you doing all of this research?" The question took us so by surprise that I had no answer at all. The interviewer pressed on, in his heavy Germanic way. "I mean to say, what is it you hope to learn?"

"Oh!" The words came unbidden. "The meaning of life. We are searching for the meaning of life."

"Do you think you will find it?" He was serious.

At the time, a huge joke.

But now...something wondrous. The meaning of life had become, for me, slowly and elegantly clear during the cleansing of the lab as we made way for the rats that were to come into the isolation booth for study. I had traveled a maze of blind alleys and had felt frustration and a desperate lack of patience; had enjoyed occasional bursts of fireworks. Now, just when the work seemed rich in promise, it was stopped. Not by committee, not by academia. The work was stopped because our small part of the tapestry was finished. There are other pieces being woven in Bucharest, in Alma-Ata, and in other places visited and unvisited. For the work goes on, even if those who do it never meet. For we are, all of us, interconnected. And for me, this sense of interconnection—with the K.J.s, the Jack Grays, the Dumitrescus, the Hubachers and the Hubers, etc., etc.—this was the meaning underlying the Search.

CODA

Summer, 1979. The International Kirlian Research Association has its third annual conference at New York University. Attendance is not large. The delegates are doggedly working for proofs that the bioenergy of Reich, the bioplasma of Inyushin, and the life fields of Harold Saxton Burr are reflected in Kirlian photography. Their papers are interesting but inconclusive. I notice there is to be a special panel of Kirlian projects on Sunday, with persons whose names I do not know. These prove to be students of several high schools, presenting their research, some of which had been supervised by Edward Graff, executive director of the association.

It was a breathtaking panel.

New Directions out of the Old

It was stunning to hear those seventeen- and eighteen-year-olds as they discussed their findings in controlled studies, which had received top scientific awards.

One rich research was by Robert Klinger, who had set out to learn if living matter photographs differently than non-living. To do this, Robert had compared the coronas of liquid bacteria cultures (the living) as against liquid barium sulfate (the non-living). And he showed that by increasing the amount of bacteria in the liquid culture, there developed far brighter and larger coronas; but increasing the amount of barium sulfate showed no change of corona at all. Here was firm support for the idea that the Kirlian technique is photographing a *bio*energy—an idea for which our UCLA lab had been many times censured. Instead of censure, Robert had been awarded major prizes from Kodak and the Navy Science Project.

Another research, by Adam Dicker, had begun in a familiar way. For Adam had gone from hospital to hospital in New York, being turned down by doctor after doctor in his request to do research in medical diagnosis. He reported how the doctors seemed interested until he mentioned Kirlian photography as his tool. And one doctor, standing up when he heard the offensive words, said, "That's garbage!" Which was when Adam changed his tactic, never again mentioning Kirlian photography but saying instead he would use "an electrical technique." Not long after that, a well-known doctor, head of orthopedics in a major hospital, agreed to take him on.

That doctor's gamble paid off, for clear and prominent changes in corona pattern were seen in patients with certain kinds of arthritis—supporting the idea that Kirlian photography was a potentially useful diagnostic technique. Adam also reported that he had photographed several patients with *sclero derma* (an illness involving hardening of the skin), but could detect no differences from normal people. (Jack Gray had worked in the lab for two years with a *sclero derma* victim, of whom we took hundreds of pictures. And though we could see her coronas radiating more and more brilliance as she improved, we could not, just as Adam Dicker could not, distinguish her *sclero derma* pictures from the Kirlian images of normal people.)

Adam was now being courted by several hospitals, which were offering research facilities and summer jobs. But the doctor who gambled on him won't let him go and introduces him as his brilliant protegé, who has won top honors from New York's science fair awards and one from the Society of Nuclear Medicine. Adam seemed a very wise eighteen-year-old, for he remarked that he probably wouldn't have been permitted the research if he were five or ten years older.

Another twice-honored report came from Andre Pilevsky, a junior in high school, who had already completed two Kirlian projects, both of them winning many awards, to the delight of Ed Graff, his supervisor. Andre's first exploration had been to examine tumors in tobacco plants. In a beautifully designed study, he contrasted healthy Control plants with Experimental plants infected by virus. It was strikingly clear, in the Kirlian images, which were the infected plants—*days before* any pathology was visible to the eye or by any other means. How? Simply, the diseased sections of the leaves did not show up at all. (As I listened to this and saw the pictures, I realized that with Bill Emboden we had done research with plant tumors—and we had once seen that a tumorous leaf did not photograph in the section where the tumor was. But we had not followed up that one photographic clue in a well-controlled study. Andre had.)

For that original research, Andre had received the top award from a New York City science contest and prizes from the International Science Fair and the United States Navy.

Thus encouraged, he went on to another study. In his first trials —Andre smiled as he spoke—he had looked at possible differences in human blood serum between cancer and normal samples and had found no difference at all. But then—and it was riveting to hear him say this—he decided to try a few more samples, *on a different Kirlian device,* and found striking differences, differences which continued to appear for a large number of samples of serums both cancerous and normal. And again, I remembered when, years ago, our lab had reported how different instruments record differently, and that an effect—such as human eye contact—which might not be seen on one device can be vividly seen on another. It is one thing to report a strange finding, but quite another to have it proved so richly in an important cancer study. (And with a twinge of chagrin, I realized that a UCLA student, for her Master's thesis, had also tried to find differences between healthy and cancerous blood but had found none. Wrong device?)

Fig. 13-4. High school student Allen Detrick's phantom leaf, showing its phantom from both sides, front, and back.

For this second project, Andre had already received several top awards, among them from the Society of Nuclear Medicine and the American Society of Women Engineers.

Finally, and I confess this was my special joy, there was Allen Detrik, a sophomore from a midwestern high school who had written me, more than a year before, when he had photographed a phantom leaf. I wrote back my delight and interest in his work. He had replied by sending not only a copy of the phantom photograph, but also the actual cut leaf, preserved in a special way so that it could be compared for size and shape with its photograph. (The actual leaf had shrunk a bit, he apologized.)

Now, at this IKRA conference, Allen was presenting his large collection of phantom leaves, both in black and white and in color, for which he had already received the state science fair award with the highest possible grade. His father, an electronics engineer, stood in the background beaming and telling anyone who would listen that he had not believed there was anything to this Kirlian stuff—until he had seen a phantom photographed before his eyes. I laughed, for I had done the same thing and had received the same comeuppance. The rationale is something like, "I'll believe it when I see it."

Allen brought down the house when, after having shown a special study in which he had photographed the surface and undersurface of one cut leaf, getting phantoms from both (Fig. 13-4), he picked up another photograph—and said, as he put it down without showing it, "Oh, that one is just an ordinary phantom."

There it was. What had been a miracle for one generation had become "just ordinary" for the next.

More important, this panel had shown that the Kirlian research which had been demeaned and ridiculed and kicked out the back door of academia was now being beckoned through the front door in the guise of these young people with their penetrating, clear minds. And better still, the very backbone of the establishment—the American Medical Association, the U.S. Army, the U.S. Navy, International Science Fairs—all had rewarded them for their research.

Kirlian photography—it was hard for me to digest this—was on its way to becoming respectable.

But even that was not the chief "meaning of life." For it struck me that my joy, my excitement, was directed toward one special idea, which seems to have caught fire in imaginations the whole world over. That idea, which probably lay at the source of my Search, is simply that none of us, none of us, is made completely of matter.

And now these young people are showing, with their fine studies, that there is an energy in and around us that can tell us more about ourselves. Here, perhaps, is the essence: to explore fully our self-awareness. For ultimately, for each of us, the thing of value, the pearl of great price, is our own awakening. Which may include the awakening of science from its long sleep in a bed of matter.

Index of Names

(Page numbers in *italic* refer to illustrations)